DANCING UNDER AN AFRICAN MOON

DANCING UNDER AN AFRICAN MOON

PAGANISM AND WICCA
IN SOUTH AFRICA

DONNA DARKWOLF VOS

ZEBRA

Published by Zebra Press
PO Box 1144, Cape Town, 8000

First published 2002

1 3 5 7 9 10 8 6 4 2

Publication © Zebra Press 2002
Text © Donna Vos 2002

All rights reserved. No part of this publication may be reproduced,
stored in a retrieval system or transmitted, in any form or by any means,
electronic, mechanical, photocopying, recording or otherwise,
without the prior written permission of the copyright owners.

PUBLISHING MANAGER: Marlene Fryer
MANAGING EDITOR: Robert Plummer
EDITOR: Martha Evans
COVER ILLUSTRATION: Natascha Adendorff

Set in 9.5 pt on 14 pt Hiroshige

Reproduction by Hirt & Carter (Cape) (Pty) Ltd
Printed and bound by CTP Book Printers

ISBN 1 86872 653 3

www.zebrapress.co.za

DISCLAIMER
Every possible care has been taken in compiling this book.
However, the publisher and/or the author cannot be held
responsible for any loss, damage or injury that occurs as
a result of following the advice contained therein.

ACKNOWLEDGEMENTS:

Pagan Africa for the following poems: 'The Storm' by Fiery Oak, 'Primal Lover' by darkwolf, 'Pagan Protest' and 'The Triad' by Dayala Stardancer, 'My Moon Child' by Amber Moon, 'The tear' by J Isen, 'Should I end up in heaven' by rainspider, 'Dawn and Dusk' by Debbie de Villiers, 'Black' by epona moondancer, and 'Untitled' by Dee.

This book is dedicated to my mother,
Who taught me what courage is.
You will always be the wind beneath my wings
Until you are born again.

CONTENTS

ABOUT THE AUTHOR		ix
ACKNOWLEDGEMENTS		xi
INTRODUCTION		xiii
1	What is Paganism?	1
2	Paganism in South Africa	17
3	Traditional African Paganism	31
4	Paganism versus Satanism	39
5	Pagan Beliefs and Practices	47
6	Magick and Ritual – The South African Scene	55
7	Southern Hemisphere Musings	71
8	Let the Witches Speak!	87
9	Little Book of Shadows	131
10	Poetry and Pathworkings	179
11	The Spirit of Afrikaans	219
CONCLUDING THOUGHTS		227
REFERENCES		231

ABOUT THE AUTHOR

DONNA DARKWOLF VOS has been a practising Pagan and Wiccan for a number of years. As founder of the Pagan Federation of South Africa, she has been instrumental in pioneering the public Pagan movement in South Africa. Donna is the arch-priestess of the Aquarian Tabernacle Church in South Africa, and is founder and arch-priestess of the Circle of the African Moon.

She has a master's degree in theology from the University of South Africa, a Biblical Diploma from the Kalk Bay Bible Institute and a Post-Graduate Diploma in Library and Information Studies from the University of Cape Town. She is also a traditional medical practitioner, registered with the Traditional Medical Practitioners, Herbalists and Spiritual Healers Association.

She has appeared on numerous television and radio shows, and in magazine and newspaper articles. She has published a number of articles in various esoteric magazines, in South Africa and abroad.

Donna lives in Cape Town, and is a full-time priestess, spiritual counsellor and teacher of Wicca.

ACKNOWLEDGEMENTS

This book would not have been possible were it not for the relationships forged with the many Pagans, closeted and public, the legal system, the media, the police, worried mothers and proud practitioners.

A tribute to Bev Nowikow, who was brave enough to teach the first Wicca class publicly in South Africa, and who dared to dream the Pagan reality that now is.

My special thanks to the high priest of the Coven of the Wheel, who at the risk of being banished from the coven, came out of the closet and joined the first Pagan movement to get off the ground and establish itself as a legal entity.

My thanks to the 21 signatories who dared to append their signatures to the official constitution of the Pagan Federation of South Africa at the Winter solstice, June 1996, thereby giving legal status to the first Pagan body that would last up until the time of publishing this book and beyond.

Also to Angela Northover and Steve Adamson, who shared the earliest vision with me, and stomped where angels dared not dance. And to Angelique Raeven, strategist and militant protagonist of the public Pagan movement.

I wish to pay the highest respect to the legal firm Bouwer and Cardona, and in particular Trevor Bouwer. Though not a Pagan, his commitment to what he calls an 'obscure' cause, and his integrity and farsightedness in dealing with our religious and moral issues, have ensured that Paganism as a movement has upheld its credibility despite some savage storms it has had to weather.

My respect to the media, who have been nothing but polite to me and always ensured that their research had been done – whether for fear I would hex them or because totally enchanted by the glamour of this seemingly new movement, I will not know.

My thanks to Colonel Kobus Jonker, head of the Occult Unit of the South African Police. Still today, ignorance tars Paganism and Satanism with the same brush, and Colonel Jonker is doing a sterling job to help set the record straight.

My thanks to all those who have worked closely with me over the years in an official capacity on various Pagan committees.

My gratitude to Papillon for typing this manuscript, leaving me more time to write, where I felt inspired best.

Special thanks to Pat Hopkins for being the karmic link, and to the Zebra team – the visionary Marlene Fryer, the astute Robert Plummer and, above all, the dedicated Martha Evans.

My thanks to all who contributed to this book, by giving interviews and sending in spells, rituals and poems.

I honour my father and grandmother, who made me do this for myself.

Finally, I thank my familiar, Borg – my bull terrier – who ponders my grievances, shares my elations and sleeps in my magickal circles. (Who said only cats were psychic?)

INTRODUCTION

This book does not claim to speak for all Pagans. Nor is it the sole authority on Paganism in South Africa. It is the view of an informed individual practitioner. Whilst I am acutely aware that Pagans are a highly individualised bunch of people with well-formulated opinions, I will have to generalise fromtime to time. A book of this scope cannot hope to do justice to the richly evolving and extremely eclectic tradition that is beginning to characterise South African Paganism. This book is a bit like a patchwork quilt, a spider web, a trifle pudding.

My aim is to provide some insight into the Pagan scene in South Africa, both for the sake of Pagan South Africa and to broaden the insight of interested international Pagans. How did the neo-Pagan movement start here? What were the influences? Who were and are the major players? What is the general approach to magick? Just how eclectic is eclectic? Are there any South African traditions to speak of?

Another crucial question is the difference between the southern hemisphere and the northern hemisphere. If we claim to be attuning ourselves to the cycles of Nature, we have to do this according to the southern hemisphere rhythms. But most of us do not know how. All the books that one gets are from the northern hemisphere, with a few exceptions from Australia. I will explain the southern hemisphere cycle in the pages that follow.

This is not a scholarly work; anecdotes are used by way of explanation. It does not attempt to rehash the myriad of excellent Pagan books already on the shelves. Where it explains Pagan concepts, paths or magick, it does so in the context of South Africa.

The book is enlivened by interviews with practising Pagans, and by spells and rituals that they have contributed. Herein lies the essence of South African practitioners' thoughts and approaches. All the practitioners in this book are highly individual, as are all Pagans everywhere. Their spells and rituals are a reflection of this. There are recipes, for example, that use herbs that are unknown to the authors of books from the US and Britain. South African practitioners have had to improvise, and many have been witches (wise women – and men) without knowing it.

CHAPTER 1

WHAT IS PAGANISM?

Paganism can be broadly defined as a Nature-based spiritual path or belief system. It dates back to the old religions and gods of ancient Europe, but also includes the pantheons of Egypt and, arguably, the cosmologies of all ancient tribal peoples.

Pagans are people who, from early times, have understood the sacrosanct feeling of bare feet on warm earth, the cleansing drops of an angry outburst of rain, the chill of the wind reminding them to prepare for leaner times, or the comfort of a blazing fire when the darkness of the underworld seems to be closing in. Pagans strive to attune themselves to the tides of Nature and its effects on their inner selves. Such harmonisation with Nature, which is the Pagan form of spiritual union with the Divine, is achieved through reverence of solar and lunar phases, which are acknowledged at the turning points of each season.

As with the evolution of any religion, Paganism has adapted certain, perhaps more primal, values to the more sophisticated needs of the modern urban human being. For instance, many modern Pagans are vegetarians, whereas, almost certainly, their ancient forebears were not. The current revival of the ancient Nature religions, known as neo-Paganism, seeks to create order from chaos through an understanding of Nature. A 'return-to-roots' or 'back-to-basics' approach typically describes the modern Pagan's search for spiritual meaning amidst the existential and environmental mayhem of the new millennium. The grand ventures into the great unknown, into black holes and into the deep abyss of space have become more commonplace, and have lost their romantic grip on humanity, and in particular the 'earthy' Pagans whose feet are planted firmly on the ground. Feeling the sand barefoot on an unspoilt beach or smelling the grass in a beautiful garden is more important in the fight against the loss of natural resources and the inevitable search for new dimensions with which to replace them.

A great variety of traditions (or paths) can be found under the umbrella term 'Pagan'. Some Pagans are pantheistic and follow multiple gods and goddesses (such as the Roman or Greek pantheons); others follow their understanding of the single life force (consciousness) – Great Spirit; while others quest for a religious understanding of the Divine couple – the God and the Goddess. (Divinity manifests equally in male or female form, and masculine and feminine values and activities are of equal importance.) You'll often come across terms such as 'Druidism', 'Shamanism', 'witchCraft' and 'Wicca'. All are essentially ways of trying to connect with the Divine through Nature-oriented spirituality. Practice and worship occur on a solitary basis or in small informal groups or sometimes both.

Paganism does not seek to convert – either believers of other religions or those who do not follow any particular path – and it does not preach, evangelise or recruit in any way. Pagans practise tolerance and request tolerance in return.

Because Paganism is a religion that celebrates mystery, it stresses individual spiritual experience. The conscious mind, with all its structured thought, is allowed to give way to unconscious personal experience. Myth and allegory then cement these initiatory experiences.

But this is not to say that Paganism is completely esoteric. It is defined by a set of ethics, as is any religion that seeks self-actualisation. All Pagans are bound by something referred to as 'the law of three', which says that that which is sent out shall return to the sender three times. This is similar to the Hindu principle of karma, or the Christian sense of reaping what you sow. The modern revival of traditional witchCraft, known as Wicca, elaborates on this principle in the Wiccan Rede: 'An it harm none, do what ye will.'

DEFINITIONS

The terms 'Pagan', 'Wiccan' and 'witchCraft' will often be used interchangeably, so they require some defining. The popular meaning of the word 'Pagan' comes to us from the Latin 'Paganus', meaning 'country dweller' or one who lived in the lowlands or country. This was to distinguish them from those who lived in the highlands – the city dwellers. The country dwellers were the folk who worshipped the old gods, the gods of the 'pagus' (meaning 'locality').

In fact, this is where the difference between Art and Craft comes in (a debate still raging with artists today). The aristocratic city dwellers practised the 'sophisticated' arts; while the country dwellers practised the more simple folk magick, called craft.

When first used, the term 'country dweller' was not a negative term, and it was later adopted by the Romans to separate the urban and rural folk. The word 'heathen' was also not a negative term at first. It is derived from the Old English word 'heath' meaning 'uncultivated land', and means quite simply 'one who dwells in the heath or country'. So, originally, it had a very similar meaning to the word 'Pagan', designating someone of the heath who worshipped the gods of the land.

When Christianity shifted its focus and became more forceful about conversion, people living in the cities were far more accessible and therefore more likely to be converted than those in the outlying rural areas. From then on, the terms 'Pagan' and 'heathen' began to take on negative connotations, and became associated with simple-mindedness (akin to a 'country bumpkin' or 'hick'). Anyone who was not a Christian automatically received the title 'Pagan' or 'heathen', which meant, at that time, 'unbeliever'.

However, a Pagan is not, as most modern dictionaries will tell you, an unbeliever or a non-Christian. A Pagan is someone who believed or believes in the old gods predating Christianity.

To emphasise this fact, today we use the term 'Pagan' with capital letters when referring to those who follow the now-recognised religion of Paganism or neo-Paganism. Neo-Paganism, which is the more correct term, refers to the modern social and religious movement that is based on the reconstruction and adaptation of beliefs and practices of ancestral polytheistic and Nature-oriented religions – a movement that can be traced back to around the 1960s. However, for ease of reference, the term 'Paganism' is used in this book.

The word 'witch' is a complex term that has caused much controversy. Unsurprisingly, it has an interesting etymology.

The *Oxford English Dictionary* states that the root word 'wiccan' ('to practise witchCraft') is 'of obscure origin'. However, we can trace its origin back to the Anglo-Saxon word for 'wisdom'. 'Witan' means 'to see' and 'to know' and it would seem that 'Wicca' is a corruption of 'witga', commonly used as a short form of 'witega' – 'a prophet, seer, magician or sorcerer'.

The Old English 'wita' means 'counsellor', and 'wis' means 'wise'. 'Wicca' and 'wicce' are themselves Old English words for 'witch'. 'Wicca' was masculine; while 'wicce' was feminine. During medieval times these became 'wicche', both masculine and feminine, denoting both a witch and a wizard.

There is also the Welsh term 'gwyddon', which means 'wise one', 'witch' or 'wizard', and the Slavonic 'vjestica' and Russian 'viedma' – both meaning 'witch'. The Icelandic 'vitki' is a wizard, derived from 'vita', meaning 'to know'.

Still another Old English term 'wiccan' means 'to bend', and the German derivative is 'hekse', meaning 'fence-rider' and denoting one who rode between fences or the worlds.

But if we look back further, the root word behind all of these terms is the Indo-European 'wid' – 'to know', 'to be wise' – and also 'wat' – 'prophecy, inspiration, ecstasy'. There also seems to be a link to the Indo-European term 'weik' – meaning 'sorcery and religious matters'. From 'weik', theorists derive the Anglo-Saxon 'wicce/wicca' and 'wiccian' – 'to cast a spell' – as well as 'wicce-craft' – 'witchCraft' – and the Old High German 'wikkerei' or 'witchery'.

Today, 'Wicca' (with a capital W) has been adopted as an alternative and often preferred term for the religion of neo-Pagan witchCraft. Many witches prefer to call themselves Wiccan rather than witches and say that they practise Wicca rather than witchCraft, because the word does not carry the negative stereotypes attached to 'witch' and 'witchCraft'. Instead, 'Wicca' signifies an organised religion with a set of beliefs, tenets, laws, holy days and rituals. The modern Wiccan movement has no bearing on alleged practices in medieval witchCraft. However, a debate still ensues, with 'traditional' witches not wanting to associate with the term or concept of Wicca precisely because it has become an organised religion.

I often ask my students to think if they want to be witchy Wiccans or Wiccan witches. There is a generally accepted saying: 'I am a witch; Wicca is my religion'– although a witch who is not a Wiccan would not accept this.

There are definitely differences between witches and Wiccans. Wicca is a religion about fifty years old with claims that it has roots dating back to ancient times. Witches have probably existed since early Shamanic times. Wicca is a religion with a hierarchical system, complete with high priestesses and novices, degree systems and ritual. WitchCraft will have none of that. Most witches are solitary and abhor any type of structure or authority. They are extremely eclectic (i.e. their beliefs and practices derive from various sources), anarchic and creative. Mostly, they are what we would term 'kitchen witches' – working alone without fancy ritual garbs, fabulous altars or temple structures. Instead they make use of basic implements, herbs and books (perhaps handed down from family to family).

WitchCraft is difficult to define; Wicca is not. Wicca has been popularised by its founders going public, by the array of books to be found in all major bookstores, by the masses of Internet sites and by the public gatherings of Wiccan communities. Wiccans by nature are more social, more coven-oriented. Not all witches shy away from small covens, but they certainly shy away from large group gatherings.

Witches do not necessarily hold the same ethics as Wiccans, leaving them free to practise magick in a way that Wiccans cannot. In other words, a witch's magick can border freely on grey, and sometimes even black, because their interpretation of the law of three hinges on their individual understanding of 'karma'. The Wiccan ethic is extremely strict and very clear, leaving no loopholes for grey activities. Wicca's appeal is very broad, and, at a glance, it appears that it appeals to all generations. On the other hand, I would guess that witchCraft in South Africa is generally not practised by youngsters, simply because it is not easily available, unless it is hereditary.

The term 'Craft' is commonly used in opposition to 'Art'. They were originally words used by the aristocracy to distinguish their practice of the finer arts of mathematics, music, poetry, astronomy, etc. from the practice of craftwork, such as smithing. WitchCraft is seen as low magick because the country dwellers lived in the lowlands – the rural areas – while the aristocrats lived on the high lands – the fortresses on hills. Most Pagans in South Africa now use the word 'Craft' synonymously with 'witchCraft' and 'Wicca'.

PAGAN PATHS

Let's now look at some of the paths that fall under the umbrella term 'Paganism'.

Shamanism

Shamanism has been defined as the first religion of humankind. However, it was an extremely basic practice that probably constituted the roots of early magick rather than religion. Shamanic practices date back to Palaeolithic time (about 30 000 years ago). They were and are 'medicine people' who wrought magick and spoke to their ancestors and the Nature spirits.

Today, Shamanism is growing in popularity in Western culture, especially in North America where the Europeans are trying to reconnect with Nature through Native American practices. The word 'Shaman' is Russian and was originally a term applied to all ecstatic healers throughout the wider area of inner Asia and northern Siberia. It comes from the Siberian Tungus 'hamman', meaning 'one who is excited about' or 'raised'. Following this is the Manchu 'saman', which means the same. Both derive from the Pali 'saman', meaning an 'ecstatic philosopher or wanderer'.

Shamanism is still regarded as a 'method' or 'approach' rather than a religion. It is ecstatic in nature – as opposed to the austerity of Buddhism, for example. The Shaman is a type of priest, magician and medicine person, who suffers for the interests of the clan. It is very difficult to characterise and pinpoint specific characteristics of the Shaman.

A person cannot simply decide to be a Shaman, and neither can they decide to be 'initiated' as one. If you are 'called', you will usually be identified by your community. This usually happens with the recognition of some sort of mental illness, which is characterised by nervousness, anxiety, nausea, sensitivity, sweating or bleeding through the nostrils, convulsions and dreams that involve death and rebirth. There may also be bouts of violence followed by long periods of silence and reclusiveness.

There is frequently an initial resistance to the calling, but inevitably a Shaman has no choice but to yield to their destiny. The acceptance period is characterised by mystical experiences in which the individual gives up their personality to be 'born again' into another person. Then comes the initiation, which is an enactment of the special relationship that the Shaman has with the realm of spirits. Intuition is used rather than ritual, and solitude and suffering are the Shaman's constant companions. The Shaman must travel alone and is known as 'the wounded healer' because of their ability to relate to the suffering of others. Consciousness is reduced, and trance is achieved through breathing, chanting, singing and drumming. With experienced Shamans, certain herbal substances may be used. There is deliberate desensitisation to external and internal circumstances, and acute concentration skills are essential.

Shamans are Pagan in that their world view is deistic, pantheistic, animistic and polytheistic. They believe in the necessity of cosmic and environmental harmony (polarity) and see little distinction between the natural and supernatural spheres. Life is seen in circular dimensions.

In South Africa there are many would-be Shamans, but, of course, we have many true Shamans as well: our Sangomas. Of late there have been some visiting Shamans, from Peru and Brazil particularly, who have been initiating people into their Shamanic tradition. It is true to say that there are many people who live Shamanic lifestyles. They live fairly reclusively, usually on plots of land, following ancient native traditions. Their religious world views are Nature-oriented, with no great attachment to pantheons and formal ritual. Spontaneous ritual such as chanting, drumming and singing accompanies their movement into altered states of consciousness.

Druidism

The meaning of the word 'Druid' is elusive, but the closest interpretation is 'wise man of the oak'. Druids were originally an intellectual and religious cast among the tribal peoples of Pagan Europe; they were the custodians of the cultural and spiritual heritage in the centuries before the Common Era (BCE). Practising their rites in urban shrines and woodland groves, Druids hold the natural world as sacred, and honour, in particular, certain trees, plants, animals, streams, lakes and springs. Mistletoe is treated as sacred, because the berries are seen as semen with the seed not yet having touched the ground. Cutting the mistletoe at Yule enacts the moment of conception and incarnation.

Historians generally associate Druids with the Iron Age Celtic culture that spread out from central Europe between 800 and 200 BCE; yet the Celtic people of Gaul maintained that Druidism originated in Britain, and that Druids from continental Europe came to Britain to study. Archaeological evidence suggests that many aspects of Celtic ritual sites echo those of the Neolithic period, with similar bank and ditch enclosures, internal settings of posts and astronomical alignments.

Remnants of Druidic teachings surfaced in the Bardic colleges in Wales, Ireland and Scotland. These remained active until the seventeenth century in medieval manuscripts and in oral tradition, folklore and ritual.

Three traditional areas of Druidic practitioners are recognised. These are the Bard, the Ovate (Ofydd) and the Druid (Derwydd).

In the Story of Taliesin, the Bard receives three gifts from the Cauldron of Inspiration brewed by the Goddess Cerridwen: poetry, prophecy and shape-shifting. These gifts typify the roles of the Bard, the Ovate and the Druid respectively. Each area of study is a process of discovery and healing – for the individual, society and the land. Though aspects of work done in each area overlap, the journey through the Druidic tradition takes us through each of the three facets. Initiation into any of these areas is seen as an individual process, which must result from a personal spiritual quest. Tree lore or Ogham (much like the Kabbalah) is the essence of Druidism.

The Bard of old was an inspired poet, musician and storyteller, as well as a seer, diviner, dream-weaver and word-magician who sang the world alive, and who, through the exercise of skills, perpetually renewed the living spirits of the gods and heroes of their people. To become a Bard could take up to twelve years.

The Ovate combined the power of the word with Shamanic practice and travelled between the living world and the realms of the spirits of dead ancestors. Contact with the plant kingdom was vital in the quest to understand the mystery of death, life and transformation.

The Druid is the philosopher, adviser, teacher and judge.

Today, Druids are solar-oriented, while Wiccans focus on lunar movements. Druidism has also traditionally been male-dominated, focusing on logic and philosophy; whereas Wicca has been more female-oriented, focusing on the process of intuition.

To study to become a Druid takes many years. Students are carefully monitored by one of the few Druidic orders that exist, none of them in South Africa. However, there is one qualified Druid in South Africa who is currently teaching others wanting to follow this path.

The Norse traditions

These are also known as Odinism (after its chief god, Odin), the Northern tradition (as in Northern Europe) or Asatru (from words meaning 'a faith in the gods'). Our perception of the Norse Viking has been rather unfair. Images of rape, pillage and plunder spring to mind – especially the image of the horned helmet, which incidentally was used only in ritual. Remember, however, that history is always coloured by the politics of its writers.

In Norse mythology there are as many gods as there are goddesses. The divine feminine is equal to the divine masculine. The appeal, however, appears to be because its approach to life is very linear. Black is black and white is white; there is no grey. This is a warrior tradition, and as such is highly disciplined.

The deities are divided into the Vanir (or Nature Gods) and the Aesir (or Sky Gods). Central to the Northern tradition is the symbol of the tree of life called Yggdrasil. It has nine worlds: Midgard, Land of Ordinary Mortals; Asgard, Land of the Aesir; Hel, World of the Dead; Vanaheim, Home of the Vanir and Freya's Hall; the Land of Fire; the Land of the Light Elves; the Land of the Dark Elves; the Land of the Ice Giants; and the Land of Fog.

The runes are magical symbols that are used, much like the tarot, for divination. Odin underwent a Shamanic experience by hanging on Yggdrasil for nine days to learn the secret of the runes.

The Asatru celebrate the seasonal festivals as well as the full moons. In Iceland Asatru is one of the two official religions, alongside Christianity. However, there do not seem to be many people who follow this path in South Africa. Unfortunately, as in Europe, there is a link between Odinism and neo-Nazism, due to the perversion of Norse myth and magick by Hitler's SS. Perhaps this is why we do not hear from these people publicly.

Eclectic Paganism

This is a form of Paganism that borrows imagery, ritual and meaning from a number of different Pagan traditions. Unlike Druidism, for example, it does not follow one particular path. You may find an individual calling him- or herself a Pagan, and having strong leanings towards Shamanic methods while simultaneously interpreting the universe in terms of the Wiccan approach.

Eclectic Paganism is probably a more accurate representation of the Pagan experience in South Africa. Today, it is becoming a respected pathway, but it still has a long way to go in proving its legitimacy to Druidism, for example, which can claim a revival from at least 300 years ago.

Goddess spirituality

Goddess spirituality has grown naturally from the feminist, neo-Pagan and New Age movements. 'Goddess spirituality' and 'the Earth Mother' are terms familiar to most people who are in any way inclined towards New Age ethics or involved with popular esoterica. But they are certainly not just terms or concepts to those women actively involved in reclaiming their womanhood.

The term 'Goddess' is generally used to describe the 'Feminine Divine' and it is this Feminine Divine that is at the root of the rediscovery of the link between the spirituality of women, women in general and the Earth (Nature).

Women involved in Goddess spirituality are coming to terms with their own feminine divinity. They are throwing off their second-class status, questioning the patriarchal aspects of their religious beliefs and realising their power as women.

Because of this, many feminist covens are emerging. A number of these feminist witches reject certain Craft tenets, such as lineage, initiation and structured ritual. Instead, they focus on gender issues. Patriarchy is vehemently rejected, and blamed for the dualism present in Western thinking as well as the split between body and mind. Goddess spirituality seeks to reintegrate the two. So, its approach is philosophical or psychological rather than religious.

Often, as a reaction to patriarchy, there are a large number of lesbian followers as well as asexual or celibate women. Because of this, Goddess worshippers are often accused of 'hating' men. However, the public needs to realise that this stigma often has to do with individual adherents' personal issues and not with the movement itself. At the same time, women involved in the movement need to understand that the fight against patriarchy doesn't imply that all men are the enemy.

When we speak of Goddess spirituality we do so within a Western context. Hindu, Chinese and Balinese goddesses are all venerated but are placed in a

Western dimension. It is not a single cohesive movement, but a movement based on Goddess-oriented spiritual practice.

The word 'goddess', in contrast to the word 'god', has suffered a systematic breakdown at the hands of Western patriarchal society. Even today, many so-called 'Goddess worshippers' are unaware that all the different deities and pantheons (i.e. systems of gods and goddesses such as the Roman or Greek) evolved from a victorious overthrow of the One Great Mother principle. Her degeneration and depletion into a plethora of goddess deities, all representing some archetypal function of the Great Mother, did not have the same intent as the many male gods or deities by which we are now also surrounded. The gods, especially their names, were and still are used as secretive communication for the one true God, the omniscient, almighty, omnipotent God the Father.

This spirituality actually goes back to the Pagan religions of prehistoric times, when goddesses were worshipped. Patriarchy didn't exist, and people lived in peace. There is a great deal of evidence that marks female figurines as sacred to these communities, and attempts to tout Palaeolithic female figurines as toys or pornographic 'dolls' are a product of the patriarchal approach to history.

The many goddess deities and all their virtues can be traced back and related to a single nurturing Earth Mother. The image of the wild, untamed and unnatural woman is an invention in direct contradiction to the laws of Nature, which are nurturing, fair, creative, sustaining and destructive, all at the same time. Research also indicates that this Goddess figure is usually more powerful than any god. Because She was life-giver, Mother, sustainer, etc., the gods were prone to succeed if they heeded Her wisdom and adopted Her powers.

There are no doctrines in Goddess spirituality. It is eclectic and loosely structured. Women are honoured as priestesses, and healing, especially self-healing, is encouraged. Groups and their rituals often develop spontaneously. Self-discovery is encouraged, and the inherent powers of the feminine are explored. Rites of passage for menstruation, childbirth, menopause, etc. are held, and celebrations of cycles and seasons are honoured.

Male mysteries

The term 'male mysteries' is commonly used to refer to practices that have become popular with modern male Pagans seeking to explore their own sacred manhood. Some say that the 'male mysteries' are a reaction to feminine spiritual movements.

To be male, other than in the traditional sense that masculinity has allowed, is a challenge to the Pagan man. Naturally, patriarchy has made many men feel alienated and rootless, and in dire need of reconnection with their own true power – 'it's-okay- to-cry' power, as opposed to the warrior status imposed by patriarchy.

Men who subscribe to the 'male mysteries' are starting to acknowledge their feminine side and are becoming more nurturing and gentle. A new masculine identity is emerging as the Goddess concept overthrows primal masculinity and its destructive ways. Many 'male mystery' adherents are learning new ways of relating to each other, to women and to the world. They also seek to transcend the dualism of mind and body and spirit and world; rid themselves of homophobia; redefine their sexuality, particularly the relation between power and sex; review the dangers of patriarchy; and assimilate myth and archetype into their religious beliefs.

Most Pagan men are quite sensitive to feminine dynamics. Since the priestess generally takes on a more assertive role, there is wholesome respect for the role of women in this spirituality. The position of the Goddess is highly respected and is visibly seen in the daily lives of Pagan men in one way or another as they attempt to manifest this spirituality. However, there is a reaction against total emphasis on the Goddess, and deeper exploration of God archetypes is encouraged.

Wicca

Wicca is probably the most popular of all Pagan traditions, especially in South Africa. It is certainly the most modern. However, most modern Wiccans claim to belong to traditions that go back many centuries, right back to the ancient Shamanic period in fact. Of course, the distinctions seem to blur when we use the word 'witch' and 'Wiccan' synonymously.

But Wicca itself emerged as a religion and system after the last laws against witchCraft were repealed in Britain in 1951 with the publication of two books by the retired colonial civil servant Gerald Gardner – *Witchcraft Today* (1954) and *The Meaning of Witchcraft* (1959).

As is the case with other religious paths, as Wicca became more and more popular, so it diversified. Here is a brief outline of some of the most widely known traditions.

The Gardnerian tradition

Gerald Gardner was a Freemason who claimed to have been initiated into a coven by a priestess known as 'Old Dorothy' (Dorothy Clutterbuck). The New Forest Coven claimed to have origins dating back to prehistory. That the coven operated and that Dorothy Clutterbuck existed are not in dispute. What is in dispute is whether Gardner founded Wicca or simply publicised an existing tradition. Academics tend to consider Gardner as the founder of Wicca, dismissing the New Forest Coven's claims to prehistoric roots.

Whatever the case may be, Gerald Gardner's rituals soon found their way into print. With these, and with the publication of his two books, covens all around England began to get in touch with him. His rituals were written with the aid of magician Aleister Crowley. However, his high priestess Dorianne Valiante objected to the Crowlean flavour of the rituals and rewrote most of them. Much of Gardner's material has been published in Janet and Stewart Farrar's *Eight Sabbats for Witches* and *The Witch's Way*.

Gardner was a nudist, so his coven practised skyclad (naked). He was also asthmatic and raised energy by scourging. Because of this, Wicca has picked up some rather negative connotations. The scourging has commonly been misinterpreted as some sort of 'S & M' practice. Naturally, new initiates have followed suit, some with great excitement, but Gardner never meant for his version of Wicca to be taken so literally by everybody.

The Gardnerian tradition places emphasis on the Goddess, and having an equal number of males and females present is encouraged. It does not allow for self-initiation and has a hierarchical system of advancement.

Today many groups call themselves 'Gardnerian', but their Book of Shadows (i.e. their book of spells and rituals) bears little resemblance to Gardner's original.

The Alexandrian tradition

The Alexandrian tradition started shortly afterwards. Alex Sanders sought initiation into the Gardnerian tradition but was turned down. It appears that he invented his initiation by his grandmother mentor, claiming a family lineage and copying from Gardner's Book of Shadows. Sanders was very media-oriented and chose the very beautiful Maxine Morris as his wife and high priestess. Together they initiated many people, the most famous being Janet and Stewart Farrar, who later formed their own coven.

Alexandrian and Gardnerian Wicca are very similar, the main difference being that, since he was a ceremonial magician, Sanders's form of Wicca had a more formal outlook, while the Gardnerian version was more folklore-oriented. It is probably true to say that their rituals are interchangeable.

The Seax tradition

From these two systems the tradition of Wicca spread, and soon the Seax tradition of Raymond Buckland found its way to the USA in 1973.

Seax-Wicca was founded by Raymond Buckland in the 1960s, and although it has a Saxon basis, it is a new denomination of Wicca in that it does not wholly continue or recreate the original Saxon version.

Buckland left the Gardnerian tradition after more than ten years of activity in order to found and promote the Saxon tradition. His new tradition is very carefully constructed as an answer to the corruption that seemed prevalent in some sectors within Wicca at the time, especially the Gardnerian tradition.

Raymond Buckland's *Complete Book of Witchcraft* gives the basics of the traditions.

Seax-Wicca's main features are:
- open rituals;
- democratic organisation (to prevent 'ego trips' and 'power plays' by coven leaders);
- coven and solitary practice;
- self-initiation instead of coven initiation, if desired;
- covens led by a priest or priestess; and
- covens deciding for themselves whether to work skyclad (naked) or robed.

Seax-Wicca can be found throughout the United States and in some other countries in the world (including South Africa and the United Kingdom).

Eclectic Wicca

The *Oxford English Dictionary* defines 'eclectic' as 'deriving ideas or style from a broad and diverse range of sources'. An Eclectic Wiccan is a type of 'modern' witch who has realised that belonging to a 'tradition' is not essential. What is important is a proper connection between the witch and the God/Goddess in the witch's subconscious.

Eclectic Wiccans are mostly individuals who have studied most of the Wiccan traditions available, and have come away with the aspects they find best suited to them. Being eclectic is stylising Wicca to complement the individual. It is Wicca freed from its traditional cage – a path suited to solitary individuals who are not averse to sharing knowledge and experiences with others. Though most eclectics prefer to work alone, groups often prove to be very creative and interesting.

A lot can be said about Eclectic Wicca, but two things are essential: the first is that Eclectic Wicca cannot truly be defined; the second is that its practitioners all agree with the Wiccan Rede: 'An it harm none, do what ye will.'

Dianic Wicca

This is not an all-female Wiccan tradition as is commonly assumed. It is also not lesbian-oriented, although there are many lesbian practitioners. There can be both male and female practitioners; however, in certain streams men are excluded. Feminine leadership is encouraged and a priestess should be present to lead ritual.

The Dianic tradition can be seen as a healing path for victims of male abuse. Although there might be a strong sense of militancy, most of the personal rage is attributed to the practitioners' personal experiences and relationships; it is not an inherent feature of the tradition itself.

The Goddess is seen almost monotheistically, but in her triple aspect as Maiden, Mother and Crone. The God takes his place beside the Mother aspect of the Goddess.

In most of the all-female circles, male deities are not invoked. Gender polarity is not seen as the answer to all things. Asexuality and hermaphroditic qualities are seen in the same light as polarity. To Dianic Wiccans, priests are seen as an interference – like the intervention of a priest between Christ and his flock.

Dianic Wicca draws on the classical concept of Diana – the independent Maiden huntress, linked to no man. This principle of belonging to no man is the essence of the tradition, even if some practitioners are married. Instead, relationships are based on love and choice.

There are no known public groups of Dianics in South Africa. There are, however, a few practising individuals who have militant feminist views.

Hereditary witchCraft

Also known as traditional witchCraft, as mentioned earlier, this is Craft knowledge and law – the old religion and the old ways that have survived Christianisation – passed down from generation to generation. Hereditary witchCraft has nothing to do with Wicca and is wrapped up in the definition of witchCraft given earlier: it has probably existed since early Shamanic times. Its practitioners are solitary, anarchic and eclectic, practising practical magick with basic implements. Most importantly, they are not ethically bound by the 'law of three' or the Wiccan Rede.

Like Shamanism, traditional witchCraft is not necessarily a religion. It can be practised as an Art or as a Craft. In fact, some practitioners even claim to be

Christians. Secrets, rituals, spells and knowledge handed down from previous generations are the domain of the hereditary witch – unlike the Wiccan, who finds these on the Internet or in bookshops.

A small number of hereditary witches are starting to come to the fore in South Africa. (See Nissa's story in Chapter 8.)

PAGANISM AND THE NEW AGE MOVEMENT

Pagans detest being associated with the New Age movement. The latter's obsession with 'the light' makes the average Pagan reach for their sunglasses. Pagans have long understood the need to be careful of the light, for it might blind them. Since Pagans subscribe to polarity, the 'dark' is venerated equally. What makes Paganism different is the profound understanding that life is enshrined in death, that there is no light without darkness, and that too much love and light cheat one out of one's full experience.

Paganism is practised across the board by old and young, poor and rich, the philosophically adept and the philosophically poor. The New Age movement has a particular profile – middle class and up, people who have the luxury of debating whether their spirit guide is channelling Bruce Lee or Joan of Arc. Endless series of regression serve no purpose for people who are practical and entrenched in the Now. Pagans must feel the earth and get their hands dirty, and they seek solace in that which is obvious – such as the sun on your body and the rain on your face. There are no places for gurus, which the New Age movement is spewing out.

Typically, New Age spirituality is linked to health and financial success. Healing is a lucrative business. Sickness and poverty are seen to be the result of an inability to be positive or somehow being on the wrong spiritual path. Pagans do not see illness or poverty as signs that they have gone wrong. Once all avenues have been exhausted in terms of changing them, such conditions are creatively fused with the living process.

Margot Adler, a respected Pagan author and academic, has pointed out that one of the most fundamental differences between New Agers and Pagans is a decimal point. A New Age teacher would charge R3 000 for a course on, say, basic meditation, while a Pagan would charge R300.

New Agers seem to enjoy creating an air of mystery and otherworldliness. Certainly both groups harness supernatural creatures like elves and faeries, but in a New Age context faeries are pretty little things that tap you on the head with little silver wands. Within Paganism faeries might be that too, but they are also tricksters who wreak havoc through their mischief.

There is a tendency among New Agers to shy away from anything sexual and sensual, linking a vague asceticism with greater spirituality. Pagans interact with the world around them quite sensuously.

Certainly there are a number of similarities between the two movements. Both are Western phenomena, and both are represented almost exclusively by the white population. But Paganism has a legacy; the New Age movement is creating it.

CHAPTER 2

PAGANISM IN SOUTH AFRICA

Most South African folk brave enough to call themselves 'Pagan' have reached this position through reading. It is therefore no mystery that so many South African Pagans have romantic aspirations to Celtic forms of Paganism or, sometimes, North American Shamanism. As children of a mixed South African soil, our naivety compels us to search for our 'roots' in foreign traditions, but South African Paganism must guard against being colonised by European forms, and, equally, not wanting to be colonised.

That Pagan practices in South Africa are not as defined as they are in the United Kingdom or the United States is of no great concern. A unique Pagan strand is evolving, and, though it is eclectic in nature, South African Paganism is beginning to articulate a precise form, not through creeds, councils or apologetics, but from a profoundly experiential South African consciousness. A new South African Pagan lineage is being born.

As with Paganism worldwide, it is a religion from the heart, born out of a sense of self-worth and individual spiritual identity connecting with the life force that Nature has to offer.

Paganism is therefore a subjective philosophy and religion. But this doesn't mean that certain principles of objectivity are not employed in its reasoning system. Subjectivity doesn't necessarily imply anti-reason, but is in fact reason from the heart. Pagan truth is simple. It comes from within – from the general to the particular, from the objective to the subjective, from the abstract to the concrete.

It's a shift from detached observation to involvement, from reaction to pro-action. This consciousness becomes a liberating experience.

But as with all religions, Pagan spirituality also begins with the actual joys and struggles of individuals within communities. In South Africa, the situation is still complex and we cannot talk about Paganism without referring to the racial divides of our past. Our world views are clouded by our political history. We live in a country that has undergone massive psychological and spiritual transitions, and because of this, it is impossible to separate any discussion of religion, and Paganism in particular, from these circumstances.

Our Paganism does not fall under any other country's interpretation of Paganism, and no true Pagan identity can be founded solely on either a white (Celtic) or black (traditional) religious perspective. South African Paganism must find a new spiritual path, one that does not organise cultures hierarchically.

A major difference between South African Paganism and Paganism elsewhere in the world is that South African Paganism draws on traditional African healing and divination methods. (A similar situation exists in North America, where many whites are trying to find their 'roots' through interaction with Native Americans.)

White South Africans who take on this powerful aspect of Paganism do so only with full permission of the tribal leaders and elders involved in this process. Permission to enter the practice of South African Shamanism is in fact determined by the 'call of the Ancestors'. Full empowerment and healing teachings are shared, and once a person is accepted, talk moves beyond black or white. This is truly a sign of a common consciousness and the healing powers of reconciliation. The similarities between traditional African beliefs and neo-Paganism will be dealt with in the next chapter.

The origins of neo-Paganism are obscure in this country. No individual can lay claim to its formation. That certain pioneering individuals have led the way, however, is certainly true. This is testimony to their conviction, courage and deep desire to explore individual religious freedom and mutual consciousness within the new post-apartheid South Africa.

While Pagan South Africans acknowledge the global influences of millennium mania, it is the dissolution of the apartheid system and the resultant crumbling of all other barriers that is the main reason for the revival of Paganism in this country.

This is the primary impetus for a new South African consciousness, the setting for a new interpretation of post-apartheid spirituality. Comprehension, analysis and judgement arise out of individual and community experiences. When people begin to understand their own situation, they start to ask questions. The situation in which South Africans now find themselves profoundly influences their desire for a more adequate 'communion' with the concept of God.

The recent 'war' where white sons, husbands and brothers were forced into conscription, in the name of a god they hardly knew or did not care to know, was utterly incomprehensible. It was a war fought for white male supremacy, a war where all black South Africans were denounced as enemies by the government. These black South Africans now govern the country, and their situation is equally bizarre. Their only connection to whites was in the form of *'baasskap'* (white male supremacy), and many now find themselves in positions of equality or perhaps even seniority. For the average South African our history is absurd.

Absurdity here does not mean that God does not exist at all, but that the previous male, white-dominated concept of God is no longer applicable. His values and norms are unacceptable and cannot be appreciated. The resulting anxiety is leading many South Africans to seek some sort of reassurance that life still makes sense and is worth living.

However, this sense of absurdity, abandonment and even alienation is being overcome by a growing sense of community, as people who experience the same angst come together to create transformation. Experience is of paramount importance. South Africans are deliberately leaving their metaphysical systems of thought and moving beyond this sense of absurdity into a religious framework that satisfies their spiritual needs.

It is ironic that, despite the feelings of abandonment that many white South Africans may experience as the once-dominant religion crumbles before their eyes, the emerging Paganism allows them to reclaim their heritage amid this crisis: the heritage of the Ancestors (black/traditional) and the heritage of the Old Ancient Ones (white/European).

As a religion, Paganism has come home, and is beginning to reclaim the heritage of its ancestors. Pagans don't regard themselves as part of the 'New Age' movement, which is a relatively new spiritual development. They see themselves as returning to the roots of ancient Palaeolithic Shamanic times. Still, they understand that this is in a modern context, hence the term neo-Paganism.

Interestingly enough, the reclamation of an ancient Pagan heritage is severely criticised by radical black Christians, who are extremely uncomfortable when asked about their gods before they were colonised by white missionaries. The backlash against Paganism going public came from this source and not from conservative, white, middle-class South Africans, as was expected. One wonders what it is that these radical black Christians feel they may lose by abandoning the new religion and reconnecting with their old ancestral beliefs and traditions.

Paganism is a religion that has survived violent odds. It is a religion that has come out in defiance against a mainstream Christianity, which until recently dominated all religious frameworks. Its dogmatic world view still pervades South African culture.

The new spiritual consciousness can be seen most clearly in the still-Christian-bound Afrikaner youth, secretly wanting information on Paganism, and rising against their patriarchal heritage and risking their comfort zones in the process.

Paganism is emerging against the backdrop of radical black Christians (uncomfortable with our challenge to revisit their earlier religions) and the backdrop of the now-crumbling Church (which until recently enjoyed state protection).

Many black South Africans have been able to integrate these two religious world views with ease. This can be seen in the militant cry of the black consciousness movement, whose theological framework calls for a 'return to roots', for an integration of African traditional religions and Christianity. While the white-dominated churches once tried to quell this crossover, they are now bending over backwards to accommodate it, because of dwindling numbers.

Against all of these backdrops, a Pagan pride is emerging, and this new consciousness is manifest in a people who no longer care if they are misunderstood by other religions or the public at large – a people who acknowledge that they have a rightful place within the South African religious infrastructure. Its adherents are called 'Satanists', 'eccentrics' and all other manner of derogatory terms. This new (and old) religion is about a choice to self-elect, to name oneself, to arrive at a deep consciousness of the self.

Within a complex and rapidly changing South Africa and within a spiritually impoverished morass, Paganism is presenting itself as a viable and legitimate religious option.

Pagan bodies in South Africa

In the early days, there were covens operating, but in great secret. Most still operate in secret today. However, they are starting to expose themselves more and more, as each member becomes more comfortable with the status of being a Pagan, Wiccan or witch in a changing South Africa. Because of secrecy and fear of discrimination, it is impossible to estimate the number of practising Pagans or covens. But in her book *Worldviews in Transition*, Chrissie Steyn points out that the neo-Pagan movement is comparable in size to the New Age movement in the United States. It is rumoured that Wicca is the fastest-growing religion in the US, and this may also be the case in South Africa.

Ten years ago, I personally knew of only one coven that had been together for a number of years. It was known as a training coven because Craft training was its emphasis. It was Gardnerian in lineage, claiming this from a mother coven in Scotland. Their high priestess had been initiated over there and returned to initiate the high priest. It was difficult to ascertain the validity of these claims because they were very secretive about their history.

There is no doubt that before the Pagan movement became public there were other covens and solitaries operating, but what their tradition was we will never know. Certainly to a large extent eclectic, but a small proportion was Gardnerian in influence. It seems that a few individuals travelled to England and Scotland (and vice versa), received initiation and began teaching in covens in South Africa under highly clandestine conditions. This tradition still remains quite closed to the broader Pagan movements, and in the early days they made things quite difficult for the spontaneous eclecticism that would eventually shape South Africa's Paganism.

The Pagan Federation of South Africa

A watershed event took place in 1994 when a group of individuals got together and proposed the formation of an organisation for Pagans. Initially, the small group was truly concerned that there were no real Pagans out there except themselves, arrogant as that might seem. They eventually realised that if they were Pagan there must be others, and so they forged ahead with a national questionnaire that was sent to a few hundred people identified as possible Pagans.

A 27 per cent response indicated interest. All those who responded were interviewed in Johannesburg, Durban and Cape Town. I remember fearing that I had completely lost my mind in this venture, and that all sorts of sinister and weird individuals would be waiting for me. But everyone seemed to have all their brain cells intact and without exception endorsed the formation of an organisation for Pagans.

Thus began a two-year process. Was it to be a federation, an organisation or an association? How would we define Paganism, and should there be a constitution? Workshops were held in all the major centres, and a constitution emerged with the help of a dedicated team of lawyers. Individuals, although settled in their ways, were able to associate with each other because they all accepted the concept of the Divine in Nature. On the whole, they were simply people who cherished the Earth, and saw in her the concept of Mother, provider, sustainer and nurturer. They saw their own lives and those of their families reflected in this notion.

After two years, the constitution was completed and the first group of Pagans gathered officially in Cape Town for the Winter solstice of June 1996 to form the Pagan Federation of South Africa (PFSA).

The following seven principles were agreed upon, after taking into consideration the principles of the Pagan Federation in the United Kingdom, those of the Pagan Spiritual Alliance, Circle Sanctuary, the Secret Grove and others:

- A Pagan relates to the Earth as Mother, and in so doing celebrates the seasons and the cycles of the planet.
- A Pagan strives to take from the Earth only according to need and to replenish the Earth in kind.
- Pagans recognise that human intelligence requires a unique responsibility towards the environment.
- A Pagan seeks to live in harmony with the Earth and the Universe.
- A Pagan abhors the malicious and wilful destruction of life and Nature.
- A Pagan reveres the balance between the Divine Masculine and the Divine Feminine principles in Nature.
- A Pagan acknowledges all forms of spirituality and respects an individual's right to follow their own spiritual path. Paganism is a path of tolerance.

The PFSA encourages its members to network and form working circles and covens and has undoubtedly been the spearhead in achieving positive public awareness for Paganism in South Africa. It has achieved a great deal since its formation, paving the road for the modern Pagan movement in South Africa and dispelling the myths that surround Paganism.

The organisation currently publishes (although on an irregular basis) the only printed Pagan magazine, *Pagan Africa*, which is on a par with international magazines, such as the *Green Egg*, and is sold in certain leading bookshops. (To a certain extent, this magazine holds the archives of much of the Pagan activity in South Africa.)

The PFSA has bridged the gap with the Occult Unit of the South African Police. When the twenty-one signatories met at the Winter solstice to form the PFSA, one of the first mandates given to the new president was to establish a relationship with the head of the Occult Unit. Up until then, this unit had often mistaken Paganism for Satanism, especially its ritual content, because Satanism employed so much Pagan ritual in its ceremonies. In an initial groundbreaking meeting, a firm understanding was established, and since then both parties have been mutually co-operative. There have also been no negative relationships with the media, thus fostering positive media awareness.

There has been a positive response from the law commission's report and the press to the organisation's application for marriage officers.

The organisation has had a lot to do with the fact that most universities are now studying Paganism in their religious studies programmes. A number of university students have also written theses on Paganism, using the PFSA as their main source of information, and books on Paganism are now readily available in standard bookshops.

Relationships have been forged with some of the most powerful Pagan bodies overseas (e.g. the Pagan Federation of the United Kingdom and the Covenant of the Goddess). Also, a number of interfaith relations have been forged, and the PFSA participated in the World Parliament of Religions.

Several cases of discrimination against Pagans, mostly work-related, have been dealt with legally before there was any unnecessary negative exposure of either party. Certain employers have even offered their Pagan employees time off for their 'holidays'.

Prison work has been officially recognised, and Pagan leaders are allowed to act as spiritual advisers to Pagan prisoners in need of guidance.

The PFSA now takes its place alongside other creative organisations. In many respects, its original aims have been fulfilled, and it may be time for the organisation to reinvent itself, review its 'old-school' approach and regain its popular appeal, or it may well become the archive of South African Paganism.

Naturally, there have been breakaway groups; the irony being that Pagans claim to be anarchic in nature, but are very desirous of leadership, especially when first starting out. As someone wise once said: 'Getting Pagans together is like herding cats.' Such breakaway groups reflect the natural process of growth and new leadership. Since the PFSA was the only credible public Pagan body at the outset, it was the Pagan watering hole. Only too soon, inspired leaders with their individual visions, goals and aspirations found their own place in the sun, quickly understanding that there was enough work for the Goddess to go around.

What follows is a brief explanation of some of the larger, credible Pagan bodies, covens and organisations currently in operation:

The Aquarian Tabernacle Church

The Aquarian Tabernacle Church (ATC) is a Wiccan church that was founded in the Seattle area in 1979 by Pete Pathfinder Davis, and has now blossomed beyond the USA into Canada, Australia and other nations, with over thirty legally recognised congregations worldwide.

The Tabernacle ordains embody the moral and ethical system, which guides its members in their mission. They are adapted from the traditional Craft ordains, various versions of which have been handed down over the centuries. The tradition is based on English traditional Wicca.

Their goal is to practise a modern Pagan life, in the knowledge that every spiritual tradition, old and new, has lessons to offer. They teach the great principles of successful living that have been discovered and rediscovered by every religion, seeking to assimilate those truths into daily life.

The belief is that the God and Goddess are good, and that all people are fundamentally good. The spark of the Divine dwells deep within each human being. Human lives are blessed and transformed to the degree that the old gods are honoured. As one becomes aware of this in daily living and opens oneself to this Divine presence within, one's life becomes richer and more rewarding.

The God and Goddess are not sought out of a sense of guilt or obligation, but rather out of a love and respect for them and their creation.

The Aquarian Tabernacle Wiccan tradition is open and welcoming to everybody, regardless of tradition, respecting the many diverse Pagan paths popularly followed today. Membership is offered on many levels of participation, from casual attendance to formal study with a goal of ordination to the clergy. The ATC does not actively seek converts; they help those seekers who come to them.

The ATC was the first church to be established in the Pagan world, and naturally it has received a deluge of criticism from Pagans who feared that it may be hiding under Christian terminology. This argument needs to be broadened to take account of the civil society in which we live. The word 'Church' itself gives Pagans the same legal protection as mainstream religion in a free society. We must learn to use the system to our benefit.

In the United States, the church is a recognised, tax-exempt, non-profit religious church corporation that exists legally with the knowledge and blessing of the state and federal governments. They have given the ATC the power to charter other congregations and grant this recognition to them, too. Clergy are recognised and have the power to sanctify marriages. The church status and the Marriage Act are both under review in South Africa.

The ATC is represented in Johannesburg, Cape Town and Durban and is co-ordinated by its Archpriestess, the Rt. Rev. Donna darkwolf Vos.

The Correllian Nativist Tradition

The Correllian Nativist Tradition is based on the teachings of members of the High-Correll family. Though founder Orpheis Caroline High Correll called the

Tradition 'Nativist', in 1992 this was replaced by the term 'Correllian Nativist' or, as we now more commonly call it, 'Correllian'.

Lady Orpheis's Tradition was highly political, emphasising the need for the world's 'Native' or Pagan religions to unite against the colonising power of Christianity. It was also a deeply eclectic form of Pagan universalism, merging a number of different practices. Correllian Nativism claims to be a branch of what would later be called 'Wicca' on account of Lady Orpheis's claimed Scottish traditional lineage, and also because of her Aradian lineage, which she acquired in 1904 through Lydia Beckett (a student of Charles Leland). However, the Tradition's Wiccan status remains a matter of debate.

The leaders of the Tradition declared it open to the public and inaugurated a series of outreach programmes. Correspondence lessons in Correllian Wicca were also started.

A strong emphasis is put on the philosophical aspects of Wicca, and on its spirituality and inner mysteries. There is powerful commitment to increased communication and co-operation between Pagans everywhere, from all traditions.

The Correllian Tradition emphasises the need for a strong public presence and accessible public ritual and stresses the importance of Pagan clergy.

In South Africa the Correllian Tradition is co-ordinated by the Rev. Carol Nowlan (Epona Moondancer). It offers a degree system for clergy and has representatives in Johannesburg and Cape Town.

The Fellowship of Isis

The Fellowship of Isis was founded in Ireland in 1976 by Lady Olivia Robertson and Laurence and Pamela Durdin-Robertson. 'Love, Beauty and Truth' is the organisation's motto, and it honours the Goddess in all her aspects, especially as Divine Mother. However, the Gods are also recognised, and both priests and priestesses are permitted to serve.

The Fellowship of Isis was instrumental in getting Goddess religion recognised as a world faith at the Parliament of World Religion in 1993.

Membership is free, and is open to all types of religious persuasions. It is organised on a democratic basis. All members have rights, whether as single members or as part of an iseum (temple) or a lyceum (college). No vows are required, and there is no commitment to secrecy.

Sacrifice, whether actual or symbolic, is discouraged. Nature is venerated and asceticism is frowned on.

The Fellowship of Isis is active in South Africa, with a number of individual members, small iseums and lyceums. A strong iseum, the Iseum of the Rainbow

Lotus, is currently co-ordinated by Carol Nowlan (Epona Moondancer), although all iseums and lyceums are autonomous.

C.O.R.D.

C.O.R.D. is an abbreviation of a name known only to the coven. Established in 1997, this is an eclectic, extremely active and often militant coven when it comes to Craft matters. Rumours abound that they have hived off several covens in the past three years. They are a dedicated group with strong bonds and loyalties to the founder members. Based in Johannesburg, their motto is 'networking the Pagan Community'. They are intent on networking the entire Pagan community and getting them all working together for the greater good of Paganism in South Africa. Their leadership, energy and endless enthusiasm, consistency and dedication have paid off. They are well known in the Johannesburg area, and their functions are well attended. Their newsletter coincides with the Sabbats and is mailed to many interested parties.

The Celestine Circle of the Waxing Moon Coven

This coven, also based in Johannesburg, was established two years ago. A group of students on a Wicca course grew so close that they refused to part, and so a coven was born. Two natural female leaders emerged and a system followed whereby the role of high priestess rotates for three months at a time. It has worked perfectly. On the next page is a copy of the coven's constitution for interest's sake.

The coven meet weekly and for every Sabbat. In the past six months they have opened their Sabbats up to a selected public (holding their own privately).

Stara teaches Wicca classes, and other members teach aspects of Wicca such as herb lore and magick.

CELESTINE CIRCLE OF THE WAXING MOON COVEN
CONSTITUTION

1. **Name**
   1.1 The name of the Coven is the Celestine Circle of the Waxing Moon.
   1.2 The name of the Coven may be changed only through a consensus vote of all current members.

2. **Members**
   2.1 The members at this time are:
   - Stara
   - Ruby Flame
   - Dark Juniper
   - Journey
   - Silver Birch
   - Black Eagle
   - Moon Lion
   - StarLight
   - darkwolf (Coven Mother)

   2.2 It is accepted that Gimel is an 'honourary' member, with voting status, should she be present in the circle, without voting status should she not be present in the Circle, and is always welcome in the Circle.
   2.3 Members are expected to attend 3 out of 4 Coven Meets.
   2.4 Absence without communication to the High Priestess or other members is considered as a lack of interest.
   2.5 Members who are absent from 3 out of 4 consecutive Coven Meets automatically lose their membership of the Coven.
   2.6 Members are expected to contribute, where possible, to the administration and functions of the Coven.
   2.7 A new member may be accepted into the Celestine Circle of the Waxing Moon after being interviewed by at least 80% of the Coven members; the High Priestess/Acting High Priestess and Acting High Priest must be present at the interview and in favour of the new member.
   2.8 The Coven Mother must be in favour of the new member, although she does not have to be present during the interview process.

3. **The High Priestess**
   3.1 The role of High Priestess is held on a temporary basis for a period of 3 months. The current High Priestess is Stara.
   3.2 A new Acting High Priestess will be appointed as per a consensus decision.

- 3.3 A permanent High Priestess will be appointed as per a consensus decision.
- 3.4 The functions of the High Priestess are the administration of Coven Meets, Coven activities, Coven finances, facilitation of magickal workings and communication with Coven members about Coven activities.
- 3.5 It is also the function of the High Priestess to facilitate the resolution of any conflict or potential conflict between Coven Members.
- 3.6 Should the High Priestess not be able to resolve the conflict successfully, the next chain of communication is the High Priest, thereafter darkwolf.

4. The High Priest
- 4.1 The High Priest is currently Fiery Oak, appointed on a permanent basis.
- 4.2 Should Fiery Oak no longer be able to perform his duties, and another High Priest be chosen, this may be on a temporary or permanent basis, as per Coven consensus.
- 4.3 The Coven may operate without a High Priest, should the Coven Mother and High Priestess be in agreement with this.

5. Coven ethics
- 5.1 The Coven upholds the principle of 'An it harm none, do what ye will' in all workings, activities and decisions.
- 5.2 The Coven always behaves in a way that shows respect for the Goddess.
- 5.3 The Coven endorses the code described in the 'Basic principles of Wicca' compiled by the American Coven of Witches.
- 5.4 The Coven rejects the performance of 'Black Magick', Satanism and sacrifice.

6. Function
- 6.1 The function of the Coven is the collective energy used for magickal workings to attain self-mastery, to improve ourselves and the Universe, for the good of all and to the harm of none, while revering the God and the Goddess.
- 6.2 Secondary Functions of the Coven include:
  - 6.2.1 Active support for the broader Pagan Community
  - 6.2.2 The facilitation of members learning about magick
  - 6.2.3 The facilitation of members developing their psychic powers
  - 6.2.4 Emotional and magickal support for members through difficult circumstances.

7. Decision-making
- 7.1 All decisions are made on a consensus basis.
- 7.2 Where consensus is not reached, the current status quo will remain.

Circle of the African Moon

The Circle of the African Moon (CAM) is a non-profit, national, religio-spiritual organisation. It is a body of members with varying Pagan beliefs and practices. Its aim is to balance the wisdom and benefits of ancient Pagan ways with the circumstances and demands of modern Pagan life. It seeks to provide a supportive and meaningful context for the lifelong practice of Pagan faiths and ways of life. It does this through open (public) Esbats, Sabbats and other interventions. It also makes available teaching and inner workings through its strong and well-formulated Wiccan (most notably the Aquarian Tabernacle Church structure and syllabus) and Pagan-specific syllabus, and it offers short courses in Wicca and other Pagan paths, designed to take the seeker into degree or other inner training.

CAM seeks to be a proactive educational network dedicated to correcting misinformation about Paganism. It does this through careful interaction with the media and through speaking in public forums.

CAM defines Paganism as a Nature-based religio-spiritual system and way of life that draws its inspiration from Nature, acknowledging Nature as a manifestation of divinity.

CAM does not discriminate against anyone on the grounds of gender, sexual preference, race, religious belief or spiritual practice. It subscribes to the principle of tolerance, both within its membership and without. The organisation asserts its right under the Constitution of South Africa in terms of protection against discrimination, and freedom of expression, association, movement, and of conscience, religion, thought, belief and opinion.

Governance is achieved through a National Council, as per CAM's constitution.

These are possibly the main public players and networking bodies that act in legal matters on behalf of their members. The Aquarian Tabernacle Church also has strong legal interests on behalf of Pagan lives in general. It is also the teaching and worshipping body for Paganism. Both the Aquarian Tabernacle Church and the Correlian Tradition offer a lineage, that is a formal degree system. This means that the degree is internationally recognised and credited.

There are countless other covens and small bodies involved in networking and publicising Paganism. The larger bodies are not always popular with these Pagans, who interface with each other through the Internet, cybercafes, and good old word of mouth.

CHAPTER 3

TRADITIONAL AFRICAN PAGANISM

The rise of the neo-Pagan movement in South Africa is mostly a white phenomenon. To a large extent, this is because white South Africans have deep spiritual needs but few religious structures. The fall of apartheid has left deep voids, none so apparent as the religious and spiritual one. The Church icon has fallen. South Africa was, and still is, a profoundly religious country. Many black South Africans are deeply religious and, if not Christian, practise their own form of traditional religious expression, or have merged Christianity with aspects of their own religion. They have a religious infrastructure. Most white South Africans, on the other hand, are a bit lost spiritually, grabbing at anything 'New Agey'. They are searching, and Paganism as a movement and religious expression is making sense to them.

I am often asked how many black Africans are Pagan, or have joined any of the Pagan organisations. But this depends on one's definition of Pagan. If we view traditional African beliefs as essentially Pagan, then naturally there are many black Pagans. Unlike most Native North Americans, it appears that many black Africans have retained their traditional religious beliefs. In spite of modern Western influences, they have managed to keep their traditional religion virtually intact, especially their magick. In fact, it is a shame that in South Africa most white Pagans chase magick at a distance: they involve themselves in weird orders and revere anything in a book on a dusty bookshelf; yet on their doorsteps in a poverty-stricken part of town are some of the world's most powerful practitioners of magick – the Sangomas (Africa's Shamans) – untouched by modern Western hands.

I am fascinated that most white Pagans not only fail to explore the rich, natural Paganism that is available to them, but, at times, appear to be almost racist in their insistent search for a European Pagan ancestry (be it Celtic, Anglo-Saxon or Teutonic).

This yen for some sort of European root is often childish and romantically nostalgic. Most South Africans are of such mixed descent that it is impossible to trace a bloodline by only one lineage. While there are a few of us who are able to trace a direct European bloodline, most are mixed like me – of German, Dutch and obviously Khoi descent. A recent trip to Ireland dissolved my childlike dreams of running down Irish moors, windswept through timeless mists, believing that 'I had come home'. My past nostalgia was not based on racism or a lack of love for this country, but, like most Pagan folk, I suffered from a European bias coupled with the previous government's deliberate attempts to endorse that bias and separate me from my African roots.

On top of this, history has been written by Europeans. This is therefore also true of Pagan history and the literature that filters down to us. The bias isn't deliberate in neo-Pagan writing, but there is simply no one willing to take up the challenge of writing within an African Pagan context. Also, since all the literature currently comes from overseas, there is no local Pagan literature to endorse or challenge concepts.

Yet, in many ways, South Africa is the cradle of humankind. It is a country steeped in oral tradition, bound by clan, still honouring timeless traditions. Magick exists in many black communities; they have their own pantheon and their own cosmology. Certainly their Shamans (Sangomas) are Pagans. In fact, many black South Africans can be seen as Pagan, unless 'converted' by the new religion (namely Christianity). White South Africans, born into a myriad religious traditions, have a sense of 'coming home' once they see through these religions and return to their roots. Arguably, we are all Pagans from birth. In recent archaeological findings, the oldest fossil remains of *Homo sapiens*, attributed to the southern African region, show a sophisticated socio-religious system based on trance and Shamanism. This presents the earliest known occurrences of 'structured' religious systems in the world, and surely proves that Paganism is far more than a 'new' spirituality in South Africa.

An important ally in the reclamation of South Africa's Pagan heritage is the High Sanusi (prophet) Credo Mutwa (Zulu author, artist, sage, cultural historian and custodian of African spiritual tradition). He not only confirmed the need for a Pagan organisation prior to its formation, but also 'married' Paganism as practised by whites and Paganism as practised by his Sangomas and healers.

This 'marriage' was performed in no uncertain terms at an interaction at his healing village Kaya Lendaba, in the presence of his five Sangomas.

Credo Mutwa is as contemptuous of European vegetarian wannabe Pagans as he is of 'born-again' black South Africans – both rendered catatonic at, for example, the ancient custom of slaughter as a sacrificial rite. This is something to which we as Pagans in South Africa have to reconcile ourselves. Our belief in our Celtic background is misplaced. We live in South Africa. There is a Pagan crossover. This was brought to my attention in no uncertain terms when I was asked to perform a handfasting (marriage) for a couple – one was a Wiccan, the other a Sangoma. The handfasting was to be an integration of both systems and would incorporate the killing of a chicken at some point in the ceremony. For a Wiccan priestess with clear guidelines, this would be an easy decision in another country. In South Africa, the guidelines are not so clear, and the decisions not so easy.

A coven I am involved with has two members who are studying to be Sangomas. This has presented difficult and complex challenges for the whole group. They don't have the answers, but are determined to find a workable solution to the integration of black and white magickal traditions.

If we are to look for 'similarities' between neo-Pagan practices and traditional black customs, they do exist. There are many concepts that white Pagans are very familiar with. Although many of these are based on universal principles, it is easy to see them in the context of Craft and Pagan practice.

Here are some of the similarities, based heavily on the research of the psychiatrist B.J.F. Laubscher (1975), who frequently draws on a Xhosa framework.

The Earth Mother

The Earth is highly revered as Mother by both black and white Pagans. White Pagans see themselves as coming from Her and returning to Her. All their rituals are focused on Elements that make up the Earth.

The Earth Mother is also significant in black Paganism. By way of example, in the Xhosa tradition, one need only look at the ritual for male initiation. The huts used to house the young initiates are made by menfolk only, but the sacred task of the women is to make the hut habitable, lining it with soft grass to emulate womb-like features.

Furthermore, a tomb-like recess is walled off – a deliberate reminder of the passage of the womb of the female. This recess is sealed off by a stone wall, and the shaft is filled in with new life.

The circle

The circle is of profound significance in black Paganism. It is used for the same purpose that white Pagans use it – to contain the psychic forces and to ward off outside negativity. The traditional circular huts are built for the purpose of containing the flow of the energy within. The most important circle of all is the cattle kraal, where all major political and spiritual events take place. The entire clan is involved in building it, layering stone upon stone to enclose the spiritual energies that may abound when called upon. The significance of cattle may be linked to the period when Taurus was worshipped or when the vernal equinox was in the constellation of Taurus.

Certainly, the celestial offering of cattle as a symbol of eternal life and its zodiacal link remind us of the time when the Israelites worshipped the golden calf.

Initiation rites

All Western and Eastern occult traditions have their protocol, rules and procedures of initiation. Black Paganism is no different. It may range from Earth rites, such as womaning, marriage or death to deeply significant and mystical procedures towards self-actualisation. Most Wiccan or Pagan initiation rites that I know of pale in comparison to the 'ordeal' that a black initiate must undergo before 'becoming a man'.

Purification and consecration

All food prepared for a ritual feast is duly consecrated, as are gifts given for any rites of passage. Water is of particular significance in the purification and consecration process. While white Pagans may delicately spray some water around the circle to welcome in the Element, black Pagans see water as an archetype. It symbolises the world of Hades as well as the first layer of spirit life – a symbol of the oblivion of past life, of rebirth and renewal.

The Ancestors

Known as the 'amadlose' in Xhosa and the 'onomathotholo' in Zulu, we know the Ancestors as the old ancient ones. In black Paganism, Ancestors are relatives who have recently died and taken on the role of a 'guardian spirit', much like the 'spirit guide' in white Paganism. Both black and white Pagans understand the ancient Ancestors as a collection of spiritual beings who had at one time lived on this Earth and now form some hierarchy of consciousness.

The Ancestors are different from the realm of spirits. There are 'spirit people': the Xhosa, for example, have the 'abantubomlambo' or water spirits. These are half-fish, half-human, symbolising the power of humankind to live in and penetrate another substance or sphere – on Earth symbolised by water, as already mentioned. Just as a fish has a body to live in water, so a human has an inner body of spirit that can live in and go through a world that feels like water. In Zulu culture, these spirits live under the Earth. White Pagans may call these spirits 'disembodied' spirits – spirits who have not lived their lives according to certain principles and are now caught in the water and forced to live like fish.

The aura

Black Pagans do not intellectualise the energy field around the body and do not call it an 'aura'. They experience it as a power around the body that protects the spirit from evil. During all their rituals, they 'raise energy', like our raising of the cone, by chanting, clapping and group participation. In this way, they 'fuse' their auras, so that the power of the group becomes a covering around them. These unseen powers flow together to assist in the build-up of the greater power.

(Interestingly enough, Isanusis (prophets) are able to feel the presence of a person as far away as three feet, with their eyes closed!)

Ritual

Ritual is a vital part of everyday life. Even among modern urban black South Africans, rituals are adhered to everywhere. Chanting is vital. It may start as: 'Come O Ancestral Spirits and make these things clear to us', much like our: 'Queen of Heaven, Queen of Hell, lend your power to this spell.'

Chants demand responses, and in black Pagan traditions, when the Isanusi chants, the community responds with 'siyavuma', meaning 'we agree'. In white Pagan traditions, the response is: 'As we will it so mote it be.'

In traditional African Paganism, there are no observers, and group participation is vital. They work as a large circle, without the stringent rules of a coven.

To my mind, the Xhosa 'umtendeleko' is one of the most beautiful rituals. It is much like the Christian sharing of the Eucharist or the Pagan 'cakes and ale' ceremony. The umtendeleko is practised at almost every ritual: beer is passed from mouth to mouth, much like the Christian communion goblet.

The umtendeleko is also often held as a great rite on its own. The entire ceremony is then dedicated to the Most High, a supreme form of worship, with an emphasis on union through fellowship. These are some of the characteristics:

- It is left to the conscience of each individual whether or not he or she is 'fit' to participate.
- Where transgressions are known, the person is prohibited from participating.
- It is required that the person be free from 'sin' for at least three weeks before the ceremony. There should be no ill feeling against anyone, only harmony, charity, goodwill and kindness – virtues that are actively cultivated before the rite.
- Group consciousness or 'at-oneness' is vital. This is a deliberate attempt to 'tune into' a cosmic consciousness.
- Brewed beer is set apart, and corn belongs to the consecrated first fruits.
- It is performed at full moon.
- Purification rituals are performed beforehand.
- On entering, the leader calls for full participation from all present. All participants must be fully aware of why they are there and what they are there to do.

The whole performance is a concentration of minds and intense desire and the acting out of this need by consuming the beer and corn. It is a presentation to Creation, providing the conditions that bring about the production of the harvest and its first fruit, and the obvious sympathetic magick that goes with that.

Sympathetic magick

Sympathetic magick, also called low magick, refers to the ritualistic use of physical objects or gestures as a representation of the event or person over which influence is sought. Much of black Paganism's magick is sympathetically based. Certainly, the Isanusi may work at a higher magickal level, but for most the relation is at a lower magickal level. We see several principles emerging:

- Guarding against evil or negative influences. For example, all building materials are hidden before the huts are prepared for initiation.
- Ritual is done mostly according to the moon phases. Male Xhosa circumcision, for example, identifies here with power or growth and development in the universe. The moon is acknowledged as growing from a narrow rim into a glorious globe of light, symbolising the universal power of development, which, by means of sympathetic timing, promotes the growth of the new character and the new and natural conception of life (Laubscher 1975:98). Everything is new in the making of a new person: new moon, new location and new hut. The moon also obviously has great significance in a number of white Pagan rituals.
- Hair, which is believed to contain the energies or soul imprint of a person, is used in healing or cursing rituals.

- Not only white Pagans are tree huggers! In the Xhosa tradition, there is a custom of planting two euphorbia trees at the birth of twins. To communicate with them in their absence, the trees could give the mothers answers to their questions. If the twins were ill or had died, the tree would go into decline, but if they were well, the trees would be healthy.

Magickal names

After Xhosa initiation into man- or womanhood, the leader of the ceremony bestows a new name on the initiate. This is known as 'hlonipa', meaning 'the new life has begun'. This outer act represents the inner creation of a new personality – and, of course, this new personality falls within one of the universal laws governing the development of spiritual consciousness.

This is also the case with Paganism in general as well as most occult systems. With Wicca it is usually given at first degree.

The colour white

White has always been a symbol for purity – it marked the dress of the ancient Egyptian and Celtic priests. In black Pagan practice, it is often used at any novices' initiation, and, in the Xhosa initiation into manhood, a white paste is smeared on the body and face at the third stage of the initiation. Inner purification now becomes externalised. This is the archetypal expression of the 'new spirit life'.

The colour white has always taken on archetypal meaning, particularly in terms of humankind's spiritual evolution. After the inner self has discarded its semi-physical layers by whatever means, ritual or rites, it emerges as pure and white. White Pagans call this 'soul body'.

The role of myth

As with all Pagans, the role of myth cannot be emphasised enough. It is a vehicle of journey into the deeper world of the psyche, and disperses archetypal meaning for people of all religions.

Divination

African Pagan divination incorporates the same focus as white or European Pagan divination, but its methods differ. The same para-psychological elements are present, such as the use of telepathy and precognition. The development of mediumship and the ability to divine is based on a collective unconscious memory of a psychic experience. Again, this is the view in all occult traditions.

Chi/ki energy – the universal life force

The mysterious power that dwells within us and its manifestations of particular vibrations through colour, numbers, etc. are what are known as 'energies' or 'an energy field'. This is known as chi/ki in the East, and the San know it as 'num'. For the San, num resides at the base of the spine. It is awakened through dance and ceremony and channelled up the spine. When num awakens, the San move into trance states and perform acts of healing.

White Pagans know it as the 'kundalini', and in all cultures its location is somewhere between the anal or genital area and slightly below the navel. We all raise the energy up the spinal column from the base of the spine.

The phallic cult

The Tokoloshe (a lascivious spirit in African folklore) and numerous white Pagan gods have their origins in the phallic cult. The youthful, strong and sexually potent Tokoloshe, endowed with a great phallus, was originally a symbol of procreation, germination and fructification.

In ancient Egypt, the god Seb was represented as a prepuce or phallic deity. Seb was also the Earth god and hence the father image: the one that fructified. In the Book of the Dead, we see Horus fighting the Apap (a dragon of drought and sterility) with his phallus, symbolising fructification, procreation and fertility.

And need we mention Pan, the horned Greek god associated with goats, whose prominent phallus and lusty nature so repelled the medieval Christian Church that some of their images of the devil were given horns and hooves?

Circumcision

Circumcision as an enactment of regeneration goes back thousands of years, again arguably to Africa. While Horus is changed from a child of twelve into an adult, he rises from the world of Amentia (the Egyptian Hades). Having gone through the rite of circumcision, he rises from the dead, resurrected and regenerated. The Xhosa rite of circumcision also refers to new life and spiritual regeneration in particular (Laubscher 1975:96).

Looking at all of these similarities between black and white Paganism, we must ask ourselves why most white Pagans reject their African roots. Why do we insist on buying and hoarding books on a Paganism so far removed from our experience? Why do we bother converting northern hemisphere practice, when we could emulate what's right here on our doorstep? To me, Africa and traditional African customs are the guardians of humankind's primordial spiritual life.

CHAPTER 4

PAGANISM VERSUS SATANISM

Although there is doubt as to exactly how widespread the phenomenon of Satanism is, evidence clearly suggests that the problem in South Africa is considerably larger than in Britain or the rest of Europe. And, to make matters worse, Paganism has often been erroneously linked with Satanism.

Pagans and Satanists both employ certain symbols, such as pentagrams, ankhs and Celtic knots. Both perform rituals within the confines of a circle. Both have altars with chalices, blades and pentacles. Both love the ambience and ritual drama of candles, incense and robes. The fact that Pagan activity has been very covert in the past has added unnecessary fuel to the fire.

Up until as recently as six years ago, 'Paganism' was a swear word, synonymous with the term 'Satanism'. However, Satanism refers to worship of and allegiance to the Christian concept of the devil, whom Pagans do not even acknowledge. Such practices involve the denigration of Jesus Christ as lord and saviour and the acceptance of the devil as such. Satanic practice is an outright attack on Christian virtues and beliefs. It shows disrespect to life through cruel acts of ritual killing. These killings are criminal acts and may range from cutting off the paws of cats (who are then left to find their way home) to crucifying an animal on a cross to killing a newborn baby or adult human in the most abysmal way. The use of drugs, rape and other crimes are also often linked to Satanic practice.

There is a difference between what may be termed 'academic' Satanism and Satanism per se. The former is often the intellectual pursuit of rediscovery of self through the fallen angel of light, Lucifer, in order to make sense of the 'absurdity' of Christianity. In South Africa, Satanism is guaranteed constitutional freedom, as are all religions. However, as soon as any criminal activity is linked to it, it is investigated. South Africa is the only country in the world that has an occult unit dedicated to the eradication of Satanically motivated crimes.

The practice of Satanism is obviously a natural reaction against the apartheid government's politically endorsed Christian world view. The South African media is littered with stories of Satanic acts and crimes. Whether these crimes are motivated by big business cartels, or whether they are inspired by bored, frustrated and rebellious teenagers, the fact remains that Paganism is inevitably associated with Satanism, and Pagans are routinely accused of Satanic activities.

Most dictionaries don't help either, describing a Pagan in one of two ways: either as an unbeliever/heathen or as a non-Christian. Both definitions are unacceptable to Pagans and have caused them to endure much discomfort and discrimination. People wanting to enlighten themselves have had only dictionaries to turn to, so the original bias is constantly reconfirmed. It is perhaps for this reason that Paganism is often confused with Satanism.

In the past five years, now that schools are no longer segregated, Satanism has spread its ugly tentacles into the black community.

But not only has Paganism been confused with the white Christian understanding of Satanism; black perceptions of Paganism are also confused in South Africa. It has been particularly complicated by the black practice of killing for muti (medicine) purposes. Some people believe that if they drink or rub their bodies with muti preparations containing certain body parts, they will be endowed with superhuman powers. Because of this, the sale of human brains, eyes and genitals has become a lucrative business for unscrupulous practitioners. It has been reported that customers will pay up to R10 000 for muti made with human body parts.

These practitioners are referred to as 'witches'. The Zulu term 'umthagathi' and the Sotho word 'boloi' speak of a witch in the most derogatory terms possible. The terms evoke feelings of great fear (akin to a villager who in the 'burning times' heard of a witch in the vicinity and sentenced them to a pyre). The fear is rampant, even among black city dwellers. 'Nyangas' (traditional healers who use medicinal herbs and potions known as 'muti') have important status in the community, and 'Sangomas' (healers using the techniques of the nyanga as well as those of divination) have even more powerful status. The concept of a 'witch', however, is applied to a scapegoat for the community (i.e. a suspect or criminal);

it is also the function of a person dedicated to the task of evil deeds. It is for this reason that the function of a 'witchdoctor' exists, one who 'sniffs out' witches. South Africa is currently witnessing a re-emergence of the European 'burning times', especially in the Northern Province.

Those who are deemed witches are either burnt or buried alive, sometimes with their entire families. This has become such a problem that several villages in Venda and the Northern Province have been established for those indicated as witches, as well as their families.

As neo-Pagans in South Africa, we treat this with contempt and grave concern. The South African Pagan community has a long way to go in convincing not so much white but black South Africans that Paganism is not evil, and that the thing they fear most is their traditional concept of the witch as the social outcast – evil, old and ugly.

By 'coming out', South African Pagans could, literally, be facing a life and death situation. Among other things, it requires the public to distinguish Paganism from white perceptions of Satanism, as well as to distinguish Pagans from the concept of a witch as it exists in the black psyche.

In a rapidly changing South Africa, the association of the colour black with evil, darkness, negativity and 'the shadow' (as opposed to the colour white, associated with 'goodness', 'light', positivity and spiritual upliftment) also needs to be urgently addressed from a politically correct perspective.

In the early days, anyone who was a Pagan was 'closet' and of necessity clandestine. This in itself created more misunderstanding about Paganism. The mere mention of the 'w' word was kept for inner circles only. Ten years ago, there were no 'white witches', no courses in Wicca, and certainly nobody advertising for Pagan soulmates. Although veiled adverts did appear, most of the time they attracted only fruitcakes.

At this time, there was nothing organised – no networking body with which to make contact. It was a lonely time – a time of darkness, when the wearing of our sacred symbol, the pentagram, could at best earn you a reputation as a Satanist and at worst invoke a jail sentence. The Internet was still a thing of the future, and access to books was almost non-existent. It was a time when most Pagans felt that they were the only Pagans out there. Many turned to Europe or America for role models.

Pagans let nobody know about their interest. I was engaged to a man who I thought was liberal, but when he discovered my books he went straight back to the religious structure he had evolved from, and with tears in his eyes confessed that he'd been seduced by a witch and needed forgiveness.

Paganism was naturally accused of being a cult, and its presence was feared by many. Moreover, the fact that South Africa has an occult unit did not bode well for Pagans and Wiccans. During the apartheid years, it was inconceivable that religious freedom would one day be the order of the day.

Also symptomatic of that period was Pagan and Wiccan animosity towards the Church. Since the tragic period in history known as the 'burning times' the response of Pagans has often been vehement. Some quote figures as high as nine million for victims executed for witchCraft under the tyranny of the medieval Church. (Most of these were women.) Unfortunately, the angry and bitter behaviour of some Pagans is as deploring as the behaviour of the very people they accuse. The tragic irony is that the history of the 'burning times' is hotly contested by certain academics, who say that figures are grossly exaggerated, and that any execution had to do with the civil courts, and not the Church. Moreover, being labelled as Satanist has fuelled the anger of many modern Pagans.

But neo-Pagans shouldn't hold the acts of the medieval Church against modern Christians. It must be pointed out that every civilisation has had its form of cruelty – its chance to dominate others violently and to explore the very depths of human depravity – before the climb to self-actualisation begins. Pagans are by no means innocent in their spiritual evolution, either in their actions towards each other, or towards other groups that may have had different religious or social values.

The public Pagan movement has, however, gone a long way in the past six years in educating the public. We now enjoy a solid relationship with the national Occult Unit and the heads of various Child Protection Units in several regions. When the twenty-one signatories met at the Winter solstice to form the Pagan Federation of South Africa officially, the new president was tasked with establishing a rapport with the head of the Occult Unit, Colonel Kobus Jonker. Up until then, this unit had also often mistaken Paganism for Satanism, especially its ritual content, simply because Satanists employed so much Pagan practice in their ritual processes. In a groundbreaking initial meeting, a firm understanding based on mutual co-operation was established.

Such meetings were not to the taste of all Pagans, some seeing it as a 'sell-out' to the police. Time, however, saw the wisdom of this move, and the Occult Unit is now completely unbiased in its response to the many phone calls it still receives from ignorant members of the public.

Clearly, Paganism in South Africa has the same vested interest that the police have. We have even been asked to begin an educational programme on the dangers of Satanism in the belief that the school-going audience will more readily listen to our representatives than the police. I have steered clear of this for fear of having hundreds of youngsters wanting to become Wiccans for cult-like reasons.

Still, our relationship with the police has not always been easy. Two examples involved legitimate police investigation into two Pagans' lives and homes, highlighting the vulnerability of Paganism in harbouring would-be criminals under its banner, and the police confusion in accepting our credibility.

Part of the process of going public has involved a deliberate decision to use the media only when it is of the highest tabloid calibre. To date, appearances on leading television channels and write-ups in top-quality magazines have served us well. I am thus far amazed at the willingness of the media to try to understand the phenomenon of Paganism within the broader socio-religious context.

'Coming out' has also involved using to maximum effect the protection that the law now offers. Under the new Constitution of South Africa, our inherent rights include protection against discrimination, freedom of association, freedom of expression, and freedom of conscience, religion, thought and opinion. South African Pagans are being taught their legal rights and how to use them. Ninety-nine per cent of the searches that have taken place on suspected Satanically linked grounds have been illegal, but because of fear and lack of knowledge the suspect allows the police to enter and in that instant loses his or her rights.

One of the more worrying pieces of legislation is the Witchcraft Suppression Act of 1957, which has still not been repealed. Naturally, Pagans have looked at this Act and opinions are divided as to whether to lobby against it, or simply to accept the inherent protection in terms of the Constitution. Perhaps it is because we have not been able to act as a unit, and any efforts to lobby thus far have been scattered. Up until now, Pagans have had to concentrate their energies on other areas.

The Act is a curious piece of writing, steeped in the preconceptions and beliefs of the previous government. In terms of the Act the following persons will be guilty of committing an offence:
- anybody who uses supernatural means to harm any person or thing, or accuses another person of being a witch or wizard;
- any person who claims they have used supernatural power, witchCraft, enchantment or conjuration to cause harm, injury, grief, disappearance or disease to a person or thing;
- anyone who employs a witchdoctor or witchfinder to indicate another person as a witch or wizard;
- anybody who claims that they have a knowledge of witchCraft, or the use of charms, and teaches others this knowledge or supplies them with any 'pretended means' to practise witchCraft;

- any person who claims they have used the knowledge given by a witchdoctor, witchfinder or other person to injure or damage any person or thing;
- anyone who pretends to use supernatural power, sorcery, enchantment, or conjuration for gain;
- anybody who pretends to use supernatural power to tell fortunes; and
- any person who pretends to use their skill or knowledge of occult science to find an object that has been lost or stolen.

Thus, anybody who believes that supernatural power exists, and acts on this belief in any of the above ways, is committing an offence in terms of the Act.

Punishment obviously depends on the severity of the crime, and fines range from R200 to R1 000. These would have been extremely hefty in 1956. Imprisonment periods range from two to twenty years, and, according to the Act, punishment can also include whippings. (The full Act is printed at the end of the chapter.)

The title and definitions of the Act are a little misleading, as they appear to pose many threats to Paganism. On a first read, it seems that it is intended to suppress the practice of Paganism in some way. According to attorney Trevor Bouwer, however, if we examine other legislation as well as the relevant court rulings, it appears that freedom of religion in this country will prevent this from happening. There is little evidence of the Act ever being used against Pagans (even under the previous government), and any attempted prosecution is not likely to bear fruit, as there is a constitutional protection of religion.

The criminal law prosecutions instituted in terms of the Act have been commonly used to suppress the so-called 'muti murders' and the mutilation of bodies, dead or alive, in certain areas. The Act has also been used to control certain instances of public violence against individuals who are targeted as 'witches' or persons believed to bring harm to a community.

In the light of this, and because the doctrine of freedom of religion is absolute in this country, it doesn't seem necessary to lobby for the Act to be abolished or altered. More than this, it would be an extremely difficult endeavour. Unless there are proven and concrete cases of discrimination, it is unlikely that the law will be changed.

WITCHCRAFT SUPPRESSION ACT 3 OF 1957

[ASSENTED TO 19 FEBRUARY 1957]
[DATE OF COMMENCEMENT: 22 FEBRUARY 1957]

(English text signed by the Governor-General)
as amended by Witchcraft Suppression Amendment Act 50 of 1970

ACT

To provide for the suppression of the practice of witchcraft and similar practices.

1. **Offences relating to the practice of witchcraft and similar practices**

    Any person who-

    (a) imputes to any other person the causing, by supernatural means, of any disease in or injury or damage to any person or thing, or who names or indicates any other person as a wizard;

    (b) in circumstances indicating that he professes or pretends to use any supernatural power, witchcraft, sorcery, enchantment or conjuration, imputes the cause of death of, injury or grief to, disease in, damage to or disappearance of any person or thing to any other person;

    (c) employs or solicits any witchdoctor, witch-finder or any other person to name or indicate any person as a wizard;

    (d) professes a knowledge of witchcraft, or the use of charms, and advises any person how to bewitch, injure or damage any person or thing, or supplies any person with any pretended means of witchcraft;

    (e) on the advice of any witchdoctor, witch-finder or other person or on the ground of any pretended knowledge of witchcraft, uses or causes to be put into operation any means or process which, in accordance with such advice or his own belief, is calculated to injure or damage any person or thing;

    (f) for gain pretends to exercise or use any supernatural power, witchcraft, sorcery, enchantment or conjuration, or undertakes to tell fortunes, or pretends from his skill in or knowledge of any occult science to discover where and in what manner anything supposed to have been stolen or lost may be found, shall be guilty of an offence and liable on conviction –

        (i) in the case of an offence referred to in paragraph (a) or (b) in consequence of which the person in respect of whom such offence was committed, has been killed, or where the accused has been proved to be by habit or repute a witchdoctor or witch-finder, to imprisonment for a period not exceeding twenty years or to a whipping not exceeding ten strokes or to both such imprisonment and such whipping;

(ii) in the case of any other offence referred to in the said paragraphs, to one or more of the following penalties, namely, a fine not exceeding one thousand rand, imprisonment for a period not exceeding ten years and a whipping not exceeding ten strokes;
(iii) in the case of an offence referred to in paragraph (c), (d) or (e), to a fine not exceeding five hundred rand or to imprisonment for a period not exceeding five years, or to both such fine and such imprisonment;
(iv) in the case of an offence referred to in paragraph (f), to a fine not exceeding two hundred rand or to imprisonment for a period not exceeding two years.

[S. 1 substituted by s. 1 of Act 50 of 1970]

2. Presumption

Where any person in respect of whom an offence referred to in paragraph (a) or (b) of section 1 was committed, is killed, it shall be presumed, until the contrary is proved, that such person was killed in consequence of the commission of such offence.

[S. 2 substituted by s. 2 of Act 50 of 1970]

3. Repeal of laws

The laws mentioned in the Schedule to this Act are hereby repealed to the extent set out in the fourth column of that Schedule.

4. Short title

This Act shall be called the Witchcraft Suppression Act, 1957.

CHAPTER 5

PAGAN BELIEFS AND PRACTICES

Paganism does not claim to be the only true 'way'. It has no liturgy or dogma. Although there are different traditions, many Pagans move freely between them. Followers don't worship any prophets or gurus, but there are wise people, elders and leaders among them.

Generally speaking, Pagans are non-hierarchical. Although covens, groves and kindreds must be organised hierarchically, a certain amount of flexibility is always predominant. Current organisations that seem hierarchical are often structured in this way only for administrative reasons. Other institutions setting up ordination procedures see the priesthood as a commitment to service rather than a hierarchical structure. Such priests and priestesses aren't intermediaries between Pagans and their gods and goddesses; they make a lifelong commitment to serving their community.

Pagans do not recruit, evangelise or proselytise. If you are of us, you will find us. We help those who seek us out. I am always amused at the level of frustration certain people experience in 'finding' me. They seem to think I should have a neon billboard outside my home; yet I am public enough to be found by sincere seekers.

Here are some of the more important beliefs and practices of the many Pagan traditions.

Ethics

The 'law of three', which regulates all Pagans' behaviour, states that that which is sent out shall return to the sender three times. The modern revival of old witchCraft, Wicca, elaborates on this principle in the Wiccan Rede: 'An it harm none, do what ye will.' This is an extremely strict code of conduct: while it appears to permit anything, it admonishes one not to harm anything, least of all oneself. Here is the full version of the Rede:

> Bide the Wiccan laws ye must
> In Perfect Love and Perfect Trust
> Live and let another live
> Freely take and freely give.
>
> Cast the circle thrice about
> To keep all evil spirits out
> To bind the spell every time
> Let the spell be spake in rhyme.
>
> Soft of eye and light of touch
> Speak thou little, listen much.
>
> Deosil go by waxing moon
> Sing and dance the Wiccan rune
> Widdershins go when the moon doth wane
> And the werewolf howls by the dread wolfsbane.
>
> When the Lady's moon is new
> Kiss thy hand to her times two
> When the moon rides at her peak
> Then your heart's desire seek.
>
> Heed the north wind's mighty gale
> Lock the door and drop the sail
> When the wind comes from the south
> Love will kiss thee on the mouth.
>
> When the wind blows from the east
> Expect the new and set the feast
> When the west wind blows o'er thee
> Departed spirits restless be.

Nine woods in the cauldron go
Burn them fast and burn them slow
Elder be ye Lady's tree
Burn it not or cursed ye'll be.

When the wheel begins to turn
Let the Beltane fires burn
When the wheel has turned to Yule
Light the log and let Pan rule.

Heed ye flower, bush and tree
By the Lady, Blessed be
Where the rippling waters go
Cast a stone and truth ye'll know.

When ye have a need
Hearken not to others' greed
With the fool no season spend
Nor be counted as his friend.

Merry meet and merry part
Bright the cheeks and warm the heart
Mind the Threefold Law ye should
Three times bad and three times good.

When misfortune is enow
Wear the blue star on thy brow
True in love must ever be
Unless thy lover's false to thee.

Eight words the Wiccan Rede fulfil
An it harm none, do what ye will.

With these eight words the Wiccan Rede fulfil:
'An it harm none, do what ye will.'

Pagans therefore don't have a set of commandments. There is one, which covers all that it means to be truly human. Because Pagans are Earth-positive, they operate from what they can do rather than what they can't and shouldn't.

The concept of sin

Pagans believe in personal power and accountability, which can be realised only if there is self-control. One has to take responsibility for one's actions, which means that there is no priest or intermediary to whom one can confess one's 'sins'. The concept of 'original sin' is foreign to Paganism, as is the concept of a 'devil'. You would never hear a Pagan excusing their behaviour with a comment like 'the devil made me do it'. The notion of external good and evil forces doing battle against each other (making us pawns) is alien. The concept of 'hell' doesn't make sense to Pagans either. Guilt especially, a manifestation of control over your life by another, is something Pagans abhor and actively oppose through healthy approaches to lifestyle and sexuality. South African Pagans work very hard to rid themselves of guilt, as most of them have a background that filled them with guilt for being human and living life. This is not the Pagan way.

There is also no intermediary who can absolve sinners of their so-called 'sin'. I sometimes wish there was, because, boy, I'd be the first in line – just say my ten 'Hail Hecates' and I'd be forgiven. But it doesn't work that way with Paganism. If you 'mess up', you have to clean up.

While Pagans accept certain inalienable universal laws, for example that human beings can't shift stars around from their present orbit, they believe that they can shape their own destiny. Being in control of oneself implies knowledge of oneself, which is therefore quite feasibly the shaping of one's own destiny. Pagans believe that most humans have greater good in them than bad, and that this can be shaped towards 'global goodness', not only through the Pagan belief system, but also through the many other belief systems that strive towards the global goodness of humanity. We believe that children are born holy, arriving neutrally on this plane. It is very difficult for Pagans to offend their gods. Their deities don't need believers to crusade for them; neither do they need believers to try to convert others to their religion.

Pagans tend to be very practical people: they get on with things, having little time to deal with remorse and guilt. Their feet are firmly planted on the Earth Mother. Tiresome and energy-sapping debates, such as what it will be like in heaven, or how many alien spaceships may be in the garden, tend to be replaced with discussions on more practical issues, like where to start cleaning up the Jukskei River.

Reincarnation and the afterlife

Along with the Hindu notion of karma, Pagans accept the idea of reincarnation and an afterlife. Upon death, it is believed that the soul goes to rest at a place called the 'Summerlands' – a Celtic name. Pagans don't debate how many planes there are to transcend, how exactly they will be reincarnated or in what form they will return, and they don't have a concept of eternal punishment or damnation.

While Pagans accept the notion of reincarnation, they don't have elaborate systems or explanations about the concept. Pagans revere all of the Earth's manifestations as equal, whether human, animal, vegetable, mineral or crystal. So, although Pagans believe in karma, the notion of a princess being a higher incarnation than a tortoise, for example, is of no great consequence to them. This does not mean that Pagans do not recognise the concept of complete evolution. There would be little debate that human beings are more complex than other life forms (based on acknowledgement of consciousness). However, given that all life forms are treated equally in this incarnation, the usual arrogance that often accompanies debates about reincarnation is seldom present in Paganism.

Sex and nudity

Pagan ethics are based on joy, love and self-esteem. Their religion or spiritual path is one of celebration. Pleasure, beauty, humour, good food, drink, music and sex are of value to them. They celebrate the life force, and abide by the words in the 'Charge of the Goddess': 'All acts of pleasure are my ritual, and there will be music, making love and feasting.' (The Charge of the Goddess is quoted in full on pages 220–21.)

However, this doesn't mean that Pagans are hedonists, wantonly entering the debauched orgiastic rituals of which they are all too often accused. They believe they are children of Mother Earth, and they partake of Her bounty within an ethical framework. At this point, it is important to mention the issues of sex and nakedness in ritual. I get many phone calls (from men) asking me if they can join the circles dancing naked around the fire. This is obviously a natural male fantasy – one that has been sensationalised by certain movies and books. Though certain covens practise their rites skyclad, especially in Britain, very few do in South Africa.

The argument for skyclad practice is that a lack of clothing allows for the full flow of energy, and that being naked during rites is a liberating experience. As mature adults, there should be no difficulties. Being sexually titillated by a naked body in a working context would be tantamount to sexual immaturity. The history of skyclad working comes to Pagans from the naturist Gerald Gardner, whose coven practised skyclad. But Gardner never ruled that all new offshoots of Wicca should practise as he did.

In South Africa during the early days of networking, this was a major issue. Unfortunately, some people became victims to certain naked rites, and, sadly, at the behest of male priests. Because of the ignorance of South African practitioners in general, and because of feelings of inferiority when confronted with experienced practitioners from Britain and America, it was easy to be duped by predatory priests from overseas.

Today, however, the matter has been settled, and the majority of South African Pagans work robed. If a person is invited to join a skyclad ritual upfront, they should be extremely wary.

It is a myth that Pagans engage in sexual intercourse during rituals. While I don't know what happens in private temples or between couples practising the Craft, it certainly doesn't occur in most covens or general working groups. In the Gardnerian tradition there is a ritual known as 'The Great Rite', where the high priest and high priestess have sex as an act of celebration at certain seasonal changes (Beltaine and Samhain). Sex is also participated in as a ritual act when third-degree students who are in a stable relationship in a coven are ready to form their own coven. The act is then blessed by the high priestess or priest. Both these rituals are conducted in private. On the rare occasion when a group acts as a single unit, the coupling is undertaken while the group turns their backs standing in a circle. So, it occurs under very stringent conditions. We must also bear in mind that minors are generally not permitted into covens or working groups of this nature. Other than this, sex in ritual is enacted symbolically using an athame and a chalice.

Sex is venerated as a joyous union, and conventional notions of a fixed sexuality are overturned; instead sexuality is seen as a shifting energy. Paganism attracts a significant gay following because of its understanding of issues of sexuality.

Environmental matters

Pagans can be quite militant about environmental matters. Since ancient times, they have understood the concept of 'Gaia', viewing the Earth as a vast self-regulating organism. The now-scientific notion that uprooting the rainforests in the southern hemisphere will affect the weather in the northern hemisphere makes complete sense to Pagans. The changes of the seasons are not only honoured as a symbolic representation of the changing face of the God and Goddess, but also assimilated in a way that makes sense of our being in relation to these seasonal changes. Pagans celebrate the four quarterly (and most commonly accepted) seasonal changes – these being the equinoxes (Spring and Autumn) and the two solstices (Winter and Summer). These are known as the lesser Sabbats. The greater Sabbats are celebrated at the cross-quarter points in between.

Thus, every six weeks, Pagans acknowledge the shape-shifting forms of Nature, and see reflected in this their own changes, needs and plans of action.

Pagans are highly individualistic. There is no 'one' Paganism. It is an individual spiritual quest with individual responsibilities. Pagans take on another magickal name – a custom that is not unique to Paganism. Shiva devotees also do this, as do Roman Catholics at confirmation. It is an acknowledgement to the deities – an enactment of the person that they are aspiring to become. It's also finding or tapping into the energy that Nature offers (in a tree or stone, for example) and becoming one with it.

The Earth is perceived as their 'Mother'. She is seen as a living deity, a conscious, self-regulating being. The Pagan 'holy book' is Nature, in the cycles of life and death. As such, the Divine is immanent; it exists in everything – within animal, vegetable, mineral and human. Pagans are thus pantheistic (i.e. they believe that the universe is a manifestation of the Divine). In addition, divinity is believed to be transcendent, existing externally. Pagans are also animists, believing that everything is living and has breath, and polytheistic, for they worship more than one god.

Pagans accept themselves as part of Nature and don't see themselves as having dominion over it. Everything is connected to everything else. They also see events as cyclical and not linear (e.g. death is necessary for rebirth). Pagans approach events positively, and have a life-affirming philosophy based on 'thou shalt' rather than 'thou shalt not'. By abiding by the Wiccan Rede, or, if one is not Wiccan, the threefold law, the necessary respect for Nature and acceptance of the self as part of Nature is cultivated.

Dualism and polarity

While very much ensconced in the West, Pagans reject the Western dualistic approach of opposites. Pagans generally don't see things as either black or white; they incorporate the Eastern philosophy of yin and yang into their philosophical and religious beliefs, seeing everything as a balance between night and day, male or female, and so on.

Pagans call this principle 'polarity'. They acknowledge that, although there are two sides to everything, things are not in opposition to each other. Pagans seek harmony and balance within the ebb and flow of antithesis. So Wiccans, for example, seek to find both the God and Goddess within themselves, regardless of their gender. Jung's concepts of 'anima' (female part of a man) and 'animus' (male part of a woman) play an important part here.

Archetypes are linked to this – the idea of the perfect love, an arch-villain, the perfect woman. Pagan gods and goddesses are archetypal. So Diana, Goddess of the Hunt, is summoned when they need courage to go forth; Kali becomes their avenger when they have been dishonoured, or suffer; and Pan is invoked when they want to make merry.

The Triple Goddess

The Triple Goddess is one of the main theological principles of Paganism. The Maiden, Mother and Crone (waxing, full and waning moon) are all symbols of the collective unconscious, and operate as hidden 'spiritual keys' to understanding the self. The Maiden aspect represents potential, self-realisation and affirmation; the Mother aspect symbolises compassion, nurturing and passion; and the Crone is the embodiment of realised potential and wisdom. This is an undeniable reversal of stereotypes, as it empowers the Feminine Divine, by reclaiming Her sexuality and asserting its sacredness.

There is a fourth phase of the moon – when the moon cannot be seen. This 'hidden' face of the moon is known as the enchantress/seductress face of the Goddess. Pagan leaders, particularly priestesses, are lobbying for this phase to be embraced. While Pagans claim to believe in a guilt-free existence and a healthy sexuality, many carry the burden of a past Earth-negative spirituality. Because of this, they shun the enticement, allure and excitement of this face of the Goddess. It is easier to understand her in her triple form than to explore the enchantress aspect. However, this character of the Goddess is particularly important in the healing of women today, as it is a refreshing and valid way of reclaiming feminine sexuality.

CHAPTER 6

MAGICK AND RITUAL – THE SOUTH AFRICAN SCENE

MAGICK

So what is magick? Quite simply, it is an act of will! It isn't the wand-bashing we see on DSTV. It takes skill, discipline, time and effort. It isn't about being a Cher lookalike in a sexy black dress with lots of silver pentacles and other paraphernalia. It takes responsibility and courage. Magick is about getting off your proverbial behind and 'doing it'. This involves *will*, *imagination* and *focus*.

History of magick

It is well known that magick predated religion. Earliest magick was an attempt to deal with the Elements Earth, Air, Fire and Water (landslides, thunder, lightning, and rain), which were seen as supernatural. A primal religio-magickal system evolved and these Elements came to be seen and venerated as gods. With the advent of religion, elemental forces were equated with deity.

There is evidence of magickal practice in Palaeolithic Shamanic times in cave paintings, burial sites and rock carvings. Most of these magickal rites appear to have been performed after successful hunts. The Shamans attuned themselves to the spirit of the animal or the herd. They could 'tap into' the energy of all life forms. They felt Nature closely – in thunderstorms, rain, heat or the respite of a cave. The Elements of Nature were ascribed with superhuman power, and the hunter-gatherers of the time began a primitive religious system, giving deity-type attributes to such Elements, and performing ceremonies to appease them. Sympathetic magick was also practised, where Shamans dressed in skins and horns to identify with the herd, and play out the hunt.

The transition from hunter-gatherer to agricultural societies was reflected in the reverence for the Earth Mother. Trees, birds and stars were all symbolic in some way. Worship of Nature and her Elements was continued. Previously, magick was practised to ensure the success of the hunt. Now it was practised to ensure increased crops and fertility. Rain and its concomitant rituals were of paramount importance. The land was honoured, and reverence was expressed through sacred art.

The Neolithic period saw people settling into communities. Small clans grew into villages, which grew into towns and eventually cities. Sophisticated religious systems sprang up with the great pantheons of Egypt, Greece and Rome. Magick flourished. These civilisations were indebted to the Sumerian and Babylonian religio-magickal systems. While the Babylonian system of deities, spirits and demons drew heavily from the Sumerians, the Sumerian system of magick emphasised a faith in humankind rather than deity. This polarity – appealing to self or appealing to deity – is still at the crux of magickal practice today.

Another major difference in the use of magick now appeared. While the Sumerians used magick to protect them from harm, the Egyptians used it to control both the realms of people and spirits.

It has now become acceptable to use the word 'magick' with a 'k' to distinguish it from stage magic. Modern magick attempts to deal with the supernatural through one's own internal god-force. It doesn't rely on any external deity. Magick lies embedded in the subconscious, and it unfolds and manifests through the will power of the personal conscious.

Definitions of magick

According to Madam Blavatsky, a leading nineteenth-century occultist, theosophical author and founder of the Theosophical Society, 'The art of magick consists in the ability to perceive the essence of things in the light of Nature, and – by using the soul power of the Spirit – to produce material things from the unseen universe, and in such operations the Above and the Below must be brought together and made to act harmoniously.'

Dion Fortune, one of the earliest modern magickal revivalists and co-founder of the Order of the Golden Dawn, says that 'Magick is the art of changing consciousness at will.'

Aleister Crowley, probably the most infamous magician of recent times, defined magick as 'The Art and Science of causing change to occur in conformity with will.'

Will has to do with intention and determination. Wrapped up in intention is imagination. Magick is a projection of thought. It is the ability to see your target and project your will onto something or someone. So, you need to be precise, and you must know all the factors, or at least as much as possible about the subject. In our modern society, both of these areas, will and imagination, have been seriously eroded. Certainly, imagination has dissipated, as we have been conditioned to be logical and analytical, thereby destroying the creativity that exists in our minds. A third ingredient for magick is focus or concentration.

White and black magick

The terms 'white' and 'black' magick are now popularly used. 'Good' magick is commonly termed 'white' magick, and 'bad' or 'evil' magick is referred to as 'black' magick. Practitioners would argue that there is no such thing as white or black magick, because the results are dependent on the 'intent' of the magician. So, they see magick as a neutral force, much like electricity. Put your finger in the socket and you'll get singed; switch on the light and all's fine.

White and black magick bring up the issue of the 'left-' and 'right-hand' paths. Usually, those that walk the right-hand path walk a path based on ethics (such as the Wiccan Rede), and submit to deities; those that claim to walk the left-hand path either don't acknowledge divinity or they seek to control it. They see divinity within themselves and seek personal power. This doesn't make them essentially bad, just as those who walk the right-hand path don't all have big white wings attached to their backs.

The left- and right-hand paths often overlap, and this is sometimes called 'grey' magick. All practitioners have to make individual choices regarding their stand on particular matters at certain times. For example, if a child has been molested, you know who the perpetrator is, and the mother comes to you for help, what would you do? There are several approaches. The neutral approach relies on karma to take control. The active approach calls for justice to be done, and the more radical (and I believe unethical) approach wills revenge on the perpetrator, thereby helping to alleviate the sense of suffering almost immediately. This last approach would probably fall into the category of black magick.

In South Africa, as in other countries, many witches precede their title with the term 'white' to distinguish their practice clearly. This distresses others who are attempting to reclaim the word 'witch' – to mean 'wise woman', 'healer' and 'counsellor'. However, given the political ramifications of the word, in South Africa I think that this is a complete waste of energy. It might be better to concentrate on reclaiming a concept such as 'priestess'. We have fairly successfully reclaimed the word 'Pagan', and the general public at least have an inkling that it is neither Satanic nor a fad. The use of the word 'white' to precede magickal practice also disturbs many magickal practitioners, as they don't believe in the distinction between black and white practice. And in South Africa, 'white is right' is a sentiment Pagans do not endorse.

Besides these distinctions, there is the difference between 'high' and 'low' magick. In older times, low magick was associated with people who lived on the heath, in the valleys. They practised a simple folk magick, harnessing natural energies, using Nature spirits, and being close to the Earth Mother. Low magick is also known as sympathetic magick. In other words, a physical link is formed between the practitioner and the individual with the aid of dolls, nail clippings, hair, photos, etc.

High magick was practised by those who lived above the lowlands, on hills or in fortresses – the aristocrats, who had access to geometry, astronomy, mathematics, music and the like. Pictures of Merlin are conjured up, with all his books, compasses and maps. This distinction is less apparent today, since most folk practise a mixture of the two. Practitioners, be they magicians or witches, are educated. The terms 'high' and 'low' have come to mean use of magick for higher consciousness or contact with the Divine (high), and use of magick for needs such as love and money (low). Yet another distinction is that between 'Art' and 'Craft'. Art is linked with 'high' magick and Craft with 'low' magick.

Magick in South Africa

Though this book is not about magicians or mages in South Africa, it's important to point out that they do exist. Just as there are traditional hereditary family witches, so there are magicians. They are as secretive as the hereditaries, and no doubt grit their teeth when someone on a talk show says: 'Hi, my name is so-and-so, and I'm a magician.'

These magicians are adepts who follow the maxim: 'To Know, To Will, To Dare, To Keep Silent.' Pagan magick is also practised a great deal, with an easy crossover into high magick. Would-be mages are extremely curious, and there is a tremendous amount of dabbling. Because of the amount of literature that is now freely available, South African society has opened up to magick and its practices. This process has been aided by the Internet, the growing respect for traditional healers, and the number of practitioners who have gone public.

Magickal orders have existed in South Africa since the establishment of Freemasonry and Rosicrucianism. The Golden Dawn has been represented in South Africa for a long time, and the Order of Oriental Templars (OTO) also has representatives. Both the Golden Dawn and the OTO are fairly secretive, with very few known members.

Three years ago, two orders went quite public. This was because certain practitioners started to bring them into the public arena. These were the OTO and the Illuminates of Thanateros (IOT).

They arrived publicly on the scene almost simultaneously, although there were a few isolated practitioners practising their traditions secretly before that. Their public appearance had a certain impact on some Pagan practitioners, who hastily attempted to make their current practice compatible with those of the new magickal orders.

Most Pagans and Wiccans are not involved in any of these orders. But some cross over easily. It's important to mention that a number of Pagan practitioners can also be called magicians. They walk a fine line in terms of their definition of divinity, acknowledging a force higher than themselves and also adhering to the personal god within.

In fact, many Wiccans shy away from high magickal practice, fearing its association with the negative left-hand path. They generally prefer the safety of the structure surrounding low magickal practice.

Magickal tools

When practising magick the mind needs to make an impending shift. To facilitate this shift, a large variety of occultic tools are used. These include robes, athames, swords, candles, incense, masks, staffs, wands, ritual jewellery, pentacles and altars. Most practitioners, whether Wiccan or magician, will have the tools described below.

Altars

Most practitioners have an altar of sorts at home. Some have a dedicated room in their home; others have a small, dedicated space. A small number use an outside room. All practitioners are different, and their altars may be elaborate or simple. Some may represent their deity with natural elements such as a pine cone (representing the God) or a shell (representing the Goddess); others may use statues (to represent particular gods and goddesses, such as Shiva or Kali). Some may have 'dark' altars, and use bones, for example, to represent the shadow side;

others represent the joyous celebratory side with flowers or fruits. Some use male symbols of power (knives and swords); others do not. Some altars are set up on a permanent basis; others are set up only when a ritual is about to be performed. I know some practitioners who have even set up mini-altars at work, where they burn incense and a candle, without any problems.

The robe

Most traditions have a robe of a particular colour. Some traditions have different robes that signify different degrees. Most robes are hooded, and should be made of a natural fibre. As with all working tools, they should be made by the owner's own hand (but as with most working tools, we tend to buy them). Since the robe is used for ritual work, it should be kept in a special place. Then the mere act of removing it ensures a subtle shift in consciousness, a preparation for something that is about to happen. The individual can decide how elaborate the robe should be. Working as a solitary also requires a robe. Again, the act of robing readies the practitioner for a change in the ordinary environment.

The cord

This is particular to Craft work and symbolises the witch's bond to the Goddess. Natural fibre such as cotton, silk or wool is usually used. As with the robe, cords may signify rank. They are also used in binding rituals and knot magick.

Jewellery

It's probably true to say that all practitioners, Craft or otherwise, have consecrated jewellery of sorts. It may be a reflection of the tradition they practise, or it may be something inspired and created by the wearer, having deep personal symbolism.

Candles, incense and anointing oil

Colour and smell are used as a subliminal trigger. There are no hard-and-fast rules, and individuals find what works best for them. However, any book on candle magick will give you information on colour and its correspondences and often includes a chapter on incense. Groups choose what they feel comfortable with. For example, you may be used to certain colour candles in the quarters and attend someone else's ritual where different colours are used.

Be careful when using candles, and do not leave them unattended, unless on surfaces like marble. I once did an eight-day candle-burning ritual in my bath, and discovered that a large hole had burned right down to the cement.

I had to get a new bath, resplendent with tiles. I was 'lucky' that the fibreglass didn't explode. (I can hear you asking if this was a sign that my spell succeeded or flopped ...)

Athame

This is one of the witch's basic tools. However, it is also used by most magicians. The Athame is associated with the Element of Fire (although some associate it with the Element of Air). It is a symbol of masculinity and is associated with power, strength and virility.

Sword

Although swords are usually used by magicians, witches and Wiccans also possess them, especially in covens. It is considered a tool of command, and is male in energy.

Wand

Assigned to the Element of Air, and also a masculine energy, the wand is seen as a tool of persuasion rather than command.

Pentacle

Used as a symbol for Earth, the pentacle can be made of any material and incorporates symbols that are meaningful to the practitioner.

Cauldron

The cauldron represents birth and creation, and is a female symbol. It is tied to much myth and tale and is most useful in the magickal act of burning paper sigils or for scrying (i.e. foretelling the future).

The cup/chalice

Representing the Element of Water, the cup or chalice is a feminine symbol. It is consecrated and used only for the purpose of communion with the gods and the self.

Magickal methods

By far the greatest part of magick preparation involves exercises to reinforce will and activate imagination. Most books on magick (which are becoming more freely available as interest in the topic increases) include detailed exercises with step-by-step instructions.

A lot of magickal work relies on the ability of the practitioner wilfully to shift consciousness into a non-ordinary, visionary state of awareness. Traditionally, certain methods have been used to cause this shift: dance, song, music, colours, scents, drumming, fasting, meditation, breathing exercises and forms of hypnosis. Dramatic, mystical environments, such as sacred groves, magickal circles or temples will aid this shifting consciousness.

Meditation, visualisation and pathworkings

Meditation, visualisation and pathworkings are also used. In visualisation, certain images are focused on, thereby stimulating the imagination. Pathworkings are probably the most powerful form of this. In a trance-like state, and under the guidance of someone else, the person or persons are taken on an imaginary journey. One of the primary reasons why pathworkings are so effective is because most of the imagery encountered is highly archetypal and therefore talks directly to our subconscious. From here on, the exercises become increasingly intense and vary according to the type of magick the person is pursuing.

Simple breathing techniques are learnt, enabling the process of relaxing the mind and body. It can be quite disciplined, requiring the individual to sit dead still for a lengthy period – at the same time focusing solely on the work in progress. Visualisation and pathworkings may be considered journeys of the conscious (from without), whereas meditation may be considered as a journey of the unconscious (from within).

RITUAL

The need for ritual is inherent within us all. Take, for example, the idea of feeling that you can't get up in the morning without a cigarette or a cup of coffee. This would be to define ritual in its narrowest sense – as a simple repetition of actions. Those who practise ritual as an act of divine service, or as a form of ceremony, would hotly contest this.

Today, the need for ritual seems unprecedented. The removal of rites of passage in our Western society has alienated us from our own understanding of the cycles of life. Pagan rituals are a lifeline in restoring the equilibrium of mind and spirit. They tend to emphasise rites of passage such as birth, sexual maturation, birth, war, death, divorce or separation, as well as house and animal blessings. They are also attuned to the cycles of the seasons, with festival celebrations at the equinoxes, solstices and the cross-quarter festivals.

In modern Western society, many people feel alienated and have weakened spiritual links; they are yearning to 'reconnect'. Because we are aware of this, ritual has made a big comeback in our spiritual growth. It need not be an empty show, although it can all too easily slip into the mode of pompous gatherings and elaborate theatre.

Definition

Ritual may be defined as a 'ceremony' – as a specific set of movements or the manipulation of objects designed to produce desired inner processes. Inherent in this definition, then, is the idea of magick – the use of will, focus and imagination to manipulate and/or change events.

To speak of ritual in a religious sense is to speak of it as union with the Divine. In a magickal sense, ritual is enacted to produce a specific state of consciousness to achieve a set of goals.

Ritual is something inherent in all religions. It enables us to deal with archetypes, to tap into Jung's collective unconscious. Ritual is a method, an approach for contacting the external and internal Divine within us. It is a way of understanding, or making sense of our inner psyche at its deepest level, in order that we may contact the Divine within. For the magician or practitioner who works only with the god-form within, ritual ceremony is a tool for tapping into that power.

Ritual then is a symbolic language. It is a way in which we come to terms with the processes of life and death and the cycles of rebirth at all levels of our being. Ritual is not an objective process; it is a relative and subjective experience.

Ritual in South Africa

Judging from the number of Pagans that attend public festivals and those that ask how and when and where they can attend them, South African Pagans love ritual. Some would describe themselves as 'ritual animals'. Having spoken to many at these occasions, their raison d'être is to 'connect', to find a place to 'belong', a place to be safe. Participating in the ritual aids these needs. Rituals and gatherings are a 'back-to-the-clan' concept, a natural manifestation of the spiritual healing taking place in post-apartheid South Africa.

The amount of ritual goings-on in small groups is growing rapidly. Here the meeting of minds and spirits is deeper than just connection and belonging; ritual is a bridge to the Divine. The eclecticism is profound. The fact that we are forging ahead with our own 'traditions', using what we want from British and American sources and applying our own minds, means that a new, dynamic approach and vision is developing. This is particularly evident in Wiccan circles. We may have a lot to learn from Britain, for example, particularly when it comes to discipline and respect for tradition, but South Africa has a lot to offer when it comes to creativity, impetus and new life.

Ritual locations

Now where do we do these rituals? There is much debate around this question. I once heard someone put it quite elegantly: we can roughly divide modern Pagans into two types: primal Pagans (the Celts and the nomadic Viking invaders) and temple Pagans (who worshipped the great Greek, Roman and Egyptian pantheons). These two schools differ in terms of their preference of location. The more hardy may fancy braving the cold and work hard at synchronising their chattering teeth in their quest for divine illumination. Others would rather work in the moderate temperature of their homes, allowing them the freedom to alternate between levels of consciousness more easily. I personally do not like getting up at three in the morning, climbing treacherous rocky paths up a mountain, carrying heavy food parcels and paraphernalia to see the sunrise. The idea of bugs creeping up my legs as I try to meditate puts me off. (No, I'm not so advanced that I can just switch off!) And no toilets! Give me a sunset in a beautiful garden any day.

Of course, if both sets get together and feel that the weather is moderate enough for outdoor ritual activity, and find an agreeable location, then the ritual can be highly successful.

The most powerful rituals take place where two or more of the Elements cross, for example at the sea, which is Earth, Air and Water, or on a mountain, which is Earth and Air.

Wherever you choose to do your work, you will need to have dedicated space. It doesn't matter if this is only a tiny corner in your bedroom, or the edge of your desk at the office for that matter. It may be a dedicated room in a house, or even a permanent temple. You may have a permanent stone circle in your garden, for example.

Ritual consciousness

This is a vital component of any ritual. It is usually achieved through a meditation or guided pathworking. Drumming, soft chanting or dancing sequences may also be employed. These dancing sequences should not be confused with the raising of energy. Ritual awareness or consciousness is a heightening of the senses, and expanded awareness of the non-physical world, a linking with Nature and the forces behind all conceptions of deity. It is an aid to prepare us for the energy raising and the working; until this point we might still be carrying our problems from the day into the circle.

Use of substances

This is a problematic area – one around which much debate revolves. Some highly evolved Shamans use substances during rituals; Native Americans, for example, use peyote. Similar use is evident in our traditional communities here, but substances are used under strict supervision if the person is in training. Natural substances (such as marijuana) are used here by Shamanic types and other Pagans. This is not to say that all weed smokers are Shamans (although, in my experience, they tend to like to think they are!). The use of chemical substances (such as LSD) to induce trance states is generally unacceptable, and the data collected is deemed false, no matter how mystical or ecstatic the experience may have seemed. Wiccans regard the use of any substance to induce shifts in consciousness as anathema. They prefer to reach heightened states through natural means.

Ritual guidelines

Wherever you do your rituals and whether you practise skyclad or not, there are some underlying principles for success in your ritual. By 'success' I mean obtaining the desired outcome, especially if you are using your ritual for a magickal outcome.

Ritual may be elaborate or simple. It may be exceptionally simple, such as sitting next to a tree and meditating, or as complex as a Latin High Mass. It may be tribal in nature, with drums, fires and feasting, or it may be a complex ceremonial temple setting.

There should be no random design. In other words, spontaneous ritual may occur, but this is rare and generally the domain of the more experienced practitioner. Always balance discipline with spontaneity. The concept of mirth should always be balanced with reverence. Many of us have suppressed Calvinistic backgrounds and approach ritual with trepidation; sometimes our mirth is even subconsciously feigned. We often forget the words of the Charge of the Goddess: 'And all acts of pleasure shall be my ritual, and there shall be music, making love and feasting.' There should always be an equilibrium between dogma (as agreed by the participating group beforehand) and spontaneity. Most of us must plan carefully, for the physical and visible activities that surround our ritual will impact on the invisible actuality that will happen as a result.

There must be conscious participation. In other words, you need to participate consciously and soberly and collaborate with the spirit world.

Ritual is not something that is done to you; rather it is something you do. In other words, there is full participation, not only with the spirit world, but also with your mind, body, emotions and psychology – in short, all of you.

There should be no observers, as they detract from your focus, and even if you feel that you are disciplined and focused enough not to let them affect you, they may interfere with the energies raised from their side – not your side. However, this is not to say that there can't be observers at an open Sabbat/festival, where one of the objectives is to create positive public awareness of Pagan rites.

Rituals are usually led by a priestess and/or a priest. It's important to remember that we are all priests and priestesses in the Craft, but within a ritual, someone takes the responsibility for the smooth flow of the event. This person may be the designated high priestess of the coven, or designated for that specific ritual. They should be experienced, as they need to guide and ground the flow of energy. They may need to alter or adapt the agreed-to ritual in parts on account of unforeseen circumstances. For example, a spirit guide may visit one in the group and impart a message or messages that could change the ritual working; or during a visualisation the entire group could 'see' the same thing or similar things that will alter the dynamics substantially.

Most Pagan rituals take place in a circular fashion. This is unlike the monotheistic approaches, which typically take place in a square shape, where the people sit on one side of an invisible line, and a priest mediates at an imaginary line between the people and God. The circle allows for energy flow and, of course, it is both the psychic barrier of protection and the containment of energy raised.

All members participating in any ritual should agree upon its structure. It is vital that the intent of the ritual be understood by all equally, for this will determine the method to be used by all. Not only this, but unless you are involved in a group that you trust, it alleviates discomfort and the unhappy situation of wanting to leave halfway through the event.

The following are the steps that typically take place in ritual. Some books may amalgamate these steps. Please note that these steps follow in order, although certain processes may occur at the same time. Some of these steps will be discussed in detail, while others have already been discussed elsewhere in this book.

- Preparation: This may include fasting, mental preparation and focus before the ritual. Individuals can prepare for days before the ritual, or just a few hours before (e.g. with a visualisation or chakra exercise).
- Purification: This may involve a purification or cleansing exercise (e.g. bathing in salt water), just before the ritual.
- Cleansing the sacred space: Before the ritual event, the space may be swept, anointed or smudged. This is an ancient Shamanic technique (practised especially by Native Americans). It involves the use of a smudge stick (made from selected dried herbs) or a bunch of joss sticks (incense sticks). This is set alight until it smokes profusely. With the aid of a large feather, the stick is taken around the perimeter of the circle or around a person's body, cleansing the space or the person's 'aura' of negative energies and readying the space or person for the rite.
- Casting the circle: This is covered in detail in the next chapter.
- Welcoming the Elements: This is also covered in detail in the next chapter.
- Invocation of deity: Many people use the terms 'evocation' and 'invocation' interchangeably; however, they are two different techniques. Invocation is the process of inviting an entity or spirit to take over your body. It can result in channelling and mediumship. Greater/higher beings are invoked; lesser spirits are evoked. So, deities are invoked. To invoke is to call 'in' or 'down'. In terms of the God or Goddess, it involves the 'invoker' drawing the Divine energy into his or her body. Alternatively, the 'invoker' can draw Divine energy into the body of the priestess.
- Visualisation: Visualisation is a means of attaining ritual consciousness. Certain images are focused on, in order to stimulate the imagination.
- Raising energy and grounding: Raising energy and grounding can be done in many ways – by singing, drumming, shouting, dancing or clapping. Certainly one of the most popular ways (especially if you are working in a group) is to move around in a circle, spinning faster and faster until you all fall to the ground naturally. At the time of falling, when your hands or palms touch the floor, you feel yourself connect with the Earth again, and focus on the reason for being there – the reason for spinning, falling and grounding. It involves sending your energy out into the universe.
- The working: This is the spell or ritual itself.
- Communion or thanksgiving: Known as 'cakes and ale' in Wiccan circles, this is a very practical intervention at the end of the ritual. Here, participants

'step down', as it were, from the working of the circle and back into ordinary reality. The eating and drinking is a realisation that we are still of this world. After magickal work, one tends to be a little light-headed. As well as a 'grounding' exercise, it is also an act of endorsement of masculine and feminine energies.
- Feasting: Feasting is an essential part of Pagan ritual.
- Banishing the Elements and bidding farewell to the deities: This is the 'closing' of all things invoked (opened), i.e. the quarters and the deities. Pagans bid them farewell and 'close down' the energy that they have brought in.
- Closing the circle: The energy raised during the ritual must be diffused, like snuffing out a candle or quelling a fire.

Can you get ritual wrong? It is unlikely. The worst that can happen is that nothing can happen. The ritual will simply be empty and yield no results. Young students entering the Craft are often nervous. They are worried that they may be using the wrong colour in the wrong quarter, or invoke an incorrect deity for a particular ritual. This sort of concern is unnecessary. We must remember that it is the intent that counts, and until your knowledge is more developed, there is a karmic process that will protect you. However, having said this, more experienced practitioners will know that things can go wrong. Innocent intent may yet yield undesired results if the correct 'ingredients' and questions are not applied. Calling up spirit forces of which you have little knowledge or which you intend to use for dubious purposes can work against you.

Finally, ritual should be practical. It's fine to read ostentatious books on the subject of ritual and fantasise about Egyptian or medieval temple-type layouts and misty stone groves, but if it's not practical, forget it. One of the most impractical rituals I ever attended was a beach ritual. This is a lengthy story, but I include it as it contains a number of humorous 'don'ts' that serve as lessons for what should be done.

It was a full moon, and it was assumed that the moon would light our way. Wrong! The moon was behind the sand dunes, and no one had thought to bring a torch. Getting there was an arduous task. It seemed that only the acting high priestess knew the spot, and the trek took ages. We had to negotiate our way over water-filled potholes that would have challenged even the toughest 4 × 4. We thought that finding the spot by using cellphones would be easy. It was like a spy movie: 'HPS1 to HPS2, which sand dune are you at now?' Eventually, we got there. The group in charge had their portable altar set up already. The altar was a very large and heavy kist (chest) filled with unnecessary paraphernalia.

The circle was such that we had to raise energy by running halfway up a dune and halfway down it again. I had on a new robe, and it was too long for me. This meant that I had to grab it every time I ran up the dune. Someone in the group had bad asthma and couldn't deal with the steep uphill. The chant was not a simple two- to four-liner as it should be, but a lengthy poem that nobody could or would care to remember, especially since we were focusing on ensuring that we didn't fall flat on our faces.

Two workings were done in the ritual. This is not necessarily wrong, but, since energy was completely scattered, there was hardly enough focus for one. To top it all off, the acting high priestess screamed at us to chant! After the circle was closed, there was no food or water for feasting. I had brought none myself since I was a visitor who had been told that everything would be arranged. Naturally, we were all hungry and thirsty, and the long walk back through the dunes and the drive over the potholes seemed bleak. Remember that the feasting afterwards is integral to Pagan rituals.

One of the most practical rituals I have attended was on top of a high-rise block of flats in the city. For urban Pagans, with no facilities for misty forests and standing stones, this made complete sense. The acting high priestess received the permission of the building's caretaker to perform the ritual, and about twenty-five of us gathered on a full moon. It being a Christmas Eve as well, we incorporated the Kabbalistic Tree of Life into our ritual and drew a large diagram in chalk over most of the roof. Upon entering the roof from the small stairwell, we were immediately asked to wash our feet in a large basin filled with a little neroli oil and flower petals. And so the ritual began.

CHAPTER 7

SOUTHERN HEMISPHERE MUSINGS

Debate surrounding southern hemisphere practice, particularly the inversion of the seasons, is one that involves most Pagan paths in South Africa. Magicians, however, don't seek inspiration from Nature, so they don't need to attune themselves to the differences between the two hemispheres.

But for Pagans, perhaps one of the greatest difficulties facing beginners, as well as seasoned practitioners, is the issue of northern hemisphere practice in a southern hemisphere context. Virtually all of the books on 'how to do it' come from Britain and America. Very little arrives from Australia. Recently, however, the Internet has provided some information.

With Nature as the starting point, we catch a glimpse of the Divine. Through experiencing the seasons we begin to understand the concepts of regeneration and reincarnation. Each season holds a mystical experience, and for some it is an initiatory one. I have seen many Imbolcs, but each time I celebrate it, something in me is renewed. I gain new inspiration and a fresh perspective.

I have great difficulty working to a northern hemisphere clock in the southern hemisphere. How can you celebrate a Summer festival (with all its associations of joy, plenty and light) in the middle of Winter (with all its associations of barrenness, cold and darkness)? How is it possible to celebrate Samhain at the end of October when we are welcoming in the Summer? The body, the psyche and the spirit simply cannot relate. I have been asked several times to re-enact a Halloween/Samhain ritual for television purposes when it is actually Beltaine time. Though the public popularly thinks that 31 October is Halloween, my physiological clock has great difficulty attuning itself to this, even for a TV mock-up.

Most Pagan practitioners, and certainly most Wiccans, enact their understanding of the changing faces of Nature through Celtic mythology. However, in certain South African circles, this is being rejected – for example by replacing the Holly and Oak Kings with indigenous alternatives.

This chapter will look at circle casting, the Elements and their correspondences, and how we attune ourselves to the Wheel of the Year by inverting the festivals.

IT'S ALL ABOUT THE CIRCLE!

The question of the circle, which falls into the scope of the debate, is not one that involves all Pagan paths. The two directions of movement – clockwise (known as deosil) and anti-clockwise (known as widdershins) – are specific to Wicca. These two directions are based on the movement of the sun's rising and setting, as well as its movement through the sky.

Shamans may move in a circular fashion, but they shuffle in either direction at the whim of their trance state, drawn by a different energy to that of the rising or setting sun. Druids also make use of a circle of stones – stacked and prepared before the rite – but with no concern about the direction in which the stones have been placed.

Many witches, like magicians, don't use circles at all. They are only too willing to make contact with the world of phantasm. The circle gives them protection that they don't want; they seek protection elsewhere.

But the circle, which is seen as essentially feminine, has a variety of functions in Wiccan practice. It serves to establish a boundary between the world of humans and the world of spirit, a divide between the mundane and the magickal. It blocks out unwanted energy, while containing the energy raised within the circle.

Prior to actually casting the circle there is a fairly elaborate method to purify, cleanse and consecrate the sacred space first, especially in Gardnerian and Alexandrian rites. It is not necessary to do this. Sometimes sweeping or smudging the sacred space will suffice.

Where does one cast a circle? Any dedicated sacred space will do. The circle may be a permanent feature, such as a circle of stones in the garden. It may be painted on the floor of your lounge, covered by a carpet when not in use. You may demarcate it at appropriate times with flour, petals or flowers on the grass outside. (Never use salt; it will destroy the grass.) An experienced witch or Wiccan can create sacred space at any time and any place.

The circle will always be cast in the air, with the aid of a wand, athame or sword, or you could simply use your finger. The idea is to create a sacred space by cutting through the etheric energy around the space in which you have determined to work.

Traditionally, the circle is cast three times, either for cleansing, consecration and the working, or in honour of the Triple Goddess. Some feel that casting once is sufficient; others walk around as many times as they feel necessary. The circle-caster, and the participants in the circle, should all visualise a sphere of energy forming around them. How and what one visualises will vary. For example, one can visualise golden, silver, white or blue light, emanating from the sword as it is drawn around the circle. Or perhaps you will want to visualise a wall being built around you, or a grove of thick trees veiling you. It's important to remember that this is a magickal act, and its completion should be endorsed by a signal or verbal response. No one should leave the circle once it is cast. However, it may be necessary at times, so an opening or doorway is symbolically 'cut'. It is closed immediately and re-opened should the individual return.

The next question is: in which direction do you cast the circle? The rule of thumb is sunwise. In the northern hemisphere, the sun rises in the east, moves to the south, sinks in the west and settles in the north. So, the sun moves through the southern sky from left to right. This makes it seem as though it moves in a clockwise direction. In the southern hemisphere, the sun rises in the east, moves to the north, sinks in the west and settles in the south. Here the sun passes through the northern sky from right to left and appears to move in an anti-clockwise direction. In both cases, east and west remain the same, and north and south are swapped around. This means that in South Africa we appear to cast the circle widdershins (anti-clockwise), moving from east to north to west to south. In the northern hemisphere the circle is cast deosil (clockwise), moving from east to south to west to north. However, some start from north and end in north. In other words, Wiccans work with the natural Earth energy of the sun.

There are many misconceptions about the terms 'deosil' and 'widdershins'. They don't correspond precisely to 'clockwise' and 'anti-clockwise'. They do, however, correspond accurately with the movement of the sun. In the southern hemisphere the Earth tilts, and the sun moves from east to west across the north. Thus, the sun moves in an anti-clockwise direction between sunrise and sunset. As mentioned, the casting of a circle should work with the power and strength of natural energies; therefore, deosil in the southern hemisphere refers to an anti-clockwise direction.

Similarly, widdershins doesn't refer purely to an anti-clockwise direction. Deosil is 'moving with the sun', so it stands to reason that widdershins is 'moving against the sun'. Therefore, in the southern hemisphere, this is clockwise, representing a closing or winding down, banishment and repression. Casting widdershins is sometimes used for negative magick. Therefore, casting the circle widdershins is seen as a negative act. However, in the southern hemisphere, widdershins means clockwise, and deosil means anti-clockwise.

So, simply put, deosil is sunwise. Therefore, in both the southern and northern hemispheres, the circle is cast deosil, even though in the southern hemisphere the circle is cast in an anti-clockwise direction.

Becoming accustomed to working and walking in a particular direction has interesting effects when you do circle work in another hemisphere. For example, in a large ritual I attended in Wisconsin, with about two hundred participants all walking clockwise, my companion and I could not help moving against them in an anti-clockwise movement in the opening of the circle. None of their pushing or jostling could turn us around; we were like automated machines.

Many folk in South Africa cast their circle deosil according to northern hemisphere tradition because this is what a book from, say, Britain has explained. They get used to this method and may find it very difficult to change.

Closing or 'banishing' the circle is usually done in the opposite direction to which it was cast, but in both hemispheres we generally begin in the east. So, in South Africa it would be clockwise. This is not to contradict the synergy of the energy just conjured up, but to 'shut' or 'close' it down. Energy raised must be diffused, like snuffing a candle or quelling a fire.

The trick, as always, is to make all practices, whether they are circle casting or directions, relevant and harmonious for the individual. This is a basic tenet of Paganism.

THE ELEMENTS

Before we look at the southern hemisphere effect on the directions, let's look briefly at the Elements and their characteristics.

The four Elements of Nature, Earth, Air, Water and Fire form the foundation of natural magick and the basis of Pagan magick. They are associated with the cardinal points of the magickal circle and govern lower-level spirits called Elementals. Guarding these are the Lords of the Watchtowers, the Mighty Ones and the Guardians.

What follows are some useful correspondences, in no way exhaustive:

Air

- Goddess association: Maiden
- Season: Spring
- Time of day: Sunrise
- Gender: Male
- Characteristics: Abstract thought, intellect, balance, justice, theory, change, reason, understanding, charity, speech, knowledge, the wind, new life, possibilities
- Elemental spirits: Sylphs (faeries, angels), ruled by Paralda
- Sense: Smell
- Archangel: Raphael
- Magickal tools: Athame, sword and censor
- Astrological signs: Jupiter and Mercury
- Zodiacal signs: Gemini, Libra and Aquarius
- Colour: Yellow
- Tarot suit: Swords
- Direction: East in both hemispheres

Fire

- Goddess association: Temptress or enchantress
- Season: Summer
- Time of day: Noon
- Gender: Male
- Characteristics: Will power, expansion, force, energy, aspiration, creativity, protection, leadership, intellect, detraction, absent-mindedness, favour, sexuality, explosion, warmth, optimism, purification, liveliness, activity, pleasure, rootlessness, perseverance, knowledge, courage, passion, force, self-assertiveness, joie de vivre, frivolity, virility, zeal, enthusiasm, heat, light, life force, waxing
- Elemental spirits: Salamanders, ruled by Djin
- Sense: Sight
- Archangel: Michael
- Magickal tools: Wand, scourge (or athame, sword)
- Astrological signs: Mars, Sun and Jupiter
- Zodiacal signs: Leo, Aries and Sagittarius
- Colour: Red
- Tarot suit: Wands
- Direction: North in the southern hemisphere; south in the northern hemisphere

Water
- Goddess association: Mother
- Season: Autumn
- Time of day: Sunset
- Gender: Female
- Characteristics: Emotion, contraction, intuition, cold, passivity, creativity, fertility, courage, depth, mystery, healing, ebb, sensitivity, delusion, psyche, love, infatuation, tides, pools, sorrow, clairvoyance, feeling, receptivity, self-indulgence, instability, womb, subconscious, waning
- Elemental spirits: Undines (nymphs, merpeople, sirens), ruled by Niksa
- Sense: Taste
- Archangel: Gabriel
- Magickal tools: Chalice or cup
- Astrological signs: Moon and Venus
- Zodiacal signs: Pisces, Cancer and Scorpio
- Colour: Blue
- Tarot suit: Cups
- Direction: West in both hemispheres

Earth
- Goddess association: Crone
- Season: Winter
- Time of day: Night
- Gender: Female
- Characteristics: Earthy, wisdom, focus, introspection, stability, quakes, growth, responsibility, endurance, strength, practicality, patience, commitment, hoarding, melancholy, stagnation, dullness, thoroughness, prosperity, nurturing, grounding, materialism, fertility, business
- Elemental spirits: Gnomes (dwarfs, elves, brownies, hobgoblins, leprechauns), ruled by Ghob.
- Sense: Touch
- Archangel: Uriel
- Magickal tool: Pentacle
- Astrological signs: Venus and Saturn
- Zodiacal signs: Taurus, Virgo and Capricorn
- Colours: Brown and green
- Tarot suit: Pentacles
- Direction: South in the southern hemisphere; north in the northern hemisphere

Some readers may look at these correspondences and argue that the magickal tool for Air is not a sword but a censor. Perhaps. In some traditions it is a blade. Some people feel that the Element of Air, that of intellect, is also highly intuitive. I believe it is the domain of reasoning and logic. For me, the area of intuition belongs to the area of the western Element, the dark waters of mystery.

Having said this I do not wish to compartmentalise the four Elements into four rigid blocks that cannot flow into each other. But I am saying that, throughout magickal practice, the Elements have been used in these ways.

Yet you will find individuals associating Water with Spring, or Air with Autumn, for example. Still, it is traditionally accepted that Air belongs to the east winds and is the place of the rising sun, not the place of the setting sun. So how can this be? And can Water, long associated with the mysterious waters of birth, be associated with Spring? The answer lies in finding your own truth and harmony – your own liturgy, in fact.

Enough said on the qualities of these Elements. But what do they mean to an individual? Some we aspire to acquire; some we wish to rid ourselves of. Sometimes a particular Element can be seen to dominate an individual. We could perhaps describe ourselves as 'fiery', 'watery' and so on, and, within that, pick out other characteristics that correspond to our nature. These we invoke into our circle when we call on a particular quarter. For example, if we were doing a ritual or spell for empowerment of an individual in a very stressful relationship, the eastern quarter would call on clarity of thought in the situation. The northern quarter would perhaps call on courage and perseverance. The western quarter would call on intuition in the situation; and the southern quarter would call on focus.

From early times, humankind related to Earth, Fire, Water and Air. Imagine the cave dwellers' anxiety during a great storm – when all the Elements are at play. Within the realms of magick, these four are still accepted as the categories to explain our world.

There is a fifth Element to which we also relate, known as the etheric or akashic Element – the Element of Spirit. It cannot be perceived with the physical senses. This Element is placed in the centre of the circle and is usually represented by the person participating.

THE SOUTHERN HEMISPHERE EFFECT ON THE DIRECTIONS

The directions, north, east, south and west (also known as the quarters, the Elements or the Watchtowers), are affected by the sun's travels through the sky.

So how do we call the quarters? Popularly, in South Africa, we call in the following order: east, north, west and south (Air, Fire, Water and Earth; male, male, female and female). Popularly, in the north the following order is used: east, south, west and north (Air, Earth, Water and Fire; male, female, female and male). In other words, we call in the same way that the circle is cast, deosil in the northern hemisphere, and widdershins in the southern hemisphere. But remember, in the southern hemisphere we also call the casting deosil!

However, there are a myriad variations on this theme. A group in Newcastle on the east coast of Australia start with north when going widdershins, calling on Fire because Australia is below the equator, and it gets hotter the further one travels north. West is summoned next with Earth as its Element – the logic being that the bulk of the continent of Australia is to the west. South is Air from which come the strongest winds. Water is east, and the great Pacific Ocean lies to the east.

Some folk in South Africa practise this method as well, based on the logic that this is southern-hemisphere-based rather than just Australian-based.

The Temple of the Dark Moon in Adelaide, South Australia, makes this suggestion for Pagans living in the east:

- North = Fire: The equator lies north of Adelaide, as does the Simpson Desert. Also, northerly winds are hot and dry.
- West = Water: West of Adelaide is the Spencer Gulf, which is obviously associated with water.
- South = Earth: South of Adelaide is the Antarctic. Southerly winds are cold.
- East = Air: The sun rises in the east, as in the northern hemisphere.

People living on the eastern seaboard of Australia, for example, might use the following directions:

- North = Fire: This is similar to the above example, as Australia is south of the equator.
- West = Air: This direction is used because in Australia winds blow across the continent from the Indian Ocean.
- South = Earth: As in the above example, it is associated with the Antarctic, and it is the traditional opposite of Fire within a circle.
- East = Water: In the eastern states, the Pacific Ocean is to the east.

I am a traditionalist in the area of circle casting and quarter calling. In other words, I am interested in the movement of the sun through the sky. I am not too concerned about whether the greater land or water mass lies ahead of me or behind me, from what direction the mightiest winds blow, or how far above or below the equator I am. As mentioned before, this is also the most popular approach in the South African Wiccan scene.

In the northern hemisphere the altar is traditionally placed in the north. In the southern hemisphere it is placed in the south. The north is traditionally considered home of the gods. It is also the direction in which the sun travels. In the southern hemisphere the altar faces the South Pole, for the sun travels south. However, we often place the altar in the middle of the circle for ease of participation.

THE WHEEL OF THE YEAR IN THE SOUTHERN HEMISPHERE

The seasons turn, like a wheel, moving one into the other, and our lives and psyches are inextricably linked to their ebb and flow. Without knowing it, we are drawn into Winter's dance of death and plummeted into the underworld of depression, anxiety and fear. For no reason, when the leaves fall, we feel a strange melancholia – a sadness and heaviness of heart that we cannot explain. As Spring floods our being, without understanding it, we get a little light-headed and euphoric. As Summer melts us, we tend to forget our worries, go with the flow and start thinking of our New Year's resolutions.

Yes, Mother Nature controls us. Pagans, witches and Wiccans understand this and take deliberate steps to participate in each seasonal change. We are consciously involved in the mystery of the seasons, thereby receiving our inspiration and teachings.

There are eight seasonal changes. These are divided into the four greater Sabbats (festivals), which are lunar-oriented, and the four lesser Sabbats, which are solar-oriented. The four lesser Sabbats are the two solstices (Winter and Summer) and the two equinoxes (Autumn and Spring). The greater Sabbats have come down to us in modern times from known ancient Pagan festivals. Also called the cross-quarter Sabbats, they are Samhain, Imbolc, Beltaine and Lammas.

Most Pagans celebrate the lesser Sabbats, while the Craft community adheres to both. Although most practitioners in South Africa are comfortable with inverting the seasons (especially once they know about it), there are some stalwarts who won't. Some have lived most of their life in the northern hemisphere and simply cannot adapt. Others travel extensively between the two hemispheres and get so confused in any given ritual that they decide to stick to one way, and it is usually the northern hemisphere way.

In some areas, such as Gauteng, it is very easy to see all these seasonal shifts. In the Western Cape the four lesser Sabbats apply more accurately.

The dates and their inversions for the eight festivals are as follows:

	Southern hemisphere	Northern hemisphere
Samhain	30 April	Halloween – 31 October; Samhain – 1 November
Yule (midwinter solstice)	21 June	22 December
Imbolc	2 August	2 February
Ostara (Spring equinox)	21 September	21 March
Beltaine	1 November	1 May
Litha (midsummer solstice)	21 December	22 June
Lammas	2 February	31 July
Mabon (Autumn equinox)	20 March	21 September

Note: The lesser Sabbats' dates change because of differences between the actual astronomical event and our calendar.

Where do we begin our sacred seasonal journey? It differs for every practitioner. Most Pagans in South Africa begin their calendar at Samhain, referring to it as their New Year. The exact date of the festival should be determined by the fact that you are celebrating a season. The rule of thumb here is rather to be late than early, as an early celebration is still within the ambits of the previous season.

Samhain – 30 April

Samhain, pronounced 'Sowen', is the old Celtic word for 'Summer's end'. In ancient times it was a period of great anxiety. It was known as the last harvest, and it was a harvest of blood. All livestock that could not be sheltered in the long Winter months were slaughtered and salted. Nobody could anticipate how long this meat or the cold would last.

The first months of the cold time were a time of great feasting and love-making – in simple terms, the months were lusty and full of life. The kings called council and decreed new laws. Travelling Bards were taken into the nearest village for safety. It was also a time of primordial chaos. How long would the Winter hold? When would the sun begin to ascend again? It was a time to appease the gods, a time of divination, of magick and predictions. It was also a time of fear, a time of dying and crossing over.

The popular name of 'Halloween' arrived when the Church tried to rationalise these issues by introducing the idea of All Hallows' or All Saints' Day. So,

Samhain Eve became All Hallows' Eve and eventually Halloween.

In our modern context, Samhain is no longer a time of appeasing the gods. It is a time to reflect on death and the regeneration that must follow. It is a time to pass on old things and let go. It is the end of a cycle and the beginning of a new.

In popular myth it is the time when the Goddess mourns the death of her husband/lover/king (the Sun King), struck a fatal blow by the Dark Lord of the Underworld (the Winter King) at the midsummer solstice, and finally killed by him at the first harvest. She has mourned and is now willing to give up her sovereignty and Motherhood to become the Crone and enter the Underworld. She will face her fear, the Dark Lord, in order to meet with her consort again, and to bring him back. She faces the Dark Lord, who reveals the mystery – that he is her husband. They meet, make love, and the seed of their union grows beneath the cold Winter Earth, readying itself for Spring. This, then, is a time to honour the dead. We invite their presence into our homes and circles. We lay a place for them at our tables. The veil is thin. In other words, we move between the worlds of darkness and light, fear and hope, anxiety and trust. We will meet with our departed and be born again.

As is the case all over the world, in South Africa popular belief celebrates Halloween party-fashion on 31 October. Pagans honour Samhain on 30 April.

Halloween is the one day of the year on which it's really great to be a witch. You get to be as stereotypical as you like. You can have an array of skulls on your altar for your ritual, and the police wouldn't even bat an eyelid.

Yule – 21 June

This is the Anglo-Saxon word for midwinter solstice. Originally it was the Norse word for 'wheel'. The Yule log represents the wheel of life or turning of the seasons. 21 June is the longest night and the shortest day of the year. The sun begins its ascent and the waxing year begins. It also marks the end of the waning year. The time of the Holly King is over, and the time of the Oak King begins. The Crone who descended into the Underworld has regenerated and become Mother and Goddess once again and now gives birth to the Sun King. Festivals to honour the ascendant sun at the Winter solstice were so widely spread in ancient times that the Church had no choice but to get in on the act. The Christmas Nativity story is very similar to the Pagan tale of the sun's rebirth. Since no one really knew when Jesus' birth date was, it was fixed only in AD 273, at midwinter in the northern hemisphere, bringing him in line with other sun gods.

Normal business stopped and homes were garlanded with evergreens such as holly, ivy and mistletoe. Gifts were given to all. Decorating trees with fruits, nuts and berries was an act of sympathetic magick designed to cheer on Spring. The signal for Winter, though still cold and icy, was over. The singing of Pagan solstice carols was very popular, long before Christmas was celebrated. These carols have been borrowed and adopted by the new religion, and examples include 'Deck the Halls', 'Joy to the World', 'God Rest Ye Merry Pagan Folk' and 'O Come All Ye Faithful'.

We celebrate the departure of the Dark Lord (known as the Holly King), welcome the new child of hope and promise – manifest in the sun (known as the Oak King). Although the sun has reached its weakest point, the first rays after the longest night reflect its returning powers in our lives. So, this is our 'Christmas'. Now how can we celebrate this on 21 December when it is midsummer? It is all about the first rays of the ascending sun after a long Winter, and in South Africa it occurs on 21 June. In the northern hemisphere it occurs on 21 December. The mystery, the initiation, the attunement with this cycle of Nature lies in this time.

Since Yule is a turning point, the end of the solar year and the beginning of the new one, many Pagans choose to begin their New Year here.

Some young Pagans and Wiccans enjoy being dogmatic and dramatic in their stance against the popular Christmas festivities in December. But it is nevertheless a time for family and friends. I enjoy having two Christmases very much!

Imbolc – 2 August

Imbolc means 'in the belly' and refers to the first stirrings of Spring, deep inside Mother Earth. It is also known as Candlemas because of the tradition of lighting a myriad of candles to symbolise the growing warmth of the waxing sun. It was also once known as Oimelc, as this was the time when the ewes began lactating and the translation of 'oimelc' is 'ewe's milk'. This is a time midway between the Winter solstice – when light ascends in the form of the birth of the Sun God – and the Spring equinox – when the Goddess returns from her journey to the Underworld. She returns as the waiting bride of the Sun God. It is a time for initiation into the female mysteries and the first flow of blood, i.e. menstruation. The Sun God, still a babe and growing, only beginning to show his horns, is unaware of these changes, until his time comes at the Spring equinox.

Winter's hold on the Earth is breaking, and the Earth is starting to show greenery once again. By the time the Spring equinox arrives in September, you will already see trees and flowers in full bloom. Now one notices tiny green buds everywhere, and birds building their nests. Already there is a flutter in one's being, and a promise of something to come. In Gauteng, Imbolc manifests a very clear shift between Yule and the equinox. This is not the case in the

KwaZulu-Natal area where the temperature is moderate all year long. (I suppose this is Nature's gift to Gauteng, for they don't have the mountain and sea that the Cape has, or the wonderful greenery of KwaZulu-Natal!)

This festival indicates a time of new beginnings, a renewal of old commitments. It is generally a time to spring-clean. Traditional practices at Imbolc are the weaving of candle-studded crowns by women, the making of a grain dolly, who represents a virgin, and burning any Yule greens that are left over.

Ostara – 21 September

Overt signs of life are present. Here, day and night are equal, and the sun is in the ascendant. This represents balance. The word 'Easter' comes from the word 'Oestre' – a Nordic goddess whose symbols are the egg and the rabbit, representing new life and rebirth.

Everything is flourishing and the young God is clad in his finest greenery. All around us fertility is evident. Crops are planted. Animals are active. We are active. Beneath the soil, after a long Winter, activity is evidenced all around us.

The Goddess, too, is in full bloom. Both the young Lord of the Forest and the Lady watch each other and are aware of their potential and virility. Wherever the young Lord of the Hunt goes, the forest beasts follow, turning all vegetation he touches green. She follows like a shadow, feeling a stirring in her soul. Their feelings for each other become more serious as the wheel turns to Beltaine.

Easter eggs, symbols of new life, were used to welcome prosperity, while hot cross buns and amulets, with their solar crosses, were used for protection.

Beltaine – 1 November

In Celtic tradition the beginning of Winter and the beginning of Summer (i.e. Samhain and Beltaine) are the most important celebrations. This is the sacred union of the God and Goddess, the traditional fertility festival. Almost every tradition at this time symbolises this union. Customs include filling baskets with symbols of fertility (such as eggs or nuts) and the weaving of the maypole (the pole representing the phallus, and the strands of red and white coloured ribbons symbolising the birth canal of the Goddess). The weaving enacts the sperm heading towards their destination. It is traditionally the time of year when handfastings (marriages) are pledged.

Large bale fires were made from the dross or waste of the Winter fields. It was a form of purification. Animals were herded through the fires to cleanse them of parasites. This is where leaping the bonfire comes from. It was an act of cleansing (remember, bathing was a rarity). Leaping the bonfire was also taken by a couple as a sign that they would be married before the next Beltaine, or, if already married, that a child would be on its way.

To the urban Pagan, the idea of fertility is conceptualised as a time of planting – thoughts, ideas and plans – but it is also the celebration of all the fertility within Nature. It is a time to rejoice in the new growth around us and to focus on bright, new beginnings.

Litha – 21 December

It is the height of Summer. It is the longest day of the year. The God and Goddess have joined as one. They reign as sovereigns. A great feast has been prepared for them. The Goddess/Queen is pregnant, a reflection of the blossoming and ripening land around her. The sun is at its peak. But this festival marks another turning point in the solar year. Until Yule, the year will be on the wane. It is customary to re-enact the battle between deities to represent both the dark and light halves of the year. The Oak King, god of the waxing year, falls to the Holly King, god of the waning year. In one of the myths, a dark shadow falls over the merrymaking, and the Sun King is challenged to a duel. He cannot see the face of his challenger, and is struck a fatal blow in his thigh, which does not heal, until his sacrificial death at Lammas.

The Earth is now a place of great beauty, filled with flowers that will soon become fruit and vegetables. For Pagans, it is a time of great joy and plenty – a time to bask in the splendour of the Earth's bounty and to think of no tomorrow. It is not a time to take stock or reflect, but to dance and be merry.

Lughnasadh (Lammas) – 2 February

Lughnasadh marks the beginning of the harvest. It is essentially a Druidic festival dedicated to the Celtic Sun God, Lugh. However, there were also goddesses associated with corn such as Ceres and Demeter. The harvest was seen as the fruit of the Mother. Lughnasadh was eventually Christianised as Lammas.

This festival was known as the first harvest festival, because of the harvest of first fruits, particularly grain products. Making corn dollies is traditional at this time.

The first signs of Autumn are evident at Lammas, just as the first signs of Spring are evident at Imbolc. After the Summer solstice, the sun's power begins to decline, and the Sun King dies symbolically. The God sacrifices himself to the land. As the grain is cut down, he is symbolically sacrificed so that his people may live. He will be reborn again at Yule.

This is a time to pause, reflect and open yourself to the change of the season, so that you may accomplish what is intended.

Mabon – 20 March

Mabon is the name of the Welsh God, known as the 'great son'. In Welsh mythology Mabon was stolen from his mother at the age of three, and taken to the Underworld, only to return at Spring. Like Demeter and Persephone, this is a time where the dark lauds it over the light. So it shall be until the Spring equinox.

Once again, day and night are equal, in perfect balance. This is the second harvest festival. At this time, the Goddess or Queen, in desperate anguish, unleashes the terror within herself. She acknowledges that her King and husband has been taken to the Underworld and that the only way she will be reunited with him will be to traverse the path he has gone.

And so she tears the veil apart, and faces the Dark Lord of the Underworld, her own fear, herself, and enters the cycle of Samhain.

Mabon is a time of preparation. It is a time of taking stock and summing up – a time to find balance again.

My personal favourites are Samhain and Imbolc. Samhain is a time where I feel forced to face my demons, where the Goddess gives me a cosmic kick up the proverbial behind and says, 'Get with the regenerative programme!' So even though I have this tendency to hold on to past things, this is the one time of the year I know I have to, and can, with the help of a community I trust, put issues to bed and start afresh.

Imbolc is an extension of this regeneration. Spring tends to pass me by. I see the pigeons balancing madly on anything they can, and green everywhere, and think: 'So what?' But Imbolc – that's different. Something stirs in me. A small 'tap-tap'. Something – a small green leaf – catches my eye. I smell something new; it stirs a distant memory, and I can't let go until I remember. Slowly, gently, kindly, softly, I awaken from a melancholy slumber, and a faint smile laces my wintered lips. Roll on Beltaine!

Before we conclude this chapter, a word on our Esbats. We have discussed the Sabbats in some detail. Most folk think of Pagans out and about at full moon. This may be true, but we do work on many different nights of the moon's phases.

The most common approach is to work within the ambits of the waxing, waning and full moon. These we align to our Triple Goddess. We see her in her waxing phase in her Maiden aspect. Here she is full of potential; this phase is about making plans, establishing ideas, planting, etc. The full-moon phase, that of the Mother, has to do with growing, nurturing and caring. The waning phase has to do with endings and putting things to rest. There is a fourth phase, when the moon is dark and cannot be seen. It is known as the phase of the temptress, seductress or enchantress, and certain practitioners advocate that no work be done at this time.

Moon time is work time; festivals are a time to celebrate.

CHAPTER 8

LET THE WITCHES SPEAK!

Bev Nowikow, 48 – Adept

I lost my mom at the age of nine and lived with my Nana, who was my first teacher. She showed me the ways of the old ones. The word 'witch' or 'witchCraft' was never mentioned, for it was considered a way of life rather than an elaborate philosophical and religious structure.

My Nana always said to me you can be whoever you want to be and can have whatever you want in this life, as long as it is for the good of yourself and others, and harms none. That was the best advice I could ever have been given and has stood me in good stead to this day. I pass this on to all I come into contact with. My Nana informed me about the coven back home in Scotland to which she and my mother belonged. She told me to make contact at some stage of my life when I was older and had more understanding of such matters.

It was not until 1994 that this occurred, and I was able to go home to England and Scotland and discover myself through my roots. It took me three months to find the coven. The crone who had initiated my Nana and my mother was still alive, aged 94. I was taken in and taught the ways of the old ones. Notes and books were passed on to me, as had been done with all my predecessors. They told me to start teaching in South Africa and assured me that they would always be there for me.

On my return I started teaching without knowing what kind of reaction I would get. This would be the first of such teaching publicly in South Africa. I advertised in a small esoteric newsletter, and to my amazement I received a number of phone calls and, therefore, students. Public interest grew and the demand and hunger of people searching became evident. The growth and teachings continued steadily. With Paganism and witchCraft becoming more acceptable and stabilised, as a result of certain dedicated individuals, I began to walk two other paths – the way of the Sangoma, and the Santeria.

The way of the Sangoma is different from Wicca. Wicca is a newly introduced practice, very popular today. The old ways of the 'wise one', the witch, are rarely practised, possibly because it is a family thing. The word 'magick', to my mind, is not properly understood. When you have asked for something or need something, and you receive it by 'coincidence', this is magick. Most individuals seem to need to cast spells and have elaborate rituals in order to create this kind of magick in their lives. Yes, this does work if your intentions are right and no harm to yourself or others is done. Most practitioners have a lot of chaos in their lives because they get what they want – without thinking about what they really want. They are not careful about their intent and the ramifications. They confuse the issues themselves. Learn to know yourself, love yourself, and get your life in order first. Then things will fall into place accordingly. The true essence of magick is to know yourself, believe in yourself, have a sense of self-worth and have the confidence that goes with this.

The sad thing for me is the number of people who come to me who do not want to help themselves. Healers and advisers (not magicians) are expected to produce this magickal change in their lives without them having to do anything. Our practice is therefore misunderstood and abused, often by the practitioners themselves, who prey on such needy individuals.

As a hereditary witch, I began to pursue other avenues of spirituality within a South African context. I qualified as a Sangoma in 1997 in Dobsonville, Soweto. I am still not sure how I ended up there. My experience was not a happy one. As a white person, I received training that many white Sangomas today are not privy to. It came at a price however; R15 000 later I was a qualified 'white Sangoma'.

The practice is very primal. Few questions are asked by (or permitted of) the student. The practice is based on the call of the Ancestors. If you have the 'sickness' – anything from itches to madness – then the Ancestors are with you, have called you, and you qualify for Sangoma school. If you do not go to school you are doomed; death is knocking at your door and all the bad luck you currently experience is due to this.

Santeria, which I pursued afterwards, is similar to voodoo, originating in

Zanzibar. It is not common practice in South Africa, and to my knowledge I am the only person initiated into it in South Africa. I trained in Cuba under my Padrino (teacher). I am comfortable with this practice. Much like the Sangoma tradition, the 'spirit' calls you.

All the various practices, whether Wicca or Santeria, are based on the same principles – cause and effect. Some may be modern, others primal. It depends on the person practising and their intent. In my personal journey through magick and mayhem, I have come full circle. No amount of occult law and study will make you an adept. A deep and rich understanding of yourself, a respect for life and love, and a deep honouring of your gods are the finest hallmarks of magickal prowess.

Tina (Volva Freya), 39 – Businesswoman

I have been involved in astrology, numerology, palmistry, etc. since early childhood. This is mainly due to my mother's influence. I found books on Wicca, and after devouring them was drawn to the Divine Feminine worship that Wicca subscribes to. Scott Cunningham's work really influenced me. His grasp of Wiccan spirituality really made an impression on me. I learned to know the Goddess and worship her through following Cunningham's lead in his various books.

I don't know if I'm a witch, a Pagan or a Wiccan. I am probably more of a Pagan at heart. The concept of me being a part of Nature, and of Nature being a part of me, makes perfect sense.

A witch, to me, is a woman coming to terms with her own feminine powers. By this definition, I am a witch. Stereotypically, I suppose I am very 'witchy'. I take no notice of what people say or think of me. This is the way I am. When people stare, I pay no heed. I have been like this from childhood. I am definitely very eclectic.

With regard to discrimination against Pagans or fearing coming out, I am not sure about this, as I have not experienced it. Whether it is because I run my own business and accord with appropriate behaviour at appropriate times, I do not know. But I do hear of others feeling this pressure.

Basically, I see eclecticism as a place from where a 'tradition' can start. In South Africa we are exposed to many varied forms of beliefs, such as Hindu, Muslim and indigenous African practices. We can tap into these different belief structures and adapt them to ourselves.

Do I connect with a black woman magickally? Well, she bleeds; I bleed; we can dance and cry together. Women share an innate being, and can connect no matter what culture they may come from.

I am especially drawn to the Norse tradition. A book I read on Norse goddesses triggered a deep interest in me. I have taken from both Hindu and Norse beliefs and adapted them to my own system and set of values. The value system of modern Goddess spirituality, combined with Norse mythology, really inspires me.

I practise daily. I have a dedicated temple room and combine the ritual elements of Norse, Hindu and Goddess spirituality. I lead several small groups in ritual exercise and I teach. I hold regular Esbats and Sabbats. I emphasise healing and letting go.

I am married to Derek (Thoth), but we seldom practise together. He practises with a few other individuals.

Certainly, in my opinion, Paganism (and Wicca especially) is growing in leaps and bounds. And I should know, as I live in a fairly conservative part of Johannesburg.

Derek (Thoth), 40 – Electronics

I would consider myself a Pagan, as I believe in more than one god. I have a strong Nature-based structure of belief, using herbs and crystals. I relate to Egyptian cosmology, particularly to a small percentage of Wicca, especially green witchCraft. I interchange the two systems easily, for example wearing ivy for healing, while praying to Isis. You could call my practice 'Egyptian Paganism', if you like, rather than Egyptian magick.

I came to Paganism while meeting my wife Tina. I feel blessed living with a witch, although we practise separately. However, we share common ideas. At times we come together, but call on our own deities.

South African Paganism is going through a rough patch at the moment. There is not enough information available to those who are seeking or for those who would like to get more involved in the practice of Paganism or witchCraft. 'Bitchcraft' is rife, and Pagan organisations are very competitive. Pagans in South Africa need to put away their nonsense and start sharing ideas.

Tina and I stay out of the politics. Perhaps even being interviewed for this book is 'political'. Who knows? I practise with one or two other individuals regularly and also have a dedicated temple room.

Tanya (Gimmel), 34 – Choreographer

I am very comfortable with the term 'witch' now, but I would not say that I have always known I was a witch. I have always known that I am different; the label does not matter to me. The label matters a lot to others, though.

Many people use the term witch for the glamour, i.e. power, ego and recognition. But being a witch is much deeper. WitchCraft is a way of life, a knowledge of who you are and where you are going – of being able to work on your weaknesses and acknowledging your strengths. Knowing where your strength lies does not mean you are vain, but it does mean that you are in touch with yourself.

Being a witch has empowered me. I live my life in a way that witchCraft is totally normal to me. If I want more compassion from my husband, I put a secret ingredient into his coffee, and the result is amazing. When I was pregnant, I wore a green cord around my waist to ensure the health of my baby. They actually had to cut the cord from around my waist when I was giving birth. WitchCraft is natural to me and is a major part of my lifestyle.

Essentially, a witch takes control of their own life and takes responsibility for their own actions, not laying blame on someone else – knowing how to tap into the power that is around you and 'sending' that power to do your bidding.

Jenni (Ruby Flame), 24 – Marketing manager

I believe I am a witch by intuitive knowledge. I have had a deep knowledge of my being a witch, and also sought out advice from a psychic, who confirmed this. It is not something that I believe, but something I know.

I decided to learn more about the Craft because I was feeling lost, coming out of a long-term relationship, and was pondering where I was and where I was going; as if I was driving a car, and knew that it was going, but didn't know which gear I was in at the time. My first contact with Wicca – or a Wiccan opening – came to me in my dreams. I went into a bookshop and bought some books on Wicca. What I read made me realise that I was in fact at heart a Wiccan. It was as if a long search had come to fruition.

I search for solutions in different ways. I have a say in how my life is going to turn out; I am not a slave to fate. My way of processing things has changed.

Wicca is seen as 'trendy'. There are a number of youngsters out there who would love to be the next 'Halliwell 3', flaunting Wiccan regalia and telling everyone 'I'm a witch.' But unless they have a grasp of the actual practical side of Wicca – the day-to-day living and breathing of Wicca in their own lives – it will be shallow and simply a phase.

I have opted to work in a coven because in a coven you have a sense of community and a secure place to learn, being able to work with people who think like you do. All of us are on the same level and have the same focus. We're not a group of sheep, but we do have very similar ideals and beliefs. We work well together. We all feel this way.

Chantelle (Silent Cheetah), 23 – Banker

The witch concept seemed very complex to me originally. As I delved into the Craft and Wicca and experienced things, I found myself attuning with the basic principles of witchCraft and felt totally at home with what I was learning.

I use the terms 'witch' and 'Wiccan' synonymously. I came to understand that I was Wiccan. I needed to find out more, get down to brass tacks, as it were. I signed up for a Wicca class, and during the course, as I learned about the Wheel of the Year and the Elements, I knew that I had found my path – that I had found a system of belief that made sense to me. I am more aware of Nature, and have much more self-confidence than I had before.

There are a great number of folk getting into Wicca today, mainly due to a romantic, glamorous portrayal of the Craft in the media, but the majority will not stick it out. Wicca is a way of life, not a merit badge for coolness.

I am part of a coven. It is great to get together again – with a sense of togetherness and understanding. We meet once a week, and if there are any needs that come up in between we call an emergency working. Our coven formed by a mutual agreement, reached by folk who had already worked together and who decided we wanted to remain together in a tight group. We did not want to have to go and find a coven, when we had all we needed in our group. It is also much easier to form a coven with a group like this than to have to go and find a coven and go through the whole 'Am I going to get on with them; am I going to fit in?' thing.

Cindi (Stara), 32 – Full-time priestess

I love the term 'witch'. I like the drama in the term; it gives me a platform to explain what I believe and what I practise.

I categorise Wicca and Paganism together, as Earth-based Goddess worship. There is a lot more to being a witch than the fluffy-bunny stuff you read about in most Wiccan literature. There are many varied traditions involved in the practice of witchCraft. My integrity makes me a witch. This is what Wicca and the Craft are all about: live your word as best you can.

I have always thought differently to what mainstream religion teaches. My realisation that witchCraft was my path came by reading an article on Paganism and Wicca. I then started reading as much as I could on the subject. On my second Silver Ravenwolf book, it hit me between the eyes: I had done all of this before. I started practising candle magick and visualisation, using a Buckland book; then went on a course and met my fellow coveners.

With regard to my children, I will let them learn about the path and feel they will come to a place where they will choose for themselves. I will raise them according to Pagan practices. I am constantly fighting the crèche because of the ideas that they are putting into my children's heads. I'm looking for a school that doesn't indoctrinate. I don't hide my practice; I burn candles and allow my son to come into the circle (not my daughter – she's the lady of misrule herself).

My husband is neither here nor there. He feels that Wicca is too rosy, but we communicate well. He finds the rituals a bit on the lightweight side, but he is also alternative in his way of thinking. He joins in on the Sabbats. He recently gave me a 'surprise' handfasting. I suspected a surprise birthday party but not a surprise handfasting. After an extremely lengthy breakfast we went home, and of course the coven and friends were waiting and … surprise, surprise! Then out popped the priest (from Cape Town), and I naturally asked if our coven mother was with him, but he said, no, he was up on business. So, I accepted that. Then a while later, out she popped in official regalia. Then I knew. I was very touched. Cynic that my husband is, he had tears in his eyes as he retook his vows.

I chose the path of a coven, and a major reason for not going solitary was that the group that was in my Wicca 101 class already had such a dynamic energy that solitary practice was not an option for me.

Candy (Willow), 24 – Secretary

I'm a traditional witch, like all the women from my mother's side of the family. I have always been involved in the Craft. One of my great-grannies was burnt for practising. All of this information and the lore that my family practised have been handed down from generation to generation. My mother still has my great-granny's crystal ball. Our family all seems to have worked with a strong leaning towards healing.

From the time I was very young, I have spoken to animals and faeries. When I grew older, the current monotheistic religions had no appeal for me at all. I've always known that I am a witch. I just feel that I need to gain more knowledge.

Wicca, to me, is a way of presenting the Craft in a more 'acceptable' light. People tend to have built up preconceived ideas about witchCraft, and these ideas come with a lot of baggage. Wicca, to them, is more acceptable, as it does not carry the same stigma that the word 'witch' does.

I get very upset about Satanism and Wicca/witchCraft being linked in some people's minds. We do not, as Wiccans, even acknowledge the existence of the devil; he has no place in our belief system.

I would not say that I follow a tradition. I am more of an eclectic witch, mixing the lore carried down in my family with what I learn from others around me – making my belief system a very personal and private thing.

Jean (SilverBirch), 22 – Application support specialist

What drew me to Paganism, and Wicca in particular, was the ideology, the truth of being responsible for yourself, and the effect that you have on the world around you.

I consider myself both Wiccan and a witch. The religious aspect of Wicca is how I live my life, but I also practise witchCraft, which is without any form of deity.

I worship deity in the form of the Triple Goddess. I also worship the Horned God, but am exploring the Goddess aspect more at present. There is a complex mythology behind each deity, which makes them completely unique. One has to understand this before you can truly worship them.

Worship to me means communing with the gods and goddesses at particular solar and lunar times, but not exclusively at these times. My worship usually takes place outdoors, as this helps me to connect with the Goddess and the God more. This is of course dependent on the weather situation at the time.

My father doesn't know about my religion, as he believes it is Satanic. My mother is very accepting and supportive, being into Goddess spirituality herself. At work everyone knows. I actually put down 'Wiccan' on my job application and was accepted without any problem. What I found is that if one has some trust, mixed with discernment, in people and give them a chance to get to know you, they have an amazing amount to offer. People have shown interest in finding out what I believe.

Chris (Journey), 24 – IT specialist

I had a 'calling', studying as many religions as I could, and when I had basically given up on the majority of them, having decided to become agnostic, Wicca came up and seemed to stand out more than any of the others.

I eventually bought my first book on Wicca. I saw that the ideals and practices made perfect sense to me, and I had a feeling of 'coming home'. It was almost as if Wicca was designed with me specifically in mind.

I worked my way through the book for almost a year, working myself through the Wheel of the Year and then I bought more books. I lapsed for about a year, just making sense of what I was learning. When I came back to practising Wicca, it had become very much a part of my life.

My viewpoints began to run deeper, and I began to form philosophical assumptions. My old point of view was broadened by the Pagan viewpoint. The level of responsibility for one's own actions was brought home to me.

I sought out formal training after doing everything on instinct and within my own limitations. I needed the balance of both intuition and knowledge.

My mother is amused by the path I have chosen to follow, as well as slightly concerned. My dad thinks that I am involved in Satanism.

I have a long-standing relationship with Jean, and it is great to be following the same path. It certainly gives me a better understanding of Jean, as we are both highly individualistic.

My future in Paganism is dedicated to my level of self-control and direction, which is the pinion of all magick. This is my path to enlightenment: Paganism.

Mariana (Papillon), 56 – Full-time priestess and grandmother

I have been practising Wicca for four years, but I have lived the Craft all my life, and just did not know it. I saw divinity in Nature, raised my children to understand the interdependence of the Elements, for example how compost replenishes the Earth, or the sun heats the Earth to form rain. This was divinity.

I asked questions about mainstream religion: why are women subservient to men? This to me was not acceptable. I just could not gel with the ideas that were being preached to me from the pulpit. To me there had to be a Female Divine – some form of goddess. The monotheistic, patriarchal theory left me cold.

After having read a book by Amber K., I knew that I had found my 'home' spiritually. I was apprehensive about calling myself a witch, especially because of the situation in South Africa. I slowly realised I was a Pagan, and that what I had been practising was indeed witchCraft. This began the metamorphosis within me.

I'm extremely proud to have found my womanhood, with all of its possibilities. I don't have to suppress anything. I'm proud of being Pagan – especially for the ethics and morals that we as Pagans support and live by. The Earth Mother is highly regarded in my way of life, and this fulfils me.

My children have all unknowingly (by myself) been raised as Pagans, and are all practising Pagans or Wiccans. The Goddess is as real to them as she is to me.

I consider myself Wiccan. I follow the Wiccan Rede 'An it harm none, do as ye will.' I also consider myself a witch who follows the Wiccan path. I am a Wiccan witch.

Barry (Gawain), 47 – International business consultant

I alternate easily between all the concepts of witchCraft, Wicca and Paganism, while Wicca indicates a form or type of practice. I am basically a witch in a Wiccan sense, who practises Pagan principles.

I found this path very simply. My daughter expressed an interest in Wicca. Out of a desire to encourage her, I joined her. I first joined a Pagan organisation, which fuelled my interest, but the real answer would be that it seemed to be the right 'next thing' for me. I've been on many esoteric paths, but seem to have arrived at the right one. I'm very at home, extremely comfortable. Sometimes I wonder if I'm being challenged enough because I'm so comfortable.

There's a merging/synergising of all my previous experiences, no rejection. Last night I participated in a ritual, and part of my preparation was reminiscent of preparing for a Christian spiritual experience, such as speaking in tongues. This time, however, I was calling on different deities. Being one with the Godhead was experienced by achievement of universal love.

I enjoy the tolerance I find in Pagans in general. There seems to be the ability to experience life for what it is without constantly analysing it.

I enjoy the servant/pastoral care I find as well as the serious ability to enjoy life and Nature. My need to experience life, and not just think it, is being met. Unlike Christian consciousness, the whole Pagan consciousness seems to resonate within me.

My relationship with my daughter has deepened since I began my Pagan walk. It is another thing we share. I especially want us both to grow in the Wiccan path.

I want to grow personally, within myself. My daughter is very much a part of these plans.

I'm constantly involved in 'spell work', using meditation, chanting, etc. Magick has become very real to me, and I enjoy the power I am able to tap into to work in my own life. In my own situation, I am never the sit-back-and-take-it type. I now have total say in where my life is going, and I alone have responsibility for my actions.

Nicola (Lady Aloe), 21 – Law student

My search is new, not even six months old. It is a path that feels natural to me; I can feel it in my blood. It is my birthright, to not be discriminated against, for seeing oneself as vitally interconnected to Nature. I feel that the background that I grew up in has been a lie. My family know the choice that I have made and seem okay with it at this point.

Before I discovered the path of the Goddess, life was mere confusion – no answer seemed to fit, and no religious reality was manifest to me. Society tries so hard to mould us into the 'correct' shape – and, sadly enough, most people are vulnerable enough to take the shape of what is expected of them – not of who they are.

I consider myself a Wiccan, mainly because I've explored it the most. It's not an airy-fairy ideal, but a working, vibrant belief. I feel empowered as a woman. My entire outlook on life has changed, from my actions and reactions to others, becoming more aware of the environment and the way I see myself.

Wicca has taught me not only to believe in myself, but also to believe in (and feel) the amazing energies and powers of the Earth and all its kind. In Wicca we learn to embrace Nature – how to utilise the intense magnitude of the Earth in our daily lives. By taking planet Earth and the universe for granted, millions of people all over the world are actually taking the very essence of being, the very spark of life, totally for granted.

Don't get me wrong. I am by no means claiming that Wicca is the one and only answer; nor is it the one and only path to enlightenment. At the heart of Wicca is the concept of tolerance, and this is one of the greatest beauties of the ways of the Goddess. We respect the fact that, as the universe is so complex, people are also complex and involved – therefore not all beings see the light in the same way.

Getting in touch with the Goddess has, in a way, been like a roller-coaster ride. Each day is filled with many surprises and gifts of life, love and hope. Being Wiccan has made me look at and experience the world through new eyes, from a new perspective and mindset. Along with discovering the path comes discovering one's inner goddess. This has led to my empowerment as a woman – something that is suppressed and undermined in many religions.

At this stage I don't know where I'm going, except to say I'd like to see Pagans being active and stop being such an armchair community. My rituals at this stage are very much improvised. I read up on what I need to do and then add my own touch. My practice is very personal and means a lot to me at my basest level.

Wicca makes me proud of being a woman. I am proud of what I am and what I will become.

Peter (Fiery Oak), 20 – Freelancer

Having a keen interest in religious studies, especially the esoteric, and having read widely, the appeal of the Craft was where I felt most at home. The atmosphere (not the mystery) and the people are community-based. We truly are an old people and a new people, as one Pagan song goes. This I see as a very healthy approach to life. Also, as the original religion from Europe, it just seemed natural to me, and my affinity with the festivals, such as Easter and Christmas, was a natural progression into Paganism.

In my experience, other religions were rendered inefficient, mostly because of the lack of the Feminine Divine. The female strengths are so obviously understood that it just seemed like the natural place to be – in a religion that espoused the Feminine Divine. It is the only religion that I personally found extended from my emotions without great ideology and the need to intellectualise. By this I mean it came naturally, and I feel intrinsically drawn to it.

In South Africa, with its history and culture of oppression, trampling all over anything perceived to be non-conformist, I originally felt a tremendous sense of isolation, especially when I realised that this is for me! Long walks in natural surroundings drowned my sense of isolation most of the time – feeling the caress of the wind, the kiss of the sun, the Earth beneath my bare feet. It was almost like sitting on Mother's lap again.

Sometimes, it wasn't a walk in the park; you would have to defend yourself. I eventually had to come clean with my folks, and it involved me asserting who I am, like it or not.

I had no Pagan friends, but I did have a Pagan empathetic friend. I did not believe there were any Pagans in South Africa. I knew Pagans existed, though – I had seen a Druid ceremony at Stonehenge on TV. I was very worried that if there were any Pagans out there in South Africa they'd be the 'pissed-off-with-God' type. I was further afraid that if there were any they would be kids – insincere, playing.

I don't know why I thought that at the time. I think it had to do with the general South African pessimism. I finally found a pamphlet advertising a Wiccan course and decided to attend. I doubted myself and wondered if I was really 'one of them'. Also the fear of the awful stories I'd heard about naked initiations, sex rites and drug abuse made me no less nervous to go. I knew I'd beat my way out of the situation or die trying. I was damned if I was going to take my clothes off.

The course consolidated my knowledge, cleared up my misconceptions, allayed my fears of unruly nakedness and my own self-doubt. It introduced me to a community of like-minded people. The theme of community is vital to me. It's where I can relax. We all know who we are and what we are, and don't have to explain, describe or defend. Even if you're a solitary practitioner it's good to know there's a community out there. Community is a body of knowledge, a pool of resources and mutual support – the modern equivalent of an old village.

I have now jumped from complete isolation into co-leading a coven. I feel relieved. Part of me knew this would happen all along. It's a feeling of coming home, in the most literal sense, like I've just come off a hard shift, hung my coat on the hook, and I'm going to have a bath, dinner and then we'll talk at the fireside.

Jacques (Ra-hotep), 34 – Full-time Egyptian magician

Ra-hotep is, by and large, a solitary practitioner, but on occasion he does not mind sharing his workspace with either a fellow practitioner or a witch. When faced with the question of whether he is Pagan, he at first answered no. Then he thought about it and realised how it was that he 'grew' into his magickal system. 'I suppose it depends on your view of the Egyptian cosmology and to what extent it is Nature-based as opposed to consciousness-based. I am very "anti" some of the ideas that Pagans are supposed to have – like hugging trees – and am scared I will be seen as "fluffy".'

Two serious prompts in Ra-hotep's life led him to the position he is in now. The first was that he always questioned the concept of monotheism, especially the dogma associated with it. By the age of sixteen he had a strong foundation in alternative views and was practising yoga and the martial arts. At this stage, he was also searching for his real father, because he felt that the answer to this would reveal his true identity in the universe. After finding him, his father rejected him, heralding the onslaught of a deep depression.

As an antidote to depression, Ra-hotep relied on the spiritual nature of the yoga and karate practices in which he was involved. When this did not help, he actively looked for answers – seeking externally, as he feared the depression that the internal answers could bring. For him the most external answers had to lie in the sun and the sky. He focused on the sun in particular, drawing inspiration from its constant rising and setting, interpreting this energy as Divine. The mere fact that it shone was symbolic enough for Ra-hotep to see this universal energy as a manifestation of God. 'And God was always there for me; I did not have to ask constantly for permission.'

Ra-hotep's love affair with the sun had begun. Whereas sun-consciousness had no name initially, with reading and deep reflection he began to identify with the Egyptian Sun God, Ra. The Divine energy manifested as Ra, and soon Egyptian magick found a comfortable place with Ra-hotep. He realised that the Divine in the sun could also manifest through him, and he began to understand and apply the principles of magick – will, imagination and focus. The Gods of Wind (Shu), Moisture (Tefnut), Stars (Nut) and Earth (Geb) lace his practice.

Joanne (Dragonmistt), 31 – Chemical engineer

I consider myself a Pagan, as I believe that the spirit of the Divine exists in all living matter, including ourselves, as we are all part of the cosmic universal spirit. I enjoy the sense of unity that I have with the world around me, recognising that familiar spirit in Nature and other humans alike. But I also consider myself a witch. I am not ashamed to say that I am a witch – even with the negative attitude that most secular people have towards that word. I practise a craft in order to express my religion, in the same manner as other religions have their own 'techniques' for their expression. It is a physical and mental stimulation for me when I make certain things, like talismans and poppets. But the added benefit to these creative skills that I am learning is that I do it with a religious intention, which gives it so much more meaning – it is not merely creating things, but stimulating all areas of your psyche, emotions and spirituality at the same time. I believe that certain things I do with my hands in a 'craft' sense, and with the right spiritual focus, can effect beneficial change to my life and my family's lives.

To complicate matters further, I consider myself Wiccan as well. I follow a religion called Wicca. My religion is very important to me, as I have a very strong urge to connect with the Divine and have a relationship with it. I follow a Goddess-oriented religion that incorporates polarity between male and female. But I am very passionate about the Goddess, as she symbolises all that is representative of the subconscious mind through which we grow spiritually. And, of course, I am a woman, and this helps me to bring out my own inner beauty through the worship of female deity. Polytheism is very important to me, as I can interact with various personalities of the Divine source and improve myself in all areas of my life, while focusing on these.

I used to be a member of a charismatic Christian movement. I could never identify with the concept of God, who he was and how the whole thing fitted together, and I wasn't prepared to be told that I must just accept everything. Praying was very empty. I felt like I was talking to a brick wall, and I had no personal grip on the theology. I developed my own ideas on who God was and what he was, and who I was in the universe. Then, years later, I picked up a book on Wicca, and the theological principles expressed were almost exactly my own thoughts and feelings. I felt that I could follow a path that actually meant something to me – that I can get passionate about – since it was my understanding of the universe which preceded the systems that go with religion, such as ritual, etc. I could connect with what I was doing, and finally I could connect with the Divine Spirit in a way that I could understand. Everybody is an individual and has different perceptions.

It is difficult not having Pagan groups or an organised Pagan system in KwaZulu-Natal, especially having been to Johannesburg to the Beltaine festival. I must say I am envious of the structures and support systems that they have in place. There is so much going on, and so many different people to interact with, and most of all, so many people with so much knowledge who are there to enrich each other's lives. In Durban we have nothing like that, with the exception of the small group that I have running at my home, of which I am the co-ordinator. This is easier on an organisational level, but terribly isolated from mainstream events such as Sabbats and joining covens. Sometimes I feel that we are left out of what is going on in the rest of the country, and there is no networking or communication between us and the main body of Pagans.

We try our best to do things the way that they are supposed to be done. Not having any guidance from anyone, it is an incredible challenge, especially when I have so many people in my group who are looking to me for teaching and guidance. So, we end up doing things our own way. I am continually studying from books and piecing together my own rituals. I share the knowledge that I have with my group, and we discuss topics, which gives us time to question things and piece information together ourselves. In a nutshell, we learn the hard way, which is perhaps the better way to learn. I have no one telling me how to do things or advising me on basic techniques of the Craft, but I receive guidance from the Goddess, who I can tell you is the best teacher I can ask for. I think as a group we all learn from each other, no matter what our level of experience or knowledge is. I think we are doing a marvellous job together!

I work closely with Annette (Dolphin Star). On a personal level, we are excellent friends. We have very similar tastes and styles and value systems. We have agreed to do more of the 'advanced' workings together, for which the rest of the group are not yet ready. We share the same beliefs and the same spiritual goals. We are totally relaxed around each other in perfect love and perfect trust, which enables us to work on things without those terrible feelings of self-consciousness. We are both able to totally be ourselves around each other, which is important when you are doing spiritual work where you are literally baring your soul to the other participants.

Every morning I do a ritual outside and draw in the positive components of each element that I will need for the day, including worship of the Divine. This keeps me constantly in tune with the energies – like constantly charging a battery. Then, every Sabbat I will hold a celebration that anyone can attend. All persons are given a role in the ritual, whether it is their first time or not. We have great fun, and we all enjoy it. There are normally about six to eight people and these consist of the general discussion group that I have running. Sometimes they will be included in the Esbat circle if there is no tough work or personal stuff to be done, but at this stage, that is a time for me to do some private worship and some private work on spiritual and personal transformation issues. I need to be alone in most of those rituals without distraction. I also expect the rest of the discussion group to start doing their own Esbat rituals without leaning on Annette and myself as part of their learning process. This normally sifts out the sincere ones from the couch-potato listeners. Annette and I are starting to work together in our Esbat rituals now that we have developed a trusting relationship with each other. I feel comfortable with her, no matter what I spontaneously feel like doing in my working rituals, and we help each other along by growing together.

God is an essence that is everywhere, an omnipotent being that has various characteristics, both good and bad, but all part of the dynamic balance. By doing certain things and delivering 'prayers' or invocations, we are actually positively stimulating this omnipotent essence in the cosmic universe, as well as within ourselves, since part of it dwells within us too. Now that makes more sense to me than the patriarchal hell, fire and brimstone image enforced for so many years. I work on a different level religiously – a much deeper level – through engaging my subconscious at will and training my brain to work in a different direction. Through this, I get to know myself better too. Going to church is something people do; having a ritual is something I experience!

I am engaged to a wonderful man who has a Pagan outlook on life and the universe, although he isn't very much into the religious side of Wicca per se. He is becoming more and more interested in what I do, and he is a fantastic support. He doesn't laugh or scoff at me in any way and respects my beliefs. Basically, he feels that I am a free person, and whatever I find works for me, I must do to the best of my ability, as this is no dress rehearsal – we only have this conscious life in this incarnation to fulfil our desires. He is a strong believer in that. My kids think I'm nuts! But they are starting to get involved in minor activities. They respect and love me for my uniqueness.

Derek (Silverfox), 38 – Journalist

I would consider myself a witch – I do not only practise Wiccan magick but predominantly follow the Wiccan path. I have, however, delved into other things out of fascination with the Craft and with working magick, low and high.

I came to terms with this when I was about twelve. I was taught quite a lot by a German South African witch who had fled Mozambique during their war there. We became very close friends and at the time, Wicca was extremely covert in South Africa, especially in the conservative areas in the North-West Province where we were living at the time. I knew, when Edie was teaching me about Wicca, that this was for me. So, in my teens I read a lot of books, some really hard-core stuff that she had brought from Europe. I stopped then for almost a decade before going back into the Craft in 1998, I think it was.

I am mostly a kitchen witch. I love the kitchen-witch stuff! Very à la Scott Cunningham, I would say. As darkwolf put it in one of the courses I did with her: 'Those herbs just work; don't ask me why; but they just work.' And that is so true. They take a bit of time, I find, but bring results – they do.

I also do other stuff, like high magick rituals in circle when the need arises. I feel equally at home with low and high magick and have also since studied other kinds of magick, such as African techniques, which I found quite interesting.

From the limited amount I know about the British Pagan scene, South Africa seems very similar on many levels. It is just a much smaller scene in South Africa. On the other hand, in London it's hard to meet other Pagans. You would be surprised at how covert it still is there. You very, very seldom see people wearing a pentacle, for example, and I searched high and low for one to buy! In all the magnificent markets of London, I found ONE stall with pentacles for sale! I believe in all the deities we work with in circle- or in other trance-state workings, and with some of them I have been working frequently, so I feel a close connection with them. Formerly, I followed a Christian path, and I still believe in Christ. I think he was a very, very brilliant magician. I believe in the angels and archangels, the Elementals, etc.

My principle is 'do what ye will, but harm none'. However, if someone has gone out of their way to intentionally harm you without provocation, then you have the right to hit back. Also, if someone close to you has been similarly harmed, and they were defenseless, then you have the right to lash out on their behalf.

I have worked informally in a coven in England on occasion, but ninety per cent of the time my work is solitary.

Annette (Dolphin Star), 26 – Speech therapist

I consider myself a Pagan. To me, a Pagan is someone who respects the land and honours Nature in all its perfection. And I do not see humans as having the right to be 'lords' over the rest of creation. I think one of the fundamental elements of being a Pagan is that you recognise all of creation, living and non-living, as sacred.

I think that I have been on the Pagan path to a certain degree my whole life. I only truly discovered the term 'Pagan' and related it to myself in October 1999.

Nature has always touched my spirit, and I have never been able to understand the attitude that most human beings have towards life – that they are the supreme beings and can control everything else. Since I was a child I've believed in being able to be in tune with Nature and animals. I have been fascinated by Celtic mythology and other ancient civilisations, like the Greek and Egyptian. I studied astrology and the runes and crystals as hobbies. My mother fell very ill at the end of October 1999 and I wanted to find a way to share my healthy, strong inner energy with her. I went into a bookstore and found a book that claimed to be able to teach me how to heal my life with natural energies and ritual. As I read the book, I felt as if the author was explaining to me all the thoughts and feelings I had about everything – she understood my mind. And she named this belief and attitude system 'Wicca'.

Wicca supports and confirms to me my absolute certainty that we are all one – that we are all perfect. It doesn't force me to believe or accept anything, other than that which I feel is right. It doesn't criticise other belief systems and allows me to 'customise' my own. But perhaps the strongest connection I have to Wicca is the feeling of intense joy, love and peace that I feel right in the centre of my being – that feeling that feels like it's exploding within when I smell flowers when driving through the city, or see dolphins at sea, or hear people laughing with joy.

I consider myself a witch because I perform rituals, using specific items such as various candles, herbs and crystals. in order to obtain a goal. I believe in the ability of one being able to effect change. This change is brought about by engaging the powerful energies that surround us and that are inherent in various ritual tools, and using those energies to focus on my intent. I do not, however, openly name myself a witch, as I feel most people these days are not broad-minded enough to understand what it means to be a witch. Responses range from thinking you're the local crazy to be laughed at, to the person who's following the latest fad, to being a Satanist (the label that the rest of us find the most insulting)!

I also consider myself to be Wiccan, and I feel blessed to be able to think so. Whereas Pagan is the 'Nature' part of my belief system, witchCraft is more the practice part. Wicca brings the theology and religion into it. I am Pagan and a witch because I am Wiccan. This means I acknowledge and respect the polarity of existence – that everything must be positive or negative, light or dark, masculine or feminine, or cease to exist. And I conceptualise this in my aspects of divinity: the Goddess and the God. These concepts are not used to give a 'face' to the being that I worship, but rather to represent the balance in creation, which is what I as Wiccan celebrate.

I met Dragonmistt and joined in a small discussion group. There are about six to eight members in our discussion group – all are Pagan, and we are all at different levels of our path. We discuss various topics and ideas, and it is good to be able to do this. We also celebrate the Sabbats together. In order to attend public festivals, I will travel to them.

Recently Dragonmistt and I have started participating in Esbat rituals together. We have very similar ideals and thoughts, and we work very well together. We also felt that because we seem to have embraced Wicca in the same way, which is perhaps not always the same as the others in the discussion group, we would be able to work on our growth together in a more focused way. We have also not sensed the same level of commitment to Wicca in the rest of the group, and this often comes through in our Sabbat celebrations. When Dragonmistt and I work together, it is definitely a more powerful working.

I am very lucky to have a very supportive partner. Although he is not Wiccan, he tries to explain my beliefs to others. And I think he gets a lot of joy from seeing how excited I am about this – when I run around the garden, or jump up and down on the beach. He is very generous in allowing my open practise of my religion throughout our house. How many partners would be so forgiving about the bedroom dresser being transformed into an altar? Because he doesn't have a formal religion himself, he feels that our rites of passage should be Wiccan, for example our handfasting, and that our children should be brought up being exposed to Wicca.

I usually start the day with a morning devotion. If the morning is hectic, and I can't manage the full devotion, I still take a moment outside to greet the day and give thanks. Sabbats are always celebrated by the discussion group. Esbats were, until recently, practised in solitary, as were dark moon rituals. But now Dragonmistt and I are starting to work together. It is definitely a positive step forward, as there is a lot more energy-building happening and I need to learn how to work with it. Most rituals are done at night, as we both work full time. Our rituals also tend to be quite structured. They are composed beforehand, and we go over them before we start. Even though it's quite formal, there is always some laughing and light-heartedness during the circle.

I think that a lot of positive things have been happening for us, such as public awareness, discussions on television, etc. But I also feel that there is a long way to go. There are a few very strong cultures here in South Africa, and none of them really value Nature and life. I feel that people in South Africa still think they can pollute the air, land and sea without a second thought. So, how will they ever accept a religion that opposes these practices seriously? We're just a bunch of 'hippies' to them. I think we also have a history of a lack of independent thought; it's easier to let our leaders think for us. And I think a trademark characteristic of a Pagan is that ability to think and rationalise for yourself – I won't believe something just because someone's told me I must. But each day I hope that by living the way I do, perhaps people's thought patterns will begin to change.

cajun (Amazon Wolfe), 24 – Lesbian activist

I don't like labels, but Pagan is the description that best suits who I am. I consider myself a witch far more than a Wiccan. Wicca can become very dogmatic, whereas being a witch is about who I am and what I do.

Driving in my car on my way to work, however, I can cast a spell. I don't need to be in a full-on ritual with candles and robes to do magick. I am a high priestess within a Wiccan structure. I have done this so that I can work with other people, and thereby gain a different kind of knowledge than I would by working on my own.

I am considered a guide in the Pagan community, despite my age, as I have always taken on responsibility, even as a child. I feel I bring to the community a sense of movement, of flow and youth – a breaking free of dogma.

I don't feel I fit strictly into any specific form of Paganism. I am closer to being an eclectic witch, but at times even doubt calling myself a witch. It depends on who I am talking to and what I am trying to bring across to the person I am talking to at the time. I will use the term more as an explanation, in order to bring across the information I am sharing in a clear-cut, concise manner, giving facts rather than embroidering an issue.

This is the same reason I call myself lesbian. It gives me a chance to explain things, and to correct some of the misconceptions some people may have. Being a lesbian doesn't mean I'm on a drastic feminist slant; I work with masculine energy, only because the lines are very blurred. I work with deity energy, which is neither masculine nor feminine.

I practise solitary mostly. Because my path is so eclectic, it is hard to find someone with the same way of thinking. However, I also work within a group at times, especially for healing.

Jasmine (Evalina Belcherry), 15 – Student

I have been practising the Craft for about two years. I basically found my way to the Craft through reading books. I was very depressed, and yet what I was reading made sense, and even managed to penetrate the depression. What got me most was how accepting Wicca is of differences in people. I am an outcast at school. I am different, and do what I want to do – not in a bad way. I just don't go around with the crowd; I dress funny. I'm not trendy or smooth, and I don't care either.

I did my first ritual on healing for myself. I didn't think it was going to work, but a few weeks later I stopped feeling such a victim. I did other spells for friends, and they also worked. I once tried a love spell, and the boy I did it for wouldn't leave me alone, and I realised how serious this all is.

My parents are divorced. When my mom found my books she took them away, grounded me, blamed my father and phoned the school to warn them that I might be influencing others. They sent me to a number of psychiatrists who eventually put me in an institution, blaming everything on Wicca. I was forbidden to see my dad for a while. Eventually, he was permitted to visit me. His position was difficult, and together we agreed I would go with the programme to avoid further trouble.

Eventually, I went back to school. I was unpopular because everyone thought I was a lesbian and a Satanist. I hated school, and often left class crying and sought out the school psychologist.

My transition came slowly. I started to accept myself. I talked to trees and flowers. I stopped allowing myself to be a victim. Wicca freed me to be myself. I was okay with being alone.

I hope to join a coven soon. Many people at school now appreciate talking to me about Wicca. I hope to grow much more.

Colleen (Firefox), 59 – Psychic Artist; and Derek (Wakanabee), 50 – Artist and healer

We are Colleen 'Firefox' Johnson and Derek 'Wakanabee' Johnson. Our principles are loosely based on Shamanism, but only loosely, as we do not follow any specific belief system rigidly.

We are attempting to follow a balanced lifestyle, as we believe in body, mind and spirit being equally important to be able to experience the fullness of life.

We also believe in the 'non-local mind' or the universality of all matter, spirit and thought. Together with some like-minded friends, we are working on building a centre where we will live communally and practise many different healing modalities. Our main objective is to bring people to the light through teachings and by example.

Colleen has spent a lifetime (nearly six decades) studying, attending workshops and obtaining knowledge wherever she could. Derek had a conventional Christian background, including the study of theology, counselling, Latin and Greek, before 'Bat' appeared. Neil Donald Walsh was read, and life dramatically changed!

We would like to mention that we are both trained counsellors and have worked together on occasion. Derek, as a lecturer and practitioner in Iridology, tends to have people coming to him with sick bodies but most often spends most of the consultation counselling. Colleen, when she presents her 'soul portrait' artworks and taped readings to her clients, often finds it necessary to incorporate a counselling session at the same time.

It should be mentioned that when Derek is working as a healer, he finds it very helpful to go into an almost meditative state in order to go 'within' the patient to discover the real cause of the disease. Colleen does a numerology and medicine card spread in order to get to 'know' the client and then begins the drawing process, which is done intuitively. The animals from the seven-card spread are often but not always incorporated together with any past-life information that may come through. Other beings and guides may also appear, depending on what is channelled.

We have a sacred space to where we retreat and where we meditate. The space has an altar on which are represented the Elements and Christian, Buddhist, Pagan and other religious symbols. We burn incense and smudge each other and our space when necessary. Our totem animals, bat for Derek and elephant for Colleen, are represented. The feathers of totem birds such as raven and owl are also used.

We respect all living things and are both vegetarians for this reason. We especially respect Mother Earth. We are on a mission and are attempting to give the land on our farm back to Mother Earth.

A while ago, Colleen had a very bad migraine attack (for her this usually lasts for four days). In our sacred space, I went into a meditative state. It was my intention merely to send her 'white light'. I said my mantra when, instead of a warm feeling that I normally experienced, I found myself looking at what I knew was the inside of her brain and neck. I saw a dark mass enveloping part of the area that was in front of me. I was able to project a white light at the mass. As I did so, it began to dissipate. With a great amount of concentration I was able to break up the whole mass. I then came out of trance. Within twenty minutes Colleen's migraine had disappeared.

I have been able to refine this technique and use it for the benefit of my patients. Very rarely do I discuss this method with them; instead I prescribe various herbs, minerals, exercise and nutritional regimes.

From what I understand of the Shamanic way, the respect of Mother Earth, the directions and the Elements assists in the development of magickal or 'non-local' abilities. Colleen attended a Shamanic workshop and has undergone the first initiation. Each of the four segments of the course was devoted to an Element. The students were shown how to communicate with Mother Earth, to tap into the energy of the trees. A meditation was done standing in a circle in a river. A fire ceremony was used to teach the ritual of cleansing. On the fourth day they did air and were shown, on a clear and cloudless day, how the Shamans called up the wind. Although this had a profound impact on Colleen, she did not pursue the training any further, as most of the rituals were South American and she felt that she needed to make her work more 'African'. Colleen and I have had many discussions between ourselves and with other people. Although we have both read many works on this and other subjects, we are not 'textbook Shamans', but try to live always in our truth.

How does this differ from Wicca? Quite frankly our knowledge of the ways of Wicca are very limited and we do not feel qualified to make an honest distinction. We seem to recall, though, that there are many similarities, for example the fire cleansing ritual. Another example is that, when a full-moon ceremony is held, the spirits and totems of the directions are called on to sanctify the circle (Wicca's calling of the quarters). Colleen's art is part of her life and in her works the directions and totems are honoured. We tie all aspects of our lives into our lifestyles and belief system. This, ultimately, helps us to create the 'magick'.

The core to our relationship has three legs: love, honesty and impeccability. We will not compromise any one of them. This creates a life of trust and respect. We believe these pillars are necessary for all humans, and, if scrupulously attended to, suffering, greed, abuse of power, etc. would be eliminated.

Anonymous (Niteshade), 36

From an early age I experienced my first 'familiar' in the form of a huge black and white cat. Then I discovered that I could see. By 'see' I mean that I saw the occasional faery or dead person – things that go bump in the night. This was not understood – being just a mere babe at the time. It scared the living daylights out of me. This led me to spending endless nights of torture on the floor at the foot of my parents' bed. At age fourteen my mother found me surrounded by a circle of candles. I remember the look on her face as she said, 'You are a witch.' Fortunately, I was brought up in a very liberal religious environment. My parents believed in reincarnation, masters, God, UFOs and witches. My grandmother was a true follower of theosophy and gave up her life to study her belief, even refusing to see her family. So I decided to pursue this witchiness that was in me

– only to find it would take me on an adventure of great proportions and sights. It is a truly remarkable experience and path that I have been led down.

At age sixteen I met the most important man in my life. He proceeded to stay in it for ten years. He was born a natural medium, so he introduced me to the tarot cards, normal playing cards, crystal balls and spirits. Life was one big adventure, and I just blossomed. I became really good at the tarot cards and then started learning about herbs. I had dried herbs hanging in the kitchen (you had an ailment, I could cure it). My skills became stronger and stronger. My mother and I explored most of the Eastern philosophies, spiritualism and the study of transcendental meditation. Transcendental meditation has still to this day been of great benefit to me. I learned and took what I needed from everything I had studied and experienced. The man in my life was now calling me a witch and warning me of the trappings. (I think he was a little afraid.) So, I then entered the world of reading cards, making herbal potions and using oils. Life was good.

As I matured, so did my magick. I grew out of the herbal potions and lotions, but continued to do card readings and spells. I then spotted an ad in the link-up, advertising Wicca courses. I was so excited I could not contain myself and joined up immediately.

Today, I remain a solitary practitioner. I am not a Wiccan. I have been called many names: a witch, a Satanist, etc. I am comfortable with my magick (magick is both black and white; we need to find a balance) and the way I perform it, so I guess I am a witch.

Anonymous (Ra-Shu), 46 – Businessman

My interest in the occult started at school in the late 1960s. I guess one of the contributing factors was my very negative reaction to compulsory Christian national education, but the other and more overwhelming stimulus was the age-old question: 'Who am I, and who is God?' I remember being forced to spend my compulsory religious instruction classes outside the headmaster's office because I was disruptive and asked too many questions! Possibly the only reason that the school never took a more serious view of my behaviour was that our headmaster was Jewish and perhaps secretly admired my stance.

My initial reaction to my treatment at school was to reject the possibility of deity entirely, but this tempered to understanding that our mere existence was proof of the existence of deity. I dabbled in Eastern mysticism, but was disappointed. While I have no criticism of the belief systems, they didn't seem to strike a chord with me.

My interests led to ancient Egypt, and I read almost everything I could about their society, religious beliefs and practices. Their solar-based religion intrigued me, as did their earlier polytheistic belief systems. From these studies came an appreciation of The Book of the Dead or, more correctly, The Book of Coming Forth by Day, the Pyramid Texts and the other ancient Egyptian writings, which purportedly inspired the teachings of the Kabbalah.

My interests and studies developed organically into Freemasonry, the Knight's Templar, the Rosicrucians, the Order of the Golden Dawn and, of course, the Kabbalah in some detail. I came to understand the meaning of magick, particularly ceremonial or art magick. I was aware of folk magick, but never really considered it until quite recently. I have a fundamental understanding of Wicca, which to me seems to be derived mainly from European and Nordic beliefs, but my spiritual belief system is entrenched in Africa and in the sacred tradition of ancient Egypt.

I dislike being labelled and always baulk at the question, 'So, what are you?' If I had to answer that question I would say that primarily I am a Pagan; my belief system is Earth-based, or more specifically for me, Universe-based. I revere deity through a polytheistic pantheon, which I see as individual manifestations of one. My metaphysical or magickal practice is solitary and based on the sacred traditions of ancient Egypt and the Kabbalah. I do modify traditional Kabbalistic practices based on personal experience. For example, I will substitute ancient Egyptian for Hebrew in ritual if I feel it is more appropriate, and my magickal correspondences are based on the sacred traditions of ancient Egypt.

I'm married to a witch, and while there are aspects of Wicca that I don't necessarily agree with (if I did I'd probably practise as a witch), I do respect and secretly admire them and am happy to share their circle if invited.

Kerry (7th Hawk), 45 – Herbalist

When I first started studying Wicca, I wasn't sure what I was doing. Overcoming a mindset, I realised that all I was being taught was coming to me naturally anyway. There is no major change in my life, only a label.

This is not a bad thing; the label sits comfortably with me – the label 'witch' carries, for me, respect. It is an acknowledgement of how fully human one can be, and what effect you can have on the things around you. I am more in tune with myself, and now, when asked to do something or to participate in something, I am led by my gut feeling and know immediately what is or is not right for me.

Wicca is not just a 'thing', like church on Sunday; it is a path, an entire lifetime. My Wicca training satisfied this awareness. Wicca is not something that you practise once a week for an hour; it is something that is part of your entire life – of the very fibre of your existence. I am comfortable as far as talking about being a witch goes. If there is a title involved I don't feel that I've encompassed enough knowledge to use the title. I need to feel qualified within myself.

The whole Wiccan and Pagan thing is very humbling, in that we get to realise that humans are the only living creatures that do not fulfil the natural order of things. I was watching a dung beetle and realised how all creatures are born, work with Nature and have a role in Nature. Wicca brings us back to basics and teaches us to work with Nature and the Earth, not against her. This insight has become more solid through more awareness, caused by everything that is encompassed in Wicca.

The one problem I have is that most Wiccans do not understand the Rede. This is something I see in young Wiccans. They read a book or two, do a course or two and think that they have it down pat – they are now a witch. Live by the Rede; let it be a part of you. Then, and only then, are you a witch.

Just because people label themselves as witches they think they have the power. We all have the power. My suggestion to any would-be witch is to live by the Rede. This somehow takes away the need to be called a witch.

Mauritz (SilverMoss), 23 – IT student

At first I was eclectic, not yet sure which path would work for me. So, I tried a little bit of everything. I think the aspects that placed me on the Druid path, above all, were the purity and majesty of their ways. I've always been a seeker of truth, and a Druid's most sacred pledge is: 'The truth against the world.' I first discovered Druidism while browsing the Internet for Pagan sites, and my interest was immediately sparked.

There are quite a few differences between Wicca and Druidism, but I think the most fundamental one is that Wicca is a religion with a high priest and high priestess, and Druidism is more of a theosophical philosophy. Although we have an arch-Druid and arch-Druidess, which are the same rank as a high priest and priestess, they do not teach a congregation, but each Druid is assigned an apprentice. In Druidism we also have what we call orders or groves; in Wicca one has traditions and covens.

I am the apprentice of a legitimate teacher, but do not belong to any order as yet. At the moment my training is being done via correspondence. My teacher assigns me a reading list and then answers any questions I might have. He has informed me, however, that he is formulating a more structured and formal course, which he will hand to me when finished.

My teacher does have other students as well, but I do not think the ancient law of one Druid and one apprentice is still in effect in this day and age.

Testing is done by the Druid himself. If I decide on taking the more structured course I will be tested at certain times on memory, spiritualism and poetry. At the moment, however, I'm just studying on my own. The difference is that with my current method of studying I can request to be tested whenever I feel ready and then be initiated into the next rank by my teacher. The testing for this method is the same as above. However, the informal method takes much longer than the formulated course.

Being solitary does not bother me too much, but it does sometimes get very frustrating not having any other Druidic students in my area with whom I can collaborate and practise.

So, when I'm with Wiccans, I have no problem adhering to their ways of doing, worshipping and practising. Our beliefs are very much the same; it's just our ways of practising that are slightly different. My partner is a Wiccan high priestess, and we do many rituals together. We find common ground and take great pleasure in combining Druidic and Wiccan elements. She is very involved in a strong Wiccan circle, and I attend these with her. I often do a Druidic banishing at these rites, or cast the circles using ancient Druidic terminology.

Angela (Elk), 36 – Copywriter

I first came to terms with the fact that I am a witch about five or six years ago when I met up with like-minded people. I had been a tarot card reader for some years before that, and it was only when I met some fellow witches that I felt that I had discovered more about who I was.

I believe that witches are people who are aware of their own mental and spiritual power and are highly in tune with themselves, other human beings, the universe and the natural rhythms of Nature. By this definition, I feel I am definitely in tune with myself, my powers of intuition and aspects of universal consciousness, and I feel huge amounts of empathy towards my fellow human beings. I'd like to think that the added knowledge that I am a witch makes me capable of dealing with my own reality in a more positive and powerful way.

I have been a practising witch for about five years now. I am a solitary practitioner and join large groups only to celebrate the various festivals. While I enjoy the company of fellow witches from time to time, I have always preferred doing my own thing. In addition to being a private person, I feel that I am far more focused when I practise alone. I also like to stay out of the political and emotional issues that tend to be generated within covens or working groups.

I adhere very strongly to the Wiccan Rede of 'do what thou wilt, but harm none'. I strongly believe that any wrongdoing will revisit me threefold. I don't 'follow' any god or goddess. I do, however, relate to the archetype represented by Pan, simply because of his sensual enjoyment of 'Earthly' pleasures. I'm a Scorpio!

With regard to the growth of Paganism, I see formal religion losing popularity, and more and more people are starting to investigate alternative spiritual paths and to relate to the basic tenets of Paganism.

Mark (Rainstorm), 38 – IT practitioner

I discovered the Craft through an Internet site that came to my attention: there was a discussion that piqued my interest.

It worries me to use the term 'witch'. I keep on remembering that it has connotations, for example they burn witches in the Northern Province. As far as magicians go, they couldn't be bothered to talk to us at all.

The name Pagan is too broad. It may be defined as a non-Christian. It's too broad a difference, and it is difficult to define myself. I would probably use the term 'witch' with caution.

A witch is more an active role, i.e. you raise energy, focus, intent. Wicca is more passive – into ecology. Perhaps this is a perception. Wiccan magick is very gentle. Wicca is bound with the Earth. WitchCraft is more modern, cyber-oriented – not necessarily bound to an Earth philosophy.

Although I feel a bond with Earth and there is an affinity, I'm not bound to it. I can work in a concrete environment; I don't need Earth as a basis for my work.

WitchCraft is alive and practised. If I want an outcome, I create a platform for my subconscious, throw it in the cauldron and let it spin. I was also losing some preconceived ideas, and that made me more comfortable with being a witch. It was a natural progression, spending time with the things of the Craft. It's a process; yet there was never a moment I was one thing and then another.

With regard to my children, I would raise them as Pagan. I want them to have balance, discover for themselves. It's in the explanation of things: a different perspective, various correspondences. They sing many Goddess songs. My wife is not a Pagan; she puts up with it.

I practise as a solitary, as I have no choice. Family commitments keep me solitary.

Angelique (Raeven), 27 – Full-time priestess

Ever since I can remember, witches have fascinated me. I was brought up with a 'Liewe Heksie' doll in one hand and a stuffed dog named 'Magic' in the other. My family is not your normal Christian variety either; my mother took me along each week to the Theosophical Society, where she would learn of chakras and tarot and a lot of other metaphysical and esoteric things. I would sit quietly and absorb all of this.

I remember a day when I was about eight: my cousin and I were playing in her backyard in Sunnyside. Suddenly, things became all serious, and we pondered what we would become when we grew up. It was decided then, in all sincerity, that we would become witches! I seemed to know instinctively that a witch was simply a powerful woman who was misunderstood and feared, because of her unusual powers. I have never believed that a witch would do something truly evil, like harm an animal. Maybe all the books on faeries and witches that I read compounded this. I also believe that Verna Vels's Liewe Heksie had a big part in this decision. I named my first cat Matewis (Matewis being the name of Liewe Heksie's cat). When I didn't have a name for my second cat, he too became Matewis.

I would say that I 'officially' realised that I was a witch in a Pagan context one day when my mom, my sister and I went to an esoteric festival in Johannesburg. I was thirteen years old. I was wearing a long, purple caftan and a silver, crescent-moon pendant around my neck. A group of interesting-looking young people were walking around, and I found myself drawn to them. They seemed to be glowing with a special kind of aura. Later that day, after attending many talks, I was sitting on a staircase eating (probably food made by Hare Krishnas), when one of the people from the group came to sit next to me.

He said 'merry meet' as a greeting, and I replied 'merry meet' back to him. At this stage I didn't know that this was the traditional witch's greeting. He said that they had noticed me, and we began talking. He had recognised me as a kindred spirit. I knew myself to be this, but I had no name for it. We exchanged phone numbers. The next weekend I went to visit a friend of mine who sold books at a flea market in Johannesburg. He had a copy of Scott Cunningham's *Wicca for the Solitary Practitioner*. Books on witchCraft were unavailable in South Africa in those days, so I bought it immediately. Of course, when I read it, I discovered to my surprise that my newfound friends from the esoteric fair were all witches. That book made a huge impact on my life, and gave me a sense of homecoming. That is how I learnt that I was a witch.

At this time in my life, I find myself mainly practising alone. I have practised in groups before and in a coven or two at various points in my life. However, because of the head space I am in at the moment I have not found another person with whom I would like to work. I also seem to do my rituals with more sincerity when I am alone. Then I am not concerned about how I pronounce the names of deities or if I hesitate when I cannot immediately think of what to say next. Also, if I feel like totally letting go of myself, then I can. I feel that to work in a group on a deep level there has to be a lot of trust, and you must be able to feel uninhibited when with those people. I am not talking about celebrating the Sabbats here, but about when working magick, or in a transformative ritual.

I am very eclectic, and consider myself something of a 'chaos witch', and am yet to find those kindred spirits with whom I can work in a serious, but fun, magickal context. It is my hope that I find those people soon, or that they find me!

The Craft in England is practised very much the same way as in South Africa. The public are even more used to Pagans and Wiccans, as they have been publicly visible for far longer than groups in South Africa. In the United Kingdom there are simply more public lessons, groups and pub moots. The people are very similar to the Pagans and Wiccans you would encounter in South Africa. Perhaps the major difference is the English tendency to follow strict traditions like Gardnerianism or Alexandrianism. Okay, so I guess I just invented those words, but you get my point! The Pagans in South Africa are far more eclectic; we are still busy finding our roots or reinventing new ones.

One of the main reasons I went public was because I was sick of the ignorance of the public in South Africa. Magazines like *You* published articles where they classified symbols like the ankh and yin-yang as Satanic! Of course the pentagram was on the top of the list. Going public has helped a lot, as far as mainstream white people go. However, I feel that we have simply skimmed the surface of the public in South Africa, as the wide majority of people are black and still believe that a witch is someone who is evil.

I feel that people mostly fear only what is unknown to them, and if light is shed upon what witches actually do, we might be able to resume our intended role as the healers and helpers within our communities.

I have been instrumental in the public Pagan scene since inception, and I am also busy with a book about Paganism in South Africa, and will continue to do my part in making Paganism an accepted spiritual path in South Africa.

Jade, 40 – Author

My spiritual awakening started when I woke up on the cold, white tiles of my bathroom floor after my third, pathetic, unsuccessful suicide attempt. I was very angry with God that I was still alive. At thirty-one, I was addicted to alcohol, tobacco, dagga and heartbreaking relationships. I could not understand why I had to live. In the fury of the moment I raised my fist and shouted: 'Damn you God, by magick only am I prepared to continue with life!' I had no idea how brave the decision was at the time. Then again, I had just faced death. Then I passed out. Three days later when I reached a measure of clarity again, I realised I had better find out what magick really is. I really did not know, but I had made the statement with so much conviction. Why? I also thought I should try something else, seeing that suicide did not seem to be my thing. So I thought, why not be happy and healthy? But I was ill-equipped to transform my life at the time: I had rebelled against, and with great glee cast off, a typical Afrikaner backround – NG Kerk religion, National Party politics and a BA degree at RAU. And all I had put in its place were addictions.

When I made that first, conscious, positive decision, the correct, needed information flowed into my life as if floodgates had been opened. At first, words healed me most: books on Earth rituals, alternative healing, positive intent, altered states of consciousness, including trance, drug trips, Shamanic journeys and dreams, female spirituality and Earth magick all came my way. It threw me into feverish states of remembering. Suddenly, my rebellion against my own narrow-minded culture made sense. I found proper answers and solutions.

When I experienced my first journey through time and space, guided by a regression therapist, I knew I had finally discovered the trip I had been looking for. My theology, my story, which had been causing havoc in my subconscious mind, was opening up like a flower, so that I could learn and grow up and heal and claim my magickal power as an Earthchild.

Getting rid of all my bad habits took a considerable amount of time and effort. It was worth my while every slippery step of the way. To me, anything self-destructive reeks of slow suicide and therefore messes with positive intent. So, the clean-up started on the physical plane: the drugs had to go. And finally did. The self-destructive thought patterns also had to go, along with the terrible self-pity. I'm still working on it, of course, although I am a much freer individual nine years down the line.

What made me succeed were the positive habits I put in place, like practising the seasonal Sabbats and moon rituals. For the first time in my life, I received spiritual nurture. And for me it was and still is very direct: the nurture comes straight from Mother Earth. Some Goddess worship did not replace the God worship. I also spent huge amounts of time alone in Nature. I found my Mother and reconnected with her flow of energy by becoming one with Earth time. I started communicating with her animals and elfins by going into a natural trance.

I am a very happy Earthchild. I know I cannot possibly get bored again because I live by magick now. I'm polishing up on my courage, because the more magickal it gets, the more unpredictable it becomes. And I have gained the ecstasy of expanding my consciousness the natural way. I need lifetimes to do all the travelling I want to do. The junkie in me cannot ask for more. And when I am in a more mature mood, suitable for my age (hee! hee!) I can go into stillness, and feel her awesome, silent embrace.

I consider myself a very, very lucky person. By the grace of my magickal matrix, I am happy and healthy and, every now and then, ecstatically alive.

Duncan (Morgainne Emrys), 33 – Lawyer

Finding the appropriate boxes to fit oneself into is a task that no esoteric looks forward to. For too long, the Western world has created neat little square holes into which they sought to place round pegs. If the round pegs would not fit into these neat, square holes, then, woe betide, the world would seek to destroy that which would not conform to the linear world view.

For the sake of vital record-keeping, I am forced to stand up and be counted by finding for myself labels that would not bind me, but seek to give a peep into our world.

I am an esoteric, I am a witch, and, more importantly, I am a Druid.

Having been invited by a respected scribe and fellow force, Donna Vos, I will render a short history of my experience as a Druid in South Africa, those factors that led me to my chosen path and the difficulties and rewards that crown my chosen path.

If I am to mark a 'begin' to the board game of the life of this Druid, then I must start at my confirmation into the body of the Methodist Church, as this was the catalyst that opened the many doors to those other realms that beckoned me. The Church was a catalyst in its inability to mirror what was documented as history not censored by her, and its inability to face the reality of the living world outside the so-called hallowed halls of Christendom.

My questions were met with hostility, with a subsequent request that I leave the square hole. Thus began my search.

My exploration ranged from the apparent ecstasy of that famous Americanised Hindu Movement, ISKCON, better know as the 'Krsna' movement. I even tried to embrace the compassionate calm of Buddhism. Finally, I was seduced by the freedom of the Craft – no more square holes and prescribed regulations.

I read extensively and intensively for two years, acquired much knowledge, grew spiritually and made some lasting friendships. While hungrily consuming every available piece of literature, which in the dark days of apartheid's Calvinist stranglehold was not readily available and dangerous to be caught in possession of, I came across an advertisement, innocuously nestled in the final pages of a text on Celtic magick. This advertisement invited interested parties to study the ancient and timeless doctrines of the Druids.

A chord was struck and more than just my interest was immediately awakened. Having found the temple of my familiar, I was led deep into the realms of the praxis of Celtic lore. I made the application, paid the subscription and undertook the fantastical journey into the archetypes of my own consciousness. There has not been a moment's regret. Seventeen years later, I am the only qualified Druid in southern Africa.

When I first started, there were none of these amazing quick-fix, three-year training courses offered by the many orders, which exist today. The books of Douglas Monroe were not yet in print, and my teachers were so very far away. It was difficult to conceive of a course, which was so intense on both an academic and spiritual level, where the teachers were so remote and so far away. They had no idea (or so I thought) of the person who was their student. The power of the call was strong enough to fuel the sheer determination, which drove me along this path. It was no longer clear who had made the choice – me or the path.

As I progressed through the work, which was posted to me, my appreciation for the path grew, and it became for me more than just my path, but my very way of life.

It became clearer than crystal that my teachers, who had not physically met me and only communicated through occasional letters, knew me and anticipated every obstacle that I would encounter. They knew where my difficulties lay and what my talents were. The most important factor was that they allowed me the latitude to find my own experiences and to be informed by these experiences within the framework of their teachings. If I encountered a problem, they would indulge the question and assist me in solving it, but left the rest to me. This was my adventure. But my every movement was observed, as if I sat at their feet. I realised this seventeen years later, at my initiation, which marked my first physical meeting with them.

My seventeen years of study were not lonely, as I had the most wonderful friends in the Craft. While they were all on different levels and not studying the way of the Druid, they were always there to listen to me and to assist me through difficult times. The framework, which the coursework material provided, had great depth and is extremely comprehensive. This shaped and supported my way of life.

After many years of study in the path of the Druid, I became aware of the order of Bards, Ovates and Druids, and proceeded to apply and join their ranks as a student. They offered me a comprehensive three-year course to complement my already advanced in-depth study of Druidism. On completion, this course gave me an in-depth understanding of the history, poetry, music and esoteric teachings of the Druids. This opened the door to the wonderful experience of ancient British esotericism. What is a body, truly, if we remove its soul? What is this soul, but the very chronicles of our past?

After seventeen years of study, my career permitting me the much-needed time, I took the plunge and went home, in the middle of Winter, to freezing, wet and cold Ireland. I was initiated as a Bard, an Ovate and a Druid on the sacred morning of 21 December 2000. The initiation took place after an examination that leaves you drained and yet breathless, and I was enveloped by an indescribable joy.

My path has not been difficult; nor has it been lonely. Whatever path had chosen me to walk its winding roads, I would find myself at my the journey's end, which, in reality, just marks a series of new beginnings. The final answer lies in a regimen of intense work by oneself for oneself. The final answer lies in the many doors that are opened at the end of each journey, and in the souls we meet.

Yes, I am a Druid – the only Druid currently in South Africa. While I willingly share my expertise and advice with all in the Craft who ask, I will not teach, except for a select few who are already on the path with me.

Blessed be.

Cassandra, 30 – Yoga teacher

I am a thirty-year-old witch and mother of two. I have been a practising witch for ten years and am married to a witch whom I met when we were involved in the workshops that led to the formation of the Pagan Federation of South Africa.

The moment when I realised that I could and would never be like the rest of my family is crystal clear in my mind. My cat had been killed by a car, and I asked the Sunday school teacher whether my cat would be in heaven to greet me when I died. He told me to stop being ridiculous and that it was common knowledge that animals have no souls. I was eight and my world would never be the same again. I was always interested in myths and legends, and it was through these stories that I learned of the old gods and goddesses and knew that they were closer to my heart than any other deities that I had as yet encountered. By the end of high school I was a non-practising Pagan.

In my second year at Rhodes University I met some women who called themselves witches. They wanted to put on a play at the Grahamstown Festival about the way witches have been portrayed in theatre over the years, so a group of us spent the June vacation preparing our play, which we showed at the festival. After that experience I realised that it was the path for me and began to read as many books as I could find. The problem with being open about my beliefs in those days was that it was still considered Satanic by the authorities, and I had a member of the police force babysit me on the Sabbats. Looking back on it now, it seems funny, but at the time it was no joke. Apartheid was in its dying throes, and the authorities were very suspicious of any deviation from what they considered to be the norm.

I met a fellow witch on my return to Cape Town and together we set up our own coven, thinking that we were the only ones in the Cape and the chance of joining an established coven was next to nothing. For the next four years we explored so much of the Craft and debated and challenged each other until we found common ground. It was a fantastic experience and it gave us a really good foundation on which to build our future practices. We were very keen on doing our own thing and took elements of many well-known paths to eventually create something that was unique to us.

Some of the group called themselves Wiccan, I preferred to call myself a witch, as it made me feel the connection to my most distant Ancestresses, and recalled to me a time when the Goddess was worshipped above all as the Supreme Mother. We felt that the witch needed to be brought back and honoured as the Wise One, the Healer, the Nurturer and at times the Settler of Scores. I fully understood the complex nature of the witch when I visited the Museum of Witchcraft in Boscastle, England. Here the history of the Cornish witches has been preserved, and the many items on display made it quite clear that there were those who were comfortable in their ability to either bless or curse. It showed me that the path has been walked by many different people with different ideas about what is acceptable or necessary in their Craft, just as it is today.

I am at heart a hedge witch and am happiest making a concoction that I know will help someone heal. My magick has always been simple and my rituals are too. I no longer work in an organised coven and will at times work alone or with some very close female friends. We celebrate the Goddess as she has always been honoured – under a full moon on a deserted beach, in a cool, dark forest or in our living rooms.

My husband is also a practising witch and together we are raising our children, aged two and four, in the Goddess tradition. A whole new world has been opened up for us by passing on our beliefs to our children. We make the Sabbats fun and take time to explain the stories that are specific to the festival. My family is Irish, so we tend to focus on the Celtic nature of the festivals, but this is not a hard-and-fast rule. We do not include them in rituals, but rather make our meal a special occasion. My children have both had naming rituals or blessings, but we do not presume to dictate to them how they should worship. When they are older they can make that decision for themselves.

Story of a coven

It all started when I enrolled for a Wicca course. I met a group of people who all looked as normal as I do! We all had different careers, different home situations and were, of course, different in age. After the ice had broken, we started to get to know each other more as people than as fellow students, and we were amazed at the commonalities between us, despite our differences. The course was so inspiring, and we had all experienced such incredible personal growth, that when it ended, we automatically signed up for the next course.

The experiences on the second course followed suit, and, before we knew it, we were all taking other courses at the same time. One of the members ran courses in the tarot, the cherubim and channelling. There was also an astrology course that most of the group started as well.

The next few weeks were almost euphoric. As a group, we met in different places every night on one course or the other, discovering this wonderful new world. It got to the stage where the various course facilitators had to schedule their sessions around each other; otherwise nobody could make the classes!

Our teacher warned us about the sacrifices that we were making to our personal lives – all just locking up to go to a different course every night! We were so inspired by the teaching we were receiving that we felt this a small price to pay.

All good things must come to an end, and so did the courses. I will never forget the warm, grey Winter afternoon, our last Wicca class, when we sat in the sun in our teacher's garden and chatted about what was next.

For us the move was clear: as a group we would form a coven immediately to continue working together magickally. I think our deepest fear was that the religious freedom we had found in this group of common-minded people would be lost should we walk away from the group. We also feared that we would have little to do with our talents and learning around the non-Pagan people in our lives.

So, from there we went, charging off to reach the sun, moon and stars. Darkwolf agreed to be our coven mother – there to guide us from behind and offer support, which she did. A certain member was the logical choice for the role of high priestess, having the most incredible knowledge of all things esoteric and Wiccan. The sad part was that she had an extremely busy life, with three children and a demanding job, which started affecting the energy she could give to the coven.

Another problem was that, as women generally do, we started independent friendships with the others in the coven. Our high priestess had known two of the other members before. It became a case of two 'cliques', which is not a favourable dynamic for a coven.

The universe soon presented the answers to us. Our high priestess got an exciting new job offer, which would take up more time than her current job, so she was not able to commit to the time needed for the coven. She resigned gracefully and the other two went with her. They left in a very positive spirit with an open invitation to return to our coven at any time in the future, and we are still in contact with them today.

That left three of us behind and we soon recruited another student that we had met at Sabbats and festivals. After a long interview process, we knew that this person was the right one to share our magick. We decided that two of us would alternate handling the role of high priestess. Each would carry the title for three months at a time. Although this way of doing it has been questioned by fellow Pagans, we find that it works very well. We obviously have a high priest, but our coven seems to be dominated by the females in the group!

Not long after that, we recruited another four members – two couples in fact, two 'thinkers' and two 'doers'. Although the one couple is married with three children, we set the rule in the very beginning: should a couple ever split up, the high priestess will decide on who stays with the coven and who will leave. We are incredibly lucky that these four joined us – all amazing people and superb Wiccans, sharing our desire to learn and experience as much as we can. They brought invaluable gifts with them: one has a vast knowledge of herbs; the other is really talented at making things, including pentacles and wands (you name it!); and the other two have the most wonderful, peaceful, solid energy.

The most important aspect in choosing new coven members was choosing people who would share the same ideal of retaining the dignity and sanctity of what we have. It was also important that they were prepared to put the coven first and above other Pagan organisations, for it is in the coven that you experience true growth and find true meaning in your religion.

The four newcomers blended really well with the rest of us. I think that it was at this point that we realised that we had found our 'community' – people prepared to laugh with you, cry with you, share your joys and attend what we call 'emergency rituals' at the eleventh hour when someone is in need.

Some of us are still closeted about our religion in the workplace, others have the environment in which they can be open about it. Yet we all know the drill when we bump into each other at shopping centres with new faces around.

We are also extremely lucky to have a dedicated covenstead. It is our sacred space, used for nothing else, except for when we engage in the odd tarot reading or reflexology session.

We meet, as a coven, once a week – usually to do rituals or workings, for whoever has a need at that time. At other 'coven meets', we share learning with the rest of the group. For instance, we have been taught how to make various herb oils, and someone has shared their extensive knowledge of Pan with the rest of us. Other times, one of us will specifically go and research a particular topic, so that it can be taught to the rest of the coven, for example certain deities or divination methods.

We have a coven constitution that we seldom refer to, but we hold it in high regard, as it outlines our basic manner of functioning and our basic principles of practice. We reject black magick completely, and although we are open to discover other magickal schools, it is always practised in the Wiccan way. If in doubt, the questions to ask are: Does this act show respect to the Goddess? And does it comply with: 'An it harm none, do as ye will'?

We also keep a book library so that we can share each other's books. These are kept in the covenstead, where we have also built up a great collection of magickal tools: the cauldron, athames, a chalice, crystals, herbs, swords, etc. It is wonderful to have all the instruments around you when you decide to do an impromptu ritual.

If I were to answer the question: 'coven versus solitary', my answer would be the former without hesitation. I have never experienced such a sense of community, a sense of passion and trust and such incredible personal growth. We may recruit new members shortly; we may not. The Goddess will, no doubt, show us the path. However, what I can say for certain is that the friends I have made in our coven will be my friends for life, and the experiences that we have shared have been indescribable. We have known each other before, and we will meet again in lives to come.

Kelly (Nissa), 25 – IT student

I have been and always was attracted to the unknown, especially the supernatural, goblins, gnomes, faeries and elves. As a child I lived the majority of my life in a fantasy world, whereas myths and legends were just make-believe in adults' lives. But somehow and somewhere I believed I was going to find them and show the world that they really did exist, and not just in a child's wildest fantasies.

I was born into a reborn Christian family, and I was raised to believe that there was only one God and only his way could get us into heaven. I do not wish to be perceived as knocking the Christian faith; I simply want to tell my story.

When I was thirteen and started to go through adolescence, I became fascinated with the occult. I started to rebel at this age, and for some unknown reason deep down inside I had a calling to break away from the normal regime and find out the truth for myself. I dabbled in the limited occult options of glassy-glassy. At first, it was a huge joke: we were crowded together in a small room giggling and making fun of what we were trying to do. Once we all held hands and what seemed like a seance had begun. All of a sudden the glass lifted from the table and smashed into the wall. You have never seen such a bunch of frightened teenagers, scared to bits, get up and run screaming for their dear lives. It was my first attempt to play with the unknown, and it was the last. Yet, a couple of months later, after I turned fourteen, there was still the craving for more knowledge and answers to all my questions.

When I was fifteen, my father got a telephone call from my grandfather to tell him that my grandmother had fallen ill. We drove to East London the next day and in the hospital I saw a lady lying in bed in the intensive care unit. I still remember saying to my father, as we walked down the corridors of the hospital, that that can't be Granny. As sure as sugar, the woman we had just passed was my grandmother. I never saw my grandmother with white hair. My whole life she had pitch-black hair. Her hair was long and always in a bun on top of her head. My grandmother loved to wear black, and my mother referred to her as the family's 'grim reaper'. Only now do I understand why!

On 11 April my grandmother passed away at 11:30 in the evening. The funeral was soon after her death, and it was brief. Another thing that I forgot to mention was that no one was allowed in my grandmother's bedroom except her husband, and of course her favourite, me! My mother was itching to get into her room, and I suppose that since I love to scratch and poke my nose into other people's things I could not wait either. In my grandmother's room we came across jewellery, clothes, hats, and – to top it off – magazines from the 1950s. You could say that my grandmother was a hoarder, and boy could she hoard, even cockroaches!

Then, to my amazement, I came across a Ouija board. 'What was this? Was my father's mother into something evil?' I showed my mother the board and of course, without a doubt, she immediately ran outside to burn it, while praying that no harm would come to the rest of the family.

The more I scratched, the more I found. Then, in a drawer of old papers, I found a small box. I opened the box and inside the box were tarot cards. I could hardly believe my eyes. 'So my grandmother must have been some kind of gypsy or even a fortune-teller or something exotic.' Finally, we had someone fascinating in the family! I secretly hid the cards away in between the mattresses of the bed in which I was sleeping, for fear that my mother would find these too and burn them as well. My curiosity started to grow. Wild with excitement, I started to rummage for more things. I secretly started to curse the woman who had opened the mystery and left no trail to the next clue. I found incense burners and idols of gods and goddesses, especially Chinese ones. These I am afraid to say were given away, for there were to be no idols in our house.

When we returned to Johannesburg with most of my grandmother's things, including all her books and cookbooks, I started to play with the tarot cards but soon got bored with the whole idea because I did not have a clue as to what I was doing. Again, there was no reading material on how to use the tarot.

A year later, my grandfather died, and again it was into the car and off to the coast for another funeral. Inside their house I remember my mother turned to me and said, 'Everything happens in threes; I wonder who is next?' Strange how that thought stuck in my head. I was not old enough to know my grandmother and now my grandfather was gone as well. Obviously, it was not meant for me to find out her truth.

Two years passed and, fresh out of school, I wanted to travel the world. Six months into my travels I got a call to come home. Sadly enough, my mother passed away two weeks after my arrival home. She was the third one. At this stage, I was angry, very angry, with the Church and with God! After all that praying and going to church, I woke up no better off than when I started. I asked so many pastors and preachers, and none could answer my questions. To this day, I have not returned to church except for funerals.

Now comes the good stuff: a couple of months ago, I was in a bookstore in which I had never been before, and something told me to turn right. I found myself standing in front of the esoteric section. I picked up a book by Laurie Cabot called *Power of the Witch*. Like a fool, I put it down because I had no money on me. I went to draw money and when I returned the book was gone! Typical of my luck, and so I left the store disappointed, just like a child who wasn't allowed a sweet that they had been promised. The following week I returned to the bookstore, and there was my book. I felt as if the book called me and had my name written all over it. I quickly bought the book and raced home to find out what it was all about. I started to read the book and felt that Laurie Cabot was talking to me – she had written the book just for me and for me only. Everything in this book had 'Nissa' written all over it, and I finished the book in two days flat.

For the next couple of months, all I did was buy books and read until my brain was bursting, but this was not enough; there had to be more. I came across a leading Pagan organisation and attended one of their public meetings. All I can say is that, after a few hours spent with the people, I felt that I had come home, and, after a few embarrassing situations, I could not keep away. The people invited me in and accepted me. I realised that I did not have to prove to them who I was and what I had or had not done. All I had to do was be myself and search within myself for the Goddess. This year, I decided to do the Wicca 101 course, and by pure fate or luck, before the course started, something deep inside said to me: 'Go look in the attic.' What I was looking for, I didn't know, and on a very hot, dry summer's day, I braced myself and took a ladder to go into our attic and search for whatever it was that wanted me to find it so badly.

In the attic I felt drawn towards a box with a red lid. Carefully, I lifted the lid and I came across old, torn hardcover books. The edges had either been eaten or had worn away with age. Most of the pages were stained, either from rain or just dampness over the years. I opened one box, and a musty smell enveloped me. Immediately, I was back in my grandmother's house. I closed my eyes and pictured walking through her front door. Who was the woman I was about to discover, and why did I feel guilty as I started to scratch through her things? I started to feel as if I was invading her privacy, and yet something deep inside said to me: 'Go on, look and see what lies beyond.'

The first book I pick up is our family history book. The cover leaf of the book is missing and I slowly turn over the first page. It is too late: I have gone past the point of no return. Our family tree is on the first page. Our family history dates back to King Edward II in 1312. Over the years, the tree grows and grows and finally the branches stop where my grandmother was born.

My grandmother was born on 2 October 1910. She was the oldest daughter of four children. The history of our family was not compiled by my grandmother, but by her aunt. The calling is getting stronger and I carry on with my search. The second book I pick up is a black velvet-covered book with an initial on it made out of silver – the initial is 'E'. The velvet is moth-eaten, and the book looks old. However, the edges of the book are intact. I am wondering: What does 'E' stand for? I open the book. Most of the pages are missing, and I start to wonder: Is this an old diary or is this her 'Book of Shadows'?

I finally come to some pages that have writing on them. Title: Philosophical Theories. I discover that this book does not belong to my grandmother but to her sister, whose name began with an 'E'. This was one of her sister's diaries, and she obviously had no intention of people learning the truth or she would have left the virgin pages untouched for later discovery.

I place the black, moth-eaten diary beside me and again look inside the box, which I have now decided is Pandora's Box. I pull out another book, and this book seems older than the other ones. The cover has not only been moth-eaten, but rats have also had their fair share. I open the book to the first page. The paper is brown and delicate. I feel that if I mishandle the book, the fragile papers will crumble in my hands. These pages are very old; there are no lines on the pages and the handwriting seems like a scrawl – as if things were written in haste.

It is a recipe book dated '1884' on the inside cover. Who did this book belong to? I don't think I will ever know. The writing seemed to be done with a quill and black ink. As I slowly page through this recipe book of mysteries, something catches my eye. 'To Soothe a Fresh Bump When Skin is Broken'. Now what a funny thing to be in a recipe book, I say to myself. I turn the page and see 'Remedy for Chest Cold'. Again I think to myself, why? I think that maybe she wrote it in her recipe book so she wouldn't forget. Then I notice 'eggshells' in the 'Remedy for Chest Cold'! Not only confused – things just do not add up.

I turn the pages and again see 'Pork Pie' and 'Confyt'. Just as I am about to turn another page, the word 'Candle' jumps off the page. There are short instructions on how to make a candle, and the secret to letting it burn longer. Before I put the book down, I see: 'To Get Rid of Beetles'. That was the ultimate; I then realised that this was a book passed down from generation to generation with spells and charms concealed as recipes.

My grandmother had her own catering business for years, and lastly, with great relief, I found a cookie cutter of a witch! I now knew what she was. I frantically ran down the stairs to get one of my grandmother's cookbooks that she left me. I started to page like a madwoman. Did she do it as well? Did my gran conceal things from the world in riddles and rhymes, hoping that one day they would be revealed to the people who wanted to know? Scones. Biscuits. Blah, blah. Where is the good stuff? Finally, I come across pieces of paper with recipes.

I turn over a piece of card and read 'A Recipe for Fertility'. Wow! Now this is what I was looking for. Finally the secret is starting to be revealed. On another piece of paper there is a recipe 'To Cure Warts' and 'Healing Lotion'. I am so disappointed that I cannot run to the phone and call my gran and say to her, 'Hey, guess what I just found? And why didn't you tell me? And what is this all about?' What disappoints me the most is that I cannot say, 'Teach me!'

Unfortunately, my grandmother died when I was sixteen. Her tarot cards became the start of a long journey of truth, lies, deception and joy. I regret that I never had enough time to find our more about her and the path which she chose to lead.

When I started to question my father about witchCraft, he just grinned. One day when I was in my room he walked in and saw a pamphlet lying on my table about the Wicca 101 workshop, and he started to laugh and said to me, 'Oh no, here we go again.' What did he mean by that? He would not tell me.

After finally going through all the books and diaries I went down the stairs and washed my hands. I was dazed and confused, yet happy and excited. I started to read bits and pieces of her diary, and to be perfectly honest I don't have the heart to print what she wrote. It was enough that I had invaded her past. What I can tell you is this: I cannot believe that my grandmother was a young child as well. So this is it: my grandmother was born into a witch's family and yet somewhere along the line the tradition was broken. I have read further on in her diaries and I noticed how she changed over the years. On one specific page she wrote that she was not impressed with the church they had to attend after moving to Rhodesia, and that one of the children came up with a rhyme:

> Unbutton one
> Unbutton two
> Cock your hat
> And spit in the pew.

I can just imagine what was going through her mind and why. My family converted to Protestantism when they emigrated to Rhodesia. Later I was to find that my great-uncle was excommunicated from the Protestant Church for marrying a black woman. My grandmother wrote that she never returned to church after that incident.

I look back now at what I have found out about my past family and the ways in which they led their lives. I have always been drawn to the Craft and have always been fascinated with the unknown. I now know that it must have run in the family because I have found my way home. But still I had no one to teach me. All I had was a fascination and a bee in my bonnet.

During the years I saw my grandmother I always remember that whenever I spent the evening at her house, she would put a glass of water next to my bed. However, I was never allowed to drink the water and, in the morning, she would pour the water down the drain. Again, only now do I realise it was a protection spell to keep us safe while we were sleeping.

I had harboured romantic notions of women being witches and healers. I had come to terms with the fact that my grandmother was not a perfect woman and she had her downside just like everyone else. My mother and her mother-in-law never really saw eye to eye. My grandmother wanted my father, her first-born, to marry another girl. My father, being the strong character that he is, ignored his mother and went against her wishes and married my mother. On my parents' wedding day, my grandmother walked up to my mother and said: 'I curse you, and for ten years you shall have no children.' Ten years went by and my mother finally fell pregnant. Two days after my eldest sister was born she died because of undeveloped lungs. Call it a coincidence or call it a curse, my mother never got over the death of her first child and never forgave my grandmother.

I cannot sing my grandmother's praises and I cannot say that she is my idol, but I am fascinated with my lineage. We are all human, and we all make mistakes. On the other hand, I did not get to know my grandmother. I still love her, for she did no harm to me directly or indirectly. One thing that I have learned is not to take the Craft lightly.

Left: Arch-priestess Donna darkwolf Vos during a ceremony.

Below: A typical circle gathering.

Some of the people involved. **Top left:** Arch-priest and -priestess Pete Pathfinder and Donna darkwolf Vos in ceremonial dress. **Bottom left:** Amazon-Woolfe, Thoth and Volva Freya. **Bottom right:** darkwolf meets with Colonel Kobus Jonker, the head of the Police Occult Unit.

Some ceremonies.

Top left: darkwolf petitions the Goddess for blessings at a couple's union.
Top right: Jacques and Frans 'tie the knot'.
Bottom left: Invoking the Element of Fire.
Bottom right: A circle is cast with a flaming sword during a ceremony by Amazon-Woolfe.

Beltaine maypole dance ceremony, a real family event, has everyone – from toddlers to wise old ones – gathering around the maypole with a ribbon in their hands …

Some examples of altar settings (clockwise from top left):
1. An altar for Samhain.
2. An altar for a handfasting ceremony.
3. An altar for Ostara.
4. An altar setting for an Esbat.
5. An altar for Imbolc.

Scenes from different ceremonies.
Above: The circle is prepared for a ceremony.
Right: Invoking east.
Below: Grounding energy.

More scenes from different ceremonies.
Top left: Barding.
Top right: Jumping the broom.
Above: Esbat celebrations around the lounge altar.
Bottom left: The sword is raised and a circle is cast.

Left: High priestess Dolphin Star drawing down the moon into high priestess Dragonmistt.

Below: darkwolf bestows a blessing.

CHAPTER 9

LITTLE BOOK OF SHADOWS

I have left these sections untouched as far as possible, simply dividing them into recipes, spells and rituals. Some spells are very short; others are longer. Some rituals include detailed wording for invocations; others do not.

The content of these spells differs widely, as does the nature of all spells and rituals everywhere. Approaches are also varied. The fact that some spells are super-short, while others are as long as rituals, is an indication of the eclectic nature of Paganism.

RECIPES

Nissa's grandmother's remedy for chest colds

Drop 3 drops of pure carbolic acid into half of an eggshell: put this into a small jug of boiling water and inhale. Repeat several times a day. To inhale open the mouth widely – hold it near the jug and put a towel around your head and the jug so that very little steam escapes.

Nissa's grandmother's recipe to prevent hair from falling out

Add one teaspoon of Jeyes disinfectant to a pint of cold boiled water. Apply well to the scalp every second night. This keeps the scalp healthy, stops hair from falling out and makes hair grow thicker.

Nissa's grandmother's recipe to soothe a flesh burn

This recipe works for burns when the skin is not broken. Scrape raw potato onto a piece of soft linen, and apply this as a poultice to the injured area.

Nissa's grandmother's cure for warts

Squeeze a piece of a green fig onto the warts – they will quickly disappear, leaving no trace behind.

Another very old remedy is to fill the wart with a bit of raw beef. Bury the beef and as it decays the wart will disappear.

Nissa's grandmother's recipe to get rid of beetles

Get some beer and leave it uncovered all day. At night put the beer into a basin. Put the basin on the floor and put little sticks all around it to serve as ladders for the beetles. They will stupefy themselves with the beer, fall in and drown. But the plan must be executed every night for some time if they are to be got rid of altogether.

7th Hawk's courage cream

Requirements

½ teaspoon of cohosh root
1 tablespoon lemon balm
10 drops clove bud essential oil
500 ml aqueous cream

Method

Place the cream in a double boiler with the herbs and warm it until the herbs have seeped properly. Sieve off the herbs and let the cream cool. Mix the cream well and add the clove bud essential oil. Mix well. Remember: during the mixing of the cream continuously imbue with courage energy.

This cream works as a mild sedative, and when used at night it will enable a more restful sleep.

Rub the cream into your body, and say: 'Cream of courage, work in strong. Seep in all night and day long.'

7th Hawk's attraction powder

Requirements

1 tablespoon jasmine flowers
1 tablespoon myrrh
1 teaspoon frankincense
1 teaspoon basil
½ teaspoon cinnamon
10 tablespoons cornflour

Method

Grind all the herbs to a fine powder, using a mortar and pestle. Add the herbs to the cornflour. Shake well and imbue with attraction energy. Fill a muslin bag with the powder and place it in between an orange and green candle – let them burn out. Dust in places where you know that the person you want to attract will sit, sleep, walk, etc. Do not forget to dust your clothes and your pillow – anywhere you go or anything that you carry with you. Remember to say these words: 'Each time I dust and where it falls, its power is felt.'

7th Hawk's recipe for clearing negativity

Requirements

2 tablespoons parsley
¼ teaspoon mistletoe
½ teaspoon mugwort
½ teaspoon St John's wort
½ teaspoon lemon balm
½ teaspoon ground cloves
1 tablespoon coarse sea salt

Method

Place the ingredients in a muslin bag, boil a litre of water and place the herb bag in the hot water. Let it seep. Use to wash your floors, walls or anything else where you want negativity to be removed. This mixture can also be added to a spray bottle and the area can be sprayed.

Thoth's recipe for myrrh oil

Requirements

Grapeseed oil or olive oil
Crushed myrrh

Method

Put the oil in a glass bowl and add 2 teaspoons of crushed myrrh to every 100 ml of oil. Heat on low for 12 hours.

Thoth's hyssop infusion
For those who prefer to shower instead of bath

Requirements

Small coffee filter bag
5–6 tablespoons of hyssop (the herb, not the oil)
10 cups of water
Percolator

Method

Place the herbs in a coffee filter on the percolator and percolate until the water is finished. When cool, place into a plastic spritzer. This lasts for a couple of months.

SPELLS

Volva Freya's magickal tips and ideas

Tarot cards
If you do not have a set of tarot cards, make your own by cutting 78 cards (±120 mm × 80 mm) from cardboard. Write the names and numbers of the suits of the minor and major arcana on the cards as well as their meanings. Use them as you would purchased tarot cards.

Pictures from magazines
Collect pictures from magazines and use them as 'seals' or to help with visualisation for magickal use.

Charcoal blocks
Generally, these blocks can become painstaking in ritual use, since they seldom burn. Preheat your oven to 100°C, and place the blocks on a metal tray. Leave them in the oven for approximately 15 minutes, with the oven door slightly open. Store them in airtight glass containers. Another method that sometimes works is to pour a few drops of methylated spirits on the charcoal blocks, but beware of the big flames!

To light the charcoal blocks, use tweezers or long-nose pliers. Hold the charcoal block over a candle flame until ignited. Place the burning charcoal block on a bowl of dry soil or salt.

It is always a good idea to ignite the blocks outside your working area since the blocks smoke a lot, and the saltpetre could cause breathing irritations.

Goddess image/statue
If family members are not too keen on your path, use a Mother Mary image as a Mother Goddess symbol, and it will divert their attention. It might come as a surprise to you that in Dianic Wicca Mother Mary is seen as an archetype of the Great Goddess.

Useful kitchen utensils
- Use a wooden spoon as a wand.
- Use a kitchen knife as an athame.

- Use an old cooking pot as a cauldron.
- Use a slow cooker to make magickal oils (empower some herbs and add to cooking oil, leave overnight on slow heat for ±12 hours).
- Coffee percolators make wonderful infusions.
- Electric blenders are handy for grinding herbs.

Some ideas for a pentacle

Glue or tie 5 twigs of equal length from any tree in your garden. Fill a round flat pot plant with dry soil and trace a pentacle on the soil. Carve a pentacle on the bottom of a candle, especially if you do not want others to become aware of your Craft.

The Elements

The following can be used as representations of the Elements:
- Earth: pot plants, a bowl of salt, coins, stones from your garden, a bowl of soil, flowers (dried or fresh).
- Air: a feather duster, feathers, incense sticks or burners, images of birds.
- Fire: candle wax, burned charcoal from your barbecue, a burned piece of wood, lava rocks.
- Spirit: flowers, photographs, candles, crystals.

Herbs and veggies

Make a list of the herbs you stock in your cupboard and stick it inside the cupboard door for quick magickal reference.

Some magickal applications of the common herbs/veggies available at any supermarket include the following:
- Cinnamon: spirituality, success, healing, power, psychic powers, lust, protection, love.
- Pepper: protection, exorcism.
- Allspice: love.
- Coriander: love, healing.
- Rosemary: protection, love, lust, mental powers, exorcism, purification, healing, sleep.
- Bay leaves: protection, psychic powers, healing, purification, strength, prophetic dreams.
- Basil: love, exorcism, wealth.
- Salt: purification, wealth.

- Ginger: love, money, success, power.
- Parsley: lust, protection, purification.
- Tomato: love, protection, prosperity.
- Garlic: protection, healing, exorcism, anti-theft, lust.
- Carrots: fertility, lust.
- Leeks: love, protection, exorcism.
- Lemon: purification, love, friendship.
- Potatoes: healing.
- Tea: riches, courage, strength.
- Apples: healing, love.

Scott Cunningham's *Encyclopedia of Magical Herbs* will be a valuable investment on your shelf between your recipe books.

Decorative Elemental bowl

Take a glass bowl and fill it halfway with water to represent the Element of Water. Add a few drops of potpourri oil to the water to represent the Element of Air. Float a few fresh leaves and/or flowers on the water to represent the Element of Earth. Add to the water a floating candle, or a tea candle to represent the Element of Fire.

Candles

If you run short on candles, do not despair! Take a fireproof bowl or holder, add some cooking oil, take a piece of cotton and roll it into a small ball, pull a small piece of cotton out of the ball and roll tightly into a wick. Put it into the oil and wait a few minutes until the oil soaks into the cotton ball. Add some empowered herbs, coins, etc., light the wick and voila – it works!

To create any colour candle you need, grate some wax crayons onto tea candles.

For candle holders, drop some melted wax from a candle onto a fireproof saucer. Stick your candle onto the soft wax. Or you can use a glass/cold drink/beer bottle as a candle holder. Use clean glass bottles (such as pickle bottles, etc.), paint decorative signs or symbols on the glass and add some dry soil or salt onto the base of the bottle. Place a tea candle on the soil and you have a beautiful magickal decorative candle bottle.

Incense stick holders

Add some soil to a cup or any deep saucer or bowl, and plant your incense sticks into the soil.

Ceramic floor tiles

These are very useful for controlling burning candles and dripping wax and for burning parchments of paper. The tile also becomes a 'power sink' for magickal workings.

Silverfox's spell to bring an as yet unknown lover into your life

1. In red ink, write down on a piece of paper all the qualities of your dream lover/s. If you like, you can also cut out pictures from magazines of people who resemble quite closely the individual/s you want to attract into your life.
2. Repeat positive affirmations to yourself at least three times a day, and each of those times, at least ten times. Say things like: 'I am good and I attract love into my life.' It is vital that you do this daily, without fail.
3. I dislike burning incense, so instead I use the following herbal mixture:
   - 1 handful lavender leaves
   - 1 handful rose petals
   - 1 vanilla pod
   - 1 tablespoon coriander seeds
   - 2 cinnamon sticks

   (To dry the lavender and rose petals if they are freshly picked, pop them into the microwave for a few minutes.)

   Charge the herbs, visualising your ideal partner coming into your life. Add 2 cups of water to the mixture and bring to the boil, while visualising all the time. You can repeat a chant quietly to yourself, if you wish – something like: 'Love is drawn into these rooms; it comes by the power of these blooms.'
4. Simultaneously, have a pink candle (scored with lavender, ylang ylang or rose oil) burning next to the stove. You can also have a red candle, scored with the same, for lust.
5. When your herbs have been brought to the boil, turn the heat down as far as possible so it simmers for, say, 15 to 30 minutes. All the time, keep on visualising and repeating your chants.

6. Remove the pot from the stove and extinguish the candles. Keep the paper in a safe place.
7. Repeat the spell for 9 days in a row. At the end of the 9th day, when you have finished chanting and simmering your herbs, burn the piece of paper in the candle flame. Collect the ashes and blow them into the air.

Note that it is probably best – but not essential – to start the spell on a Friday night, and to do it when the moon is waxing. If you can get another witch to do it with you at least on one of the nights (he or she does not have to be in the same place as you, geographically), then that can enhance it tremendously.

An extension of a high magick spell to attract a lover

(I would recommend this, and if you can do it with another practitioner, so much the better.)

Again, the high magick spell to attract an as yet unknown lover/s into your life is best done when the moon is waxing and on a Friday night – but this is not crucial. For instance, you might not always be able to get together with another practitioner during the waxing phase of the moon.

1. Write out your spell and address the gods and goddesses with whom you will be working (e.g. Pan, Venus and Aphrodite and, for homosexual love, Hyacinthus).
2. Use pink and red candles for love and lust. You can also use an orange candle for pure confidence, and a blue candle for healing (yourself). Some practitioners (e.g. in Egyptian magick) use green candles instead of pink.
3. Cast your circle, calling on the Elements.
4. In your cauldron, burn the same herbal mixture as above, but also cut 9 small hearts out of red or pink paper. Add the piece of paper with all the lover's desired qualities, etc.
5. Read your spell with intensity, three times, petitioning the gods and goddesses to bring the ideal lover/s into your life. This is the point in the spell when you can also use whichever technique you prefer to build up energy for the working and to direct it outwards into the atmosphere.
6. Burn the piece of paper with the lover's qualities on it.
7. Give thanks to the deities, Elemental spirits, etc. Dismiss them and open the circle.
8. Be sure to ground yourself and get rid of the energy you have built up during the working part of the spell (or you may end up being quite manic and not being able to sleep that night).

Note that these spells can take from 24 hours to 6 months to show results (although they average between 2 and 3 weeks). They are MUCH more effective when you do them for other people. One word of warning: be very clear on the qualities of the person you wish to attract into your life. This is crucial. More than once, I have seen the spells work in terms of bringing new lovers into people's lives – and quite quickly too – but because the quality lists were not completed properly, the new relationships were doomed because the people involved had fundamental differences.

Willow's love spell

1. Collect a number of stones, and charge each stone with the qualities that you are looking for in a partner.
2. Put the stones into a bottle along with the oils that correspond to love, e.g. lavender, vanilla, ylang ylang and patchouli. Add a little honey.
3. Seal the bottle and shake it up. As you are doing this, visualise your love coming to you.
4. Place the bottle under your bed and leave it there until love comes to you.

Dragonmistt's spell for sending a greeting to an absent beloved

When my children spend the weekend with their dad, I like to do this ritual when I wake up in the morning – basically to say 'good morning' to them and to let them know that I am thinking of them. I send them good wishes for the day and all the love of their mother while they are away.

Follow these simple steps:

1. Take a pink candle and, if possible, have the person to whom you would like to send the greeting empower the candle with their personal energies by kissing or holding the candle before they leave.
2. Stand in an area where you have an open view over the general direction of where the person is at the time when you would like to send the greeting.
3. Light the candle and hold it up to that person at eye level, and concentrate on sensing the person's presence with you as you focus on their energy.
4. Say words of greeting and love that you would like the person to hear, feeling the emotions of what you are saying while doing so. Wish them joy and happiness for the day, blessing them with your love, hugs and kisses.
5. Then once you have spoken your wishes for them, raise energy through the concentration of your energies into the candle flame.

6. Finally, once enough energy is raised, blow out the flame as hard as you can towards that person and allow the Air and Fire Elementals to carry your wishes to the person who they are intended for in the direction of where they are.

Angelique Raeven's spell for meeting someone special

If you have an affinity for music as I do, this spell will work well for you. Before getting dressed, but after having a bath or shower, obtain one unused blue candle. Place this in the centre of your altar, or, if you don't have one, a small table, or any surface that is readily available, and within sight.

Light some of your favourite incense, and put on a song that really moves your soul. Turn up the volume as loud as you comfortably can without having the neighbours phone the police! Light the candle and turn out the lights.

Kneel or stand in front of your altar and focus on the blue candle. Feel the music energising you, and focus simultaneously on a picture of your meeting the right person for you. Mentally open yourself for this person to enter into your life.

This process always leaves me feeling giddy and excited in a contained kind of way.

When your song is finished simply take a deep, confident breath, thank the Ancient Ones, and continue getting dressed to go out. Leave the candle burning until just before you leave your abode. Always extinguish this candle by snuffing, not blowing, as by blowing you will blow away your luck.

For some extra luck you can dab some good-quality Sandalwood oil on your wrists, as this also attracts loving energy to you. There is nothing worse than cheap Sandalwood oil, so do make sure you get a good one.

The blue candle can get used repetitively for this spell until it is finished.

It has never failed to bring interesting individuals into my life, and I hope it brings about the same result in yours.

Papillon's 'money tree' spell

Requirements
1 black candle
1 green candle
A deep bowl of earth
Full-moon water
7 five-rand coins
Patchouli incense

Moon phase: Full or waxing
Time: When the moon is in a favourable aspect with Jupiter (the Great Benefit)
Day: Sunday

1. Set up your altar with the above-mentioned items, cast your circle and open the quarters, asking for their energies to aid the spell.
2. Next, invite in the goddess of abundance, Rosemerta.
3. Cleanse and consecrate the Earth and coins.
4. Light the black candle, banishing negativity while doing so.
5. Light the green candle, inviting health and prosperity into your life. Now 'plant' the seven coins one by one in the soil, chanting: 'As I sow, so shall I reap. My goddess of abundance, bring prosperity to me. May I not go hungry and may I share my fortune with those who are less so.'
6. Visualise yourself having all you need to live comfortably, while watering the coins with the full-moon water.
7. Thank and say farewell to the goddess and quarters. Draw up the circle and send it off into the astral plane to do your bidding.
8. Every evening after that, for seven nights, 'reap' one coin.

Whenever I've been strapped for cash, I've done this spell. I assure you, somehow, in some way, I've always managed to have enough to live on in the manner I'm accustomed to.

Ra-hotep's prosperity spell

For all purposes

Heat a charcoal block and put it into a censor with cinnamon. Have an image of Isis or strongly visualise Isis and say: 'Mighty Isis, Goddess of magick, hear my plea. As the smoky incense rises, bring me lots of luck and prosperity.'

cajun's spell to obtain what you want

1. Make a dreamcatcher. Focus your intent in every knot – everything that you want, e.g. money, healing and love.
2. When you have finished, hang the dreamcatcher where you will see it every day. When your dream is 'caught' the spell has worked its course.
3. Destroy the dreamcatcher. If you want to keep the dreamcatcher, the spell must be cleared from it.

Thoth's healing spell

For all purposes
1. Prepare by taking a cleansing bath in hyssop (or smear hyssop over yourself if you are in a shower).
2. On your altar, light two blue candles.
3. Burn myrrh and healing herbs for incense (e.g. carnation, eucalyptus, gardenia, lotus, rosemary, violet, spearmint and olive).
4. Chant: 'Isis, send healing over my body.'
5. Inhale the incense with rapid, short breaths until you are slightly light-headed; then inhale the incense with four deep, slow breaths.

Silver Birch's cancer spell

When my mom was diagnosed with cancer, and went in for her operation, I set up a ritual space for her.

For clearing the negativity that surrounds the cancer, burning basil (either the incense or the oil) is useful – it binds the 'nastiness', almost like an exorcism – and sprinkling salt is essential for cleansing.

I wrote down my mother's problems and burned them. After her operation, she had chemotherapy. The negativity had gone and she recovered fully.

Journey's healing spell

For physical injury
This spell requires much mental concentration, as it relies strongly on visualisation:
1. Cast the circle.
2. Call on the Elements.
3. Call on the Goddess and the God, attuning specifically to deities connected with healing, e.g. Horus and Nephtet.
4. Lay your hands on the injured area, visualise the injury dissipating, and as it does so a cone of light expanding into a star. Put energy into the star, and then place the star on the injured area. See the light from the star entering the area of the injury. See the light filling the entire body, bringing about total healing and cleansing of the area.
5. When the working is done, thank and dismiss the Goddess or God and the Elements.
6. Close the circle.

cajun's medicine pouch spell

You will need a circle of leather. Make holes around the edge and thong it.

Pick this up and wear it every day. Place your intent into the bag – things that represent what you want to work on. You may even need to make representations of what you want.

This spell works in two ways: psychologically – by seeing it every day, you focus on your needs; and magickally – the daily release of energy draws your needs to you.

Niteshade's spell to stop a person from harming one

Light a white candle and your favourite incense. Meditate for a short while on the problem. Invoke the Spirits of Protection for you and yours. Then take a piece of brown paper, and write the name of the offending person or people in lead pencil. If unknown people are involved, also print and write 'and all persons unknown that are causing harm to me'.

Cross off each (person) forcefully and say emphatically: 'I freeze (name/s) to be bound by this spell, unable to cause any more harm to (name/s)! As I will, so mote it be!'

Then put a spoonful of used coffee grounds on the brown paper. Fold it into a small parcel and place it in the freezer. Leave it until the problem is completely resolved. I wrap a rubber band or string around the parcel to keep the coffee grounds from falling out. You can also use a ziplock bag. Be sure to burn the candle down completely and don't use it for any other purpose.

Angelique Raeven's visualisation spell

I have had a lot of success in doing spells without tools. All the magick energy you need is within you and around you in the ether.

So, simply close your eyes, and centre and ground yourself. After you feel fairly serene, begin to visualise whatever it is that you want to happen as clearly as possible.

I have found that it is more effective to hold this image clearly for only one minute and then to let it go, rather than trying to keep it up for ten minutes and losing focus.

Once you have the image, surround it with a bubble of the appropriate colour. If you're not sure of a colour, gold is a very good general choice.

Imagine yourself drawing energy from the universe that surrounds you, pulling it through you and pouring it into your image until your bubble is 'full'.

Then send your image out into the ether; you can launch it by bursting the bubble in a mighty explosion, or let it simply float away, with instructions to expire the moment that it has become a physical reality.

With this little visualisation spell, I've always managed to have a taxi come by my house whenever I've needed it. It is also very good for small-life situations, like finding parking or finding a certain item that you are looking to buy, but don't know where to find.

However, the secret to any spell working is of course the little, but difficult, trick of not thinking about it or talking about it afterwards.

A song spell

To a Druid, a simple song or poem is as magickal as a spell. In Druidism, we have what we call song spells. Here is an example of such a song spell:

> Moon Goddess, one of great beauty
> Grant me prosperity for the year to be.
> Oh great hunter and horned god
> I pray thee, bless me with thy eternal rod.
>
> Elemental spirits of the land
> Bring me health with thy caring hand.
> All the gods – I kneel to thee
> And as I will, so mote it be.

This can be done as a song or simply as an invocation within a cleared sacred space. If you want, you can also use some herbs. Use cinnamon for prosperity or wealth, St John's wort for healing, and sage for blessings and spirituality. Cast the herbs over an open fire while singing or intoning the above.

Stara's spell for learning

Reece is a post-graduate student in his second year at university studying for a BCom. He is having problems with stats and can't seem to grasp the concept of the subject.

He is very troubled by the situation because it forms an integral part of his studies, and he needs to accomplish and understand this section to continue and be successful in his year-end exams. He requests a spell.

I make an appointment to see him and pack up a makeshift altar comprising all the Elements.

Altar setup

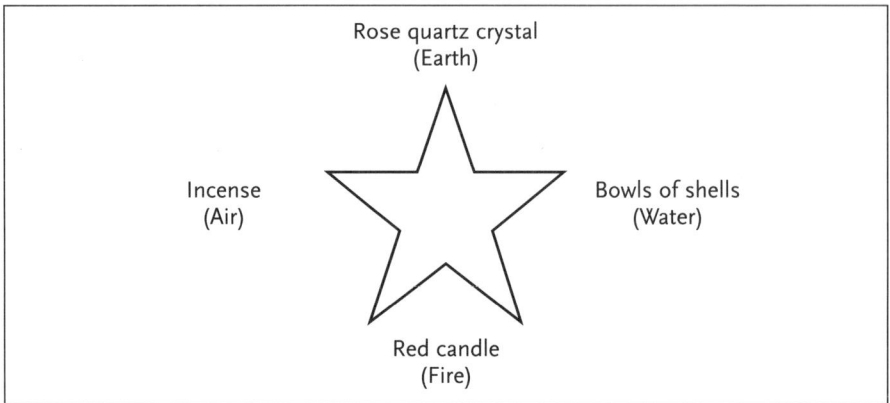

On arrival I set up my altar and prepare to do a tarot reading. This will give me an overview of the situation. During the reading it is evident that Reece is deeply troubled. He is confused and frustrated, which is hampering his clarity of thought. His aura is cloudy with dark patches.

Now that I have an idea of what I am working with, I decide on a form of spell. I cleanse and consecrate three candles and a clear quartz crystal.

With premixed oils I empower the following:

- A yellow candle: Yellow represents the Element of Air, so I empower the quality of Air for clarity and to clear his confusion.
- A red candle: Red represents the Element of Fire. He clearly has the desire and passion to get over this obstacle or he would not be as frustrated as he is. I ask the Element of Fire to encourage this desire in a positive manner, that he may feel confident about passing his exam.
- A blue candle: Blue representing the Element of Water, I empower the blue candle to keep his mind flowing and at ease while working from his textbooks and that he not get stuck on a specific problem but be able to work past it.

Lastly, I empower the quartz crystal with all the above qualities that I have asked of the Elements. He carries the quartz crystal in his pocket until he has completed his exam.

The rest is up to Reece. In order for the spell to be successful, he has to meditate each evening before he retires for the night, with all three candles burning in front of him, paying careful attention to the qualities of each Element.

The last part of the spell is to cleanse his aura. He has a salt bath every day for a week in order to do this.

I got feedback from Reece within three weeks of the spell being performed. He passed stats and managed to grasp the factor that he had been missing all along. A positive approach was all that was needed, but he had become so negative in his thinking about the subject that his attitude needed to be consciously shifted – from a negative space to a positive one. With a bit of magickal help, everything worked out well.

Papillon's travelling protection spell

I try to do this spell every time I get behind the wheel of my car. Before I turn on the ignition, I close my eyes, visualise and say the following:

> I cast my circle of protection around my car, keeping it and its occupants safe. My circle will ensure that everything mechanical and electrical will work at peak perfection. In addition to this circle, I cast a triple, purple circle that will enchant all other motorists and pedestrians casting their eyes on this vehicle. They will be imbued with a wonderful sense of well-being, love and compassion.

Quite honestly, I have never had any vehicle mishaps when I've remembered to do this spell.

Papillon's bath relaxation spell

I draw my bath and, while the water is running, add three handfuls of salt. If time permits me to have a leisurely, *long* bath, I light a few green, white and blue candles and my favourite incense. While lying in the salted bath water, I close my eyes and start visualising a golden ball of light (coming straight from divinity) above my head. It envelops me slowly from the head down. I see the divine light push the pain out, and the salt solution pulling all toxins out of my body. I have both the 'push' and the 'pull' factor. I can actually feel pain leaving my body, and I have a wonderful floaty feeling. This done, the golden ball hovers at my feet for a few seconds, then quick as a flash darts off. I pull the plug and visualise all the muck going down the drain.

After this spell, I'm usually bursting with energy!

Papillon's new moon home spell

The night before new moon, I steep some basil (for banishing), sage (for spirituality) and bay leaves (for protection) in some warm (but not boiling) water. The following day, I use a clean cloth and wipe all the entrances to my home with the solution. As

I wash the window and door frames, I chant: 'Herbs of basil, sage and bay, bring your love and protection to stay.'

I visualise all living under this roof being happy and healthy.

I mix the residual herbs with vinegar and pour the mixture down all the drains, chanting: 'May only positive thoughts, words, deeds and entities enter this home. With these herbs I banish all negativity in any shape or form.'

I kid you not: I did this at my daughter's home; she came back to tell me that that particular month she got a promotion at work and even her colleagues enquired why she looked 'different', so happy and radiant!

Silverfox's emergency contact spell

If you have to get hold of someone urgently but are unable to phone them, try this telepathic spell. You can do it anywhere and at any time, but you need to be alone in a place where you won't be disturbed for a minute or two.

Visualise the relevant person standing opposite you, almost 'mirroring' you, if you like. Imagine that the two of you are cocooned in a sphere of yellow light. Then visualise a red beam of light travelling from your forehead to theirs, and another red beam of light from your mouth to theirs, and a third light beam from your throat to theirs. Concentrate on this for a few seconds and then imagine a bolt of white lightning travelling from your forehead to theirs and, at that moment, transmit your telepathic message to the other person.

Silverfox's spell to break up an adulterous affair

If you discover that your spouse is having a clandestine affair behind your back (and you are one hundred per cent sure of this – and you yourself are definitely not guilty of having done the same), then here is a spell you can try. It can be done at any time, but it is best in the waning moon.

Follow these steps:
1. On a piece of paper, carefully draw the two people concerned in black ink. It is more powerful if you have a photo of them: cut out two pictures of them and glue them onto one page.
2. Write the names of the people on the drawings (on their chests). Pour some lemon juice or some polluted water onto the images.
3. Concentrate all the time on what you are doing and what you wish to achieve.
4. Use black candles.
5. Cast your circle and call on deities like Merlin, Thor, Hecate and the Dark Kali. (If you have been badly wronged, the deities are generally very

sympathetic and they tend to look after those who have been harmed, particularly if unprovoked.)
6. Write your spell on another piece of paper – you will be reading it three times in the circle – and then gather up your energy. Put some lemon juice on that piece of paper too.
7. Take the piece of paper with the drawings and rip it in half (or cut it with a pair of scissors), symbolically splitting up the adulterous couple.
8. Burn one half of the paper and hide the other in a secret place after the spell has been completed. Burn the piece of paper with the spell. Collect the ashes and flush them down the loo later on.
9. Dismiss and give thanks to the deities and Elementals. Open the circle.

darkwolf's never-fail ingredients for successful spells

- One good psychiatrist – to ensure that you walk between the veil, and don't fall through it.
- One successful lawyer – always handy in case your spell backfires.
- One (or several) bottle(s) of the Cape's finest wines – important to ready your strength of will (add some incense for extra results).
- One lover – active hormones are excellent for stress relief and, as a result, better focus (add some candle magick for extra results).
- A Marilyn Monroe or Zsa Zsa Gabor outfit (if you are a man, you should try it too), complete with wig and very high heels. Glamour adds to the visualisation process.
- An ABBA CD – vital for mood setting, ending with 'Andante, Andante' at the point of sending your spell into the universe.

Seriously, though, no fancy wands or swashbuckling swords are necessary – no great incantations, no swirling robes. A stress-free temple space is all that is required to guarantee a shift in conciousness.

RITUALS

Ritual for psychic development – Ruby Flame

I wrote this ritual to help myself develop my psychic abilities with the aid of divination methods. The purpose of the ritual is also to commit yourself to trying to open your third eye. The idea is to do the legwork yourself, as asking the gods to do it all would be rather passive and, in my opinion, unfair. This spell is for sustained psychic growth; it is not about asking for answers to fall from above.

I wrote it to be performed with my coven; however you could also adapt it to perform in solitary by excluding the last exercise.

The spell revolves around a question for which you are seeking an answer – something in your life that you need to understand. It involves choosing a god or goddess to walk with you on this path and a divination method for which you have a good feel. As in the numerical associations in Wiccan tradition, the threefold combination is the cornerstone of the spell.

Altar

Decorate the altar with various divination tools (e.g. tarot cards, ruins, a pendulum, a Ouija board and crystals) as well as the usual chalice, athame, Goddess and God statues, candles, flowers, etc.

God and Goddess invocations

When we performed this ritual, Isis and Osiris were invoked because the high priest and high priestess were partial to working with these deities. However, you may prefer other deities with whom you are more comfortable or familiar. As I invoked Isis, I called her for her psychic abilities, her knowledge of the underworld, her supremacy on the astral planes and her maternal qualities, so that we, her children, may be nurtured by her in our growth.

Meditation

A meditation is essential for this kind of ritual, so that everyone's minds are clear and focused. Though I did not write a guided meditation, there are many suitable ones available. We did the meditation to soft music, as is traditional.

The meditation involved opening each chakra around the body one by one, using the various colour associations and then focusing on a swelling pale blue light that descends and is absorbed by each individual.

Our meditation also involved a journey into the realms of the gods, bringing each person into a sacred temple surrounded by a garden, where the gods had left us each a gift. Chatting about our unique gifts made for an interesting discussion during the cakes and ale.

Raising energy and chanting

We always find that the best way to raise energy is to run in an anti-clockwise direction, faster and faster, chanting 'My eyes to see, my mind to grow' louder and louder until told to 'drop'. The energy is then grounded.

Working

Each person writes down their question on a piece of paper. It must be something that is answerable within a certain time frame. For example: 'Will I get promotion at work within the next six months?'

Each person then chooses a particular deity to whom their question is posed. Make a toast to your god or goddess and put your piece of paper in the cauldron.

The following words are then said:

> As paper gives way to flame, so the essences of the words remain. As I ask my question, so I shall know the answer within (number) days. So mote it be.
>
> The (tarot/pendulum/runes/Ouija/I Ching) shall be the guide to my answer. (Each person chooses the divination method that they prefer.)
>
> I shall grow as I follow my path. I shall learn about myself and the universe through the ways of the Craft and I shall be wiser because of my Craft.
>
> I am strong; I am wise; I am psychic. Blessed be. I (magickal name) thank (name of deity). So mote it be.

Before the end of the ritual the libation or cakes and ale ceremony is held.

Fun exercise

As a fun exercise I paired off the coven members. Each person then charged their cord with their particular question. Using the cord, the other person must divine the question, i.e. tell their partner what their question had been. It was amazing to see how the energy from the ritual affected people's mind states. Almost everyone managed to get it right.

Banishing and cleansing ritual – darkwolf

(This is useful for someone who has ended a long-term relationship and the lover has left the home.)

Please note that the purpose of the banishing is to end something magickally or to get rid of a bad presence, whereas the cleansing is to remove negative energy, vibrations or images from a place by using positive psychic energy. This working takes place during the dark moon.

The ritual will take the standard form:
1. Gather and smudge all present.
2. Circle will be cast around the entire working area.
3. Call on the four quarters:
    - Air (east):   Elements of the east
                      Hearken to your sign
                      Sylphs of the Air
                      Bring the Divine.
    - Fire (north):   Elements of the north
                      I bid you welcome
                      Salamanders of Fire
                      Bring what we desire.
    - Water (west):   Elements of the west
                      Hear our call
                      Undines of Water
                      Fluid is your protective wall.
    - Earth (south): Elements of the south
                      Ground us now
                      Gnomes of the Earth
                      To the Great Mother we bow.
4. Invocation of the God or Goddess.
5. Visualisation* (included below).
6. Offering.
7. Raising of energy.
8. Chant through house: 'Heal our sister. Cleanse this space. Banish all sadness from this place.'
9. Cakes and ale ceremony.
10. Dismiss the God or Goddess.
11. Close quarters.
12. Close circle.

Lover to provide the following:
- Incense that will fill the whole space.
- Two white candles on either side of the altar.
- One black candle (small or cut) – this candle must be dressed before being burnt.
- White petals in a basket of sorts.
- A white cloth to cover the altar.
- Some bread and a goblet filled with wine.

*Visualisation

It is dark moon – the night on which no work or magick is traditionally performed, unless there is work to be done. And so it is that we have gathered as a clan, as a brotherhood and sisterhood to acknowledge this night as a night to banish and cleanse.

Where once the fullness of the Mother shone on this place, and things seemed to grow in harmony, now that growth has shrivelled to a propensity sustainable only by the dark moon.

How is it that a love can blossom, grow and then die? How is it that the moon in all her phases has witnessed so much passion, so much pain? And how is it that in our pain we gather for such a purpose?

It is so because we are the offspring of the mating of the sun and the moon. It is so because we have little choice in being born, living, loving and dying. It is so because within each of us surges the will to live – despite the pain – the wish to love and be loved in return. Despite the pain, we understand that we must obey the life force, for if we don't, we will rot inside – go back to the Earth in a manner – which we know is not our karma. It is like having had a limb amputated. Still we experience the pain of the whole limb when we attempt to lift the little stump in our seemingly futile attempt to regain the control we previously had.

Likewise, we experience pain as we attempt to lift our pathetic emotional self from the crumpled heap of self-doubt into which it has sunk. But there is a reason for the pain, and even the conquering of pain, in this world and this life. When the purpose of this life is done, we will journey beyond, just as the evergreen grows and prospers in both Summer and Winter.

Year after year, so also does the soul continue from strength to strength, growing ever stronger, wiser, richer. And so the soul of the departed person in this place must go on, in peace, if that is allotted to him or her, and harmony – that is all of our destinies.

And to you, dear one: hear the words of the Great Mother:

Lift your eyes moonwards if you can; lift your head starwards in your trust; lift your beautiful torso and salute the sun; get off your magnificent feet and begin to run.

For mine is your power as I take your pain. Mine is your release as I go insane. From Maiden to Mother to Crone I go, repeating these phases, to remove your woe.

I understand the anguish, the madness, the pain. I understand the darkness, the fear, feeling lame. But now you will arise, in the dark of my moon, and make ready for your healing, as you sing a new tune.

Chant (sung by the high priestess)

Great Warrior Goddess
Mother of all
We rely on your strength
Hear our call.

I request you now
To do my will
Cleanse and banish
Our needs fulfil.

Chorus (sung by coveners)

Heal our sister
Cleanse this space
Banish all sadness
From this place.

The moon is dark
The time is sad
The veil will lift
And we'll be glad.

Chant (sung by the high priestess)

You will run
With the Maiden, be with the Crone

The Mother will comfort you
You will sit on her throne.

Make all and any presence left behind,
Depart in peace and harmony to the world
From which it came.
May the Goddess go in peace,
And may we ever bask
In her love, light and strength.

Cleansing ritual – darkwolf

Cleansing rituals can be for personal, home or business use. In this case, it was performed to cleanse a home after a particularly negative experience with a tenant.

The following procedure is useful:
1. Cast the circle with a sword.
2. Call on the quarters, emphasising the protection that these Elements offer us:
   - Air (east): using incense – Elements of the east
     Hearken to your sign.
     Sylphs of the Air
     Bring the Divine.
   - Fire (north): using a candle – Elements of the north
     I bid you welcome.
     Salamanders of Fire
     Bring what we desire.
   - Water (west): sprinkling water – Elements of the west
     Hear our call
     Undines of Water
     Fluid is your protective wall.
   - Earth (south): sprinkling salt – Elements of the south
     Ground us now.
     Gnomes of the Earth
     To the Great Mother we bow.
3. Invoke the energies of the God and/or Goddess.
4. All walk through the house and each individual choose a room that they will cleanse, both in their mind during the visualisation and on the physical walk-through that will take place.

5. All return and be seated. The visualisation* (see below) then takes place.
6. After the visualisation, and at the signal – i.e. when the bell is rung – all rise and move in an anti-clockwise direction, starting with the east Element first and others follow after east into the chosen room/s.
7. Return and present individual gifts of protection.
8. Close the deities, the quarters and the circle.

Visualisation

Visualise the house, filled with mist. See the mist everywhere, collecting around the window frames, along the window sills. See it hanging from the ceilings of every room. See it over the bed in the main bedroom; see it around the front door and the back door.

See the mists curling around the chair and table legs in the dining room, kitchen, bedroom, spare room. Everywhere. See the mist fill every drawer you try to open ...

Visualise the mists once again.

Go into the room or rooms you have chosen and see the mists swirl around the window frames, around every ornament and around the doors of cupboards. Open the door and see the mist swirl inside the shelves. See it around the light suspended from the ceiling and along the curtain rails ...

Now, start seeing yourself in the middle of that room. See yourself making the mist flee – from the cupboard handles, from inside the shelves.

See the mist vanishing from the window sills, the window frames, from under the bed, the table. See the mists start to disappear from the walls, thinning out and forming strange little circles as it moves out the door. Repeat this exercise until all the mists in the room are gone, and you see each object clearly.

Banishing ritual for unforgiveness and bitterness – Dragonmistt

The purpose of this ritual is to get rid of bitterness, an inability to forgive and emotional scarring caused by hurt. These negative emotions can seriously hamper your spiritual, emotional and personal growth, and you are far better off without that baggage!

Make a list of all the people towards whom you feel bitter or have been unable to forgive because of the way that they may have mistreated or hurt you in the past.

Use the following items on your altar:

- Tarot cards: The tower – for subconscious focus.
- Other symbols: Correspondences or symbols for Saturn.
- Colours – black.
- You will need some pins – one for each person who needs releasing.
- A tall black candle – it must be tall enough for you to be able to stick the pins down its length at regular intervals.
- Other black candles for altar purposes only (not working candles).
- A red candle (any shape).
- A green candle (any shape).
- Black obsidian crystal (cleansed and empowered for absorbing negativity).
- A piece of black ribbon and a pair of scissors.

Cast the circle in the normal way and do the following:
- Dress the black candle for use with vinegar, oil and herbs. (Buckthorn is good for getting rid of things.) Dress the candle from the middle to the ends for banishing.
- Dress the red candle from the ends to the middle with anointing oil for attracting strength and courage.
- Dress the green candle with healing oil – once again from the ends to the centre.
- Consecrate these candles in the usual way.

Step 1: Crystal meditation to release negative emotions
- Set up a meditation around the black obsidian crystal to absorb the negative feelings that you have. Imagine yourself inside the obsidian; it surrounds you completely and is sucking all the negativity out of you. Take as long as you need on this step.

Step 2: Separating yourself from a problem or a person
- Hold each end of the ribbon, naming each end, one your name, and the other the names of the people in question, and say:

    I call upon the energies of universal balance.
    I call upon the ancient energies of my people.
    I call upon the living essence of the Calliech.
    I call upon the mighty presence of Herne.
    Underworld and heaven
    Land and sea

I awaken these energies unto me.
Witness now that I renounce and sever
Break bonds and connections with the unforgiveness and
   bitterness that I harbour.
By all powers that are the One Power
May the great sisters of karma now weave anew
And separate me from you.
As I will, so mote it be.

- Cut the ribbon and chant: 'It is so!'
- Burn both pieces of ribbon.

Step 3: Candle spell to be run over several weeks

This is the preparation of the candle you will use for the spell. The actual spell will be done at various intervals not included in this ritual circle. However, don't forget to cast a simple circle every time you do them!

- Take the consecrated black candle and pierce a pin (one for each person that needs to be released from your life) down the length of the candle with equal spacing. (This is made easier if you warm up the pin in a flame first so that it presses easily into the hard candle wax.)
- As you stick each pin into the candle, name it after the relevant persons, and don't forget to keep a list of whose name belongs to which pin.
- Meditate on what needs to be changed, then say: 'Dark Lady, Ruler of Rebirth, I fully accept the responsibility of my own actions in this lifetime. I, (state name), ask for the enlightenment needed to get rid of any unforgiveness and bitterness which I harbour in my soul and that is detrimental to me.'
You have now consecrated the candle for use on a regular basis, though not in this circle.
- Close the circle in the normal way.

What to do with the pierced candle

- Every day of Saturn, which is Saturday (a good time for banishings, especially during the waning moon), light the candle and focus on the flame while visualising releasing from your life the person whose name represents the first pin. Imagine what it is like to be totally rid of animosity towards that person. Watch it burn, and concentrate on the final result. Have the red consecrated candle burning at the same time for strength and healing. Accumulate symbols relating to Saturn energy and have them on the table-top, with symbols for

Mars energy for fighting battles. Take a piece of paper with the person's name on it and burn it, releasing them to the cosmos. Watch as the flame transfers any bad feelings towards that person into light.
- When that segment has burned out and the pin has fallen out, snuff out the candle for the next week to deal with the next person.
- Repeat this every Saturday (preferably on the waning moon) until all the pins have fallen out and the candle has burned down totally.
- In addition to this, and very importantly, during the waxing period of the moon with symbols of Venus on the table (and preferably on the Friday, which is the day of Venus and healing) concentrate on the green healing candle, and focus on the scars being softened and healed completely.

Calling the four quarters – Fiery-Oak

East/Air
Guardians of the Watchtowers of the south
Attend with us this sacred feast:
Let the heavens witness here
There is nothing left to fear.
Descend the owl and birds of prey
Blue and white and black and grey
Sylphs of logic, thinking clear
All these things take presence near
Let the winds of wisdom blow
Take us where no others go
Purest nectar we now breathe
All to delight and none to grieve
Transgress the space from here to there
And thus we hail and welcome Air

North/Fire
Guardians of the Watchtowers of the north
Let thy salamanders gather forth
Burn thy light within our hearts
Sparks and arrows – burning darts
Creatures fiery and serpentine
Deep red blood and sensual wine

Red and orange – yellow, gold
Burn all chains – destroy the mould
Thy flaming energy to us this hour
Lend its warmth to conjured power
With thy heat and by thy fume
All our toils anew consume
Rising triumphant from the mire
And thus we hail and welcome Fire

West/Water

Guardians of the Watchtowers of the west
By our spells thee now be blessed
Rivers, lakes and mighty seas
None are more loved than all of these
Let thy tides bring skills of mind
Undines, fish and waterkind
Fountains spout and clouds do burst
Total quench for every thirst
Blue and azure, silver flowing
Thy cleansing wisdom leaves us glowing
Great open ocean of all life
An end to pain; an end to strife
For Mother, father, son and daughter
And thus we hail and welcome Water

South/Earth

Guardians of the Watchtowers of the south
Hear the words sounding from my mouth
Camel, saffron, brown and green
Mountains visible and gnomes unseen
Fertile fields and wealthy yield
Homes of rock and metal shield
Lend us now the gift of creation
To produce our needs through our elation
Grounded and secure we can now stand
Reaping harvests from the land
Nurturing Mother and Father Pan

Pregnant woman and virile man
With sincerest piety and joyous mirth
And thus we hail and welcome Earth.

Witch's Lesser Banishing Ritual of the Pentagram (WLBRP) – Ra-Shu and Firestar

Because my wife is a witch and, being a typical left-brain-oriented male, I like the structure of ceremonial magick, we felt we needed a banishing ritual that we could use together at Wiccan ceremonies. We've called our collaboration 'The Witch's Lesser Banishing Ritual of the Pentagram', or WLBRP for short. Please note that we do not claim this ritual as 'our own work', as we have used material from various sources, too numerous to remember and credit.

In the southern hemisphere, witches switch the Earth and Fire Elements and cast the circle anti-clockwise, so we've built in these changes. Of course, magicians would cringe at this, but then the WLBRP is really about compromise!

We've used the Egyptian pantheon, rather than the Hebrew god forms and archangels, and the original Egyptian god and goddess names, rather than the familiar Hellenised versions. Of course, you could substitute any other pantheon; although we suggest you stick to a single pantheon. If you want to use Hellenised names for the Egyptian pantheon, then go ahead. We've also substituted Enochian for the conventional Hebrew.

If ceremonial magicians cringe at what they perceive to be apparent inadequacies, and witches think it's terribly structured, complicated and unnecessary, then we've succeeded in our aim!

Clearly, both intonation and visualisation are critical to the success of the WLBRP. Certain words and phrases should be vibrated, i.e. spoken loudly using one single exhalation. We've indicated these in **BOLD CAPITAL TYPE**. We suggest that you perform the WLBRP slowly rather than quickly, and focus on the visualisation.

We've broken the ritual into several logical steps for the scatty, intuitive witches!

Step 1: Start the ritual

- From the altar, sound the bell or tap the altar 10 times in the following pattern: /// //// ///
- Circle the area anti-clockwise, wand, athame or 'power hand' aloft, and chant: 'Hekas (pronounced hay-kays), hekas, este, bebeloi!' You may repeat this if you feel it's necessary.

This is a traditional way of announcing that a ritual is about to begin, and that all those not entitled to witness it, including the spirit realm, should leave.

Step 2: Perform the Witch's Cross of Light

- Walk anti-clockwise to the centre of the circle and face east.
- Breathe in deeply and, adopting the Goddess pose (arms outstretched towards the sky) visualise a pure white ball of light descending into your third eye. Bring both hands down to your side. Touch your third eye (between your two eyes) with your right index finger. Feel the light, spirit and love of the Goddess enter your body.
- Fill your lungs with Air and, using a single exhalation, vibrate: **IO EVOE AUSET**. (Blessed be Auset (Isis), Mother Goddess.)
- Breathe in through your nose and out through your mouth. Visualise a column of pure white light descending through your body into your genitals and into the Earth. Move your power hand slowly down your body to a position over your genitals and point to the ground, grounding the energy. Using a single exhalation, vibrate: **IO EVOE ASAR**. (Blessed be Asar (Osiris), Father God.)
- Breathe in deeply. Touch your right shoulder with your right index finger and visualise a column of pure white light running up your body to your right shoulder and extending into the universe. Using a single exhalation, vibrate: **EKO, EKO AMELAK**. (Hail, hail to the Glory – Strength.)
- Breathe in deeply. Touch your left shoulder with your right index finger and visualise a pure white ball of light running across your body into your left shoulder and extending into the universe. Using a single exhalation, vibrate: **EKO, EKO AZARAK**. (Hail, hail to the Power – Mercy.)
- Breathe in deeply. Clasp both hands across your chest in the God pose. Visualise a column of light (representing the Goddess) entering your heart, forming a bright ball of light and dwelling within you. Vibrate: **IO EVOE**. (Blessed be.)
- Breathe in deeply. Adopt the Goddess pose, and chant: So mote it be! (Fellow ritualists should respond, 'So mote it be!')

Step 3: Perform the Circle of Protection

- Face east and stand slightly east of the centre of the circle. You may use your athame, wand or simply your index finger. Draw a flaming blue, Earth-banishing pentagram in the air in front of you. You should start drawing from the bottom left ray as you face the pentagram and draw in a

clockwise direction. Visualise the flaming blue pentagram. Breathe in deeply and adopt the God form of *The Enterer* by standing up straight with your hands alongside your ears with your index fingers pointed upwards, like horns. Breathe in deeply and, when you have a lungful of air, step forward purposefully with your left foot. Thrust both hands forward into the centre of your flaming pentagram and using a full exhalation, vibrate: **SHU!** Step back with your left foot and stand with your arms next to your side. Using your power hand, point to the centre of the pentagram and trace a continuous, flaming blue line from the centre of this pentagram to the centre of the next pentagram in the north. This means that you will move anti-clockwise around the circle (as is the practice with southern hemisphere witches), rather than clockwise (as is the normal practice of ceremonial magicians or northern hemisphere witches).
- Face north, and stand slightly north of the centre of the circle. Draw a flaming blue, Earth-banishing pentagram in the air. Visualise the flaming blue pentagram. Breathe in deeply and perform *The Enterer*, and vibrate: **NUT!**
- Following the same procedure, move to the west and draw an Earth-banishing pentagram. Perform *The Enterer*, and vibrate: **TEFNUT!**
- Following the same procedure, move to the south and draw a banishing Earth pentagram, perform *The Enterer* and vibrate: **GEB!**
- Trace a continuous flaming blue line back to the centre of the east pentagram, completing the circle of protection. Move anti-clockwise to the centre of the circle.

Step 4: Invocation of the Great God or Goddess
- From the centre of the circle, face east and adopt the pose of Asar slain. (Stand with your arms extended to each side, parallel to the ground, so that you form the shape of a T.) Then chant:

> Before me Shu, the four-plumed god of the wind!
> Behind me Tefnut, lioness goddess of moisture and the clouds!
> On my right the green god Geb, custodian of the Earth our home!
> On my left Nut, goddess of the sky and night, whose bountiful
>   beauty cradles the heavens!
> Around me flames the protection of the pentagram, and within me
>   dwells the light, spirit and love of the Goddess.

Step 5: Repeat the Witch's Cross of Light
- Don't overlook this step! It's important to finish with the complete Witch's Cross of Light – see Step 2.

Magicians use the LBRP to clear the space of negative influences. Remember that the LBRP is a very basic banishing ritual and that any magician worth his wand would perform at least the Middle Pillar Ritual and the Banishing Ritual of the Hexagram before possibly Opening by Watchtower and doing magick. We suggest that witches do not use the WLBRP as a replacement for any of their banishing rituals but rather as an addition to their rituals. After the WLBRP you should cast your circle and follow with your normal ritual protocol.

Hindu goddess ritual – Volva Freya

Devi (or Ma-Ha-Devi) is the oldest worshipped goddess in India. Her name simply means 'goddess'. All the Hindu goddesses are merely aspects of Devi and are always portrayed with beautiful, colourful saris. They are sometimes referred to as 'the dancing Shakti'.

Hinduism is the oldest continued religion and has millions of followers across the world. This ritual is not designed according to strict Hindu religious custom, but is based on a more personal experience of Goddess spirituality. Please feel free to adjust the ritual to suit your personal needs.

Altar

Decorate a small table with a colourful cloth of your choice. This will be your altar. Place the following upon it:
- For the Element of Earth: flowers, coins, jewels of any kind and/or an image of the goddess Lakshmi.
- For the Element of Air: incense sticks, miniature musical instruments and/or an image of the goddess Sarasvati.
- For the Element of Fire: a red candle, a picture of a lion or tiger and/or an image of the goddess Durga.
- For the Element of Water: a bowl of water and pebbles from a river to represent the Ganga Mother.
- For the Element of Spirit: a deep brass dish (or any heat-proof dish or small cauldron). Pour some cooking oil into the dish. Take a piece of cotton wool and roll it into a small ball. Pull a small piece from the ball and roll it into a

wick. Place the cotton wool into the bowl of oil. The goddess associated with the fifth Element (spirit) is Devi.

Lakshmi, Sarasvati, Durga and the Ganga Mother are all aspects of Ma-Ha-Devi.

The working

Sit or stand in a comfortable position in front of your altar, and take a few deep breaths to centre yourself and clear your mind from any outside influences. Visualise a circle enfolding you and say: 'Loving Goddess, enfold me round with your protective arms.'

Look heavenwards and say: 'Above the sun, moon and stars, your sacred jewels.'

Look down to the floor and say: 'Below your kingdom.'

Now, visualise yourself in a sacred and protective bubble.

Calling of the Elements/goddesses

- Earth: Touch the flowers, gems, coins, etc. and say: 'By the powers of Earth do I call upon thee, great Lakshmi, most beloved one, grantor of wealth, lover of jewels. Lend me your love and beauty.'
- Air: Hold your hands over the incense smoke and say: 'By the powers of Air do I call upon thee, Mother of the Vedas, Great Sarasvati. Your poetry pours forth like a flooding river. Grant me your inspiration. Lend me your music and song.'
- Fire: Hold your hands over the candle flame and say: 'By the powers of Fire do I call upon thee, Great Divine Mother Durga, protector of your children, demon slayer and obstacle remover. Grant me your power. Lend me your strength and protection.'
- Water: Touch the tips of your fingers in the bowl of water and say: 'By the powers of water do I call upon thee, Ganga Mother of rivers three, celestial one, who are heaven and Earth. Grant me your flow. Wash this temple. Purify me.'
- Spirit: Light the cotton wick in the bowl of cooking oil and slowly bring your hands together in prayer mode, touching your heart. Then move your hands to your lips and then your forehead.

Prayers

Now open your hands and, with palms down over the altar, say: 'I welcome thee, oh great Ma-Ha-Devi and all goddesses.'

Place in your left palm a mixture of your favourite herbs. Touch the herbs with your right hand and mentally pour your prayers into them.

Direct your prayers as follows:
- Lakshmi: Ask her in your own words to bless you with wealth, prosperity, etc.
- Sarasvati: Ask her in your own words to bless you with intellectual powers, inspiration, etc.
- Durga: Ask her in your own words to bless you with protection, to remove obstacles, etc.
- Ganga Mother: Ask her in your own words to bless you with intuition, spiritual development, etc.

When you feel that the herbs are empowered through prayer, sprinkle the mixture of herbs into the bowl, and feel the energies of your prayers swirling in the bowl. While doing so, chant the following:

Lakshmi gives it form.
Sarasvati sings this prayer into being.
Durga gives it strength and power.
The Gangas give life and flow.

Tap the bowl three times with your index finger, and point your finger heavenwards. While doing so feel the power of your prayer being released from the bowl, swirling into the universe and reaching its destination. Conclude by saying: 'By the love and power of Ma-Ha-Devi, and all goddesses, this prayer is alive.'

The offering and thanks

Place an offering on the altar (such as milk, honey, rice or bread) and say: 'Accept my offering with love and thanks for the blessings I know are on their way.'

Thank each goddess in your own words for their presence and for the blessings that they have granted to your prayer.

Place your palms together in prayer mode. Touch your third eye, then your lips and then your heart. Now hold your palms over your altar and say: 'My love, my thanks and blessings to thee, great Ma-Ha-Devi, and all goddesses.'

Visualise the Goddess opening her embrace and say: 'Great Goddess, as you open your embrace, may your love and protection ever stay, now and always, blessed be, one and all!'

Invite the Goddess into your life with a daily prayer; entertain her with song, dance the Shakti; and your blessings will be manifold.

Bast ritual – Ra-hotep

(This ritual was given to Ra-hotep on the astral.)

Bast, the Egyptian goddess of beauty, love and protection, is invoked in this ritual. Whatever you request should therefore be within the ambits of these graces.

Take an image of the goddess Bast and place a bronze vessel of fire in front of it. Then place two charcoal blocks and some frankincense on either side of the image.

Write down what you want six times and say the following:

> O, mighty goddess Bast,
> Goddess of love, beauty and protection,
> Grant me this wish.
> As this wish passes throughout the fire dispersion of Nephtus,
> Let it pass through the fire of the solidification of Isis
> And manifest in my life.
> Mighty Bast,
> As I will it so mote it be.
> Thank you great and mighty Goddess.

While saying this, put the paper into the fire, take a saucer of milk and pour as libation unto her. Then take the ashes and scatter them to the four winds.

Recharging personal energy with the energy from the sun – SilverMoss

1. In the morning, stand in your garden facing east, towards the sun.
2. Close your eyes and spread your arms slightly out to the side.
3. Now visualise beams of light shooting out from four points of your body – from your forehead, the palms of your hands and your feet (one beam for your feet). See the beams drawing energy from the sun into the places of your body where the beams are coming from. Visualise the energy flowing from the points of entry to the centre of your body.
4. Keep visualising until you feel completely recharged.

If done correctly, you should feel a warm sensation on the forehead, the palms of your hands and the bridges of your feet.

Samhain ritual – darkwolf and group

1. Banishing (cleansing) ritual – WLBRP.
2. Anointing ritual.
3. Cast circle.
4. Call on the quarters as follows:
   - East: 'Ancient Ones of Air, guardians of the Watchtower of the south, I invoke you to join us tonight! In this dark, mysterious time when the veil between the worlds is thin, share with us your knowledge – of prophecy, telepathy – and secrets of the dead. Sylphs of Air, we bid you hail and welcome!
   - North: 'All hail spirits of Fire, Fire of oak, heat of molten lava, Fire of the dragon. All hail spirits of Fire. I call upon thy warmth. In this cold season, hail and welcome.'
   - West: 'Spirits of the west, spirits of Waters. On the night of Samhain, we are reminded that the Land of the Dead lies across a body of water to which the soul must return before it can be rebirthed. May the power of Water rise up in us all! Spirits of the Waters, hail and welcome!'
   - South: 'Hail and welcome to the Watchtowers of the south, Element of Earth, custodians of the mystic sphere. We invoke thee and ask that you hear our petition and be here now! Protect us as we step into a darkly splendid world of unknown paths. Keep far removed all evil and unwanted phantoms whose dwelling is in the invisible. Hail and welcome.'
5. Invoke the Goddess as follows:
Great Goddess, she who is Triple, she who passed from being Maiden, potential to come, to Mother, potential realised, now to Crone. The Old One, the wise and feared one, the one who dwells in the Underworld, we honour you tonight. Hail and welcome.
6. Invoke the God as follows:
God of Death and Rebirth, King of the realm of dreams, we invoke thee. Death is no barrier, for by death is rebirth. Prepare your halls for us this Samhain night. Lord of the dance of shadows, bring to us wisdom and insight, and reveal to us the mysteries of life on this Halloween night. We bid thee hail and welcome.
7. Meditation: This should be related to inner reflection, the past year, misgivings, moving on and regeneration.
8. The head priest (HP) rises, wearing a mask. The head priestess (HPS) addresses the HP as the Dark Lord, as follows:

Dark Lord of the Underworld, I face you without fear. I come to seek my husband whom you struck at the Summer solstice, and my son and lover, whom you took at the Autumn equinox.

I cannot be without them. I relinquish myself as Maiden, Mother and Queen, and travel the final part of my journey into the Underworld to find them.

In relinquishing my fear, you cannot stand in my way. And I now become the Crone, the wise woman.

9. HP removes his mask, tenderly lays a hand on the HPS's shoulder and says:

I am not that to be feared. I am all that you seek: I am your husband, son and lover, all in one. And that is the mystery you dared to unravel. Together now we shall dwell in the Underworld for six months at a time and then you shall dwell in the Middleworld for six months in the Spring and Summer.

But for now my beloved we meet, and the union of our love will allow the seed of our love to be born as the Sun King at the Winter solstice.

I am not the darkness. I am not the terror. I am simply the Winter Earth below.

10. Both embrace.
11. One by one the quarter coven members each address the Dark Lord and Crone, saying the following:

While Samhain is a sombre time when we remember the departed souls journeying through the twelve gates of Duat on the sacred solar boat, we should also remember that the ancient Egyptian Pyramid Texts in the pyramid Unas at Saqqara reminded us of renewal. The fields of Rushes are filled with water, and I am ferried over to the Far southern side of the sky, to the place where the Neteru (gods) fashioned me, wherein I was born, new and young.

This is a time for spiritual growth and meditation. The year and Nature has come full circle. This is the time when life ends and begins anew.

At this time of Samhain we say farewell to our blessed God, but this is a temporary farewell; he is not dead, but lives within the womb of the Goddess and prepares to be reborn of her at Yule. Here at the end we begin the next spiral round. It is an ending and a beginning.

Tonight we cross the veil between the worlds and stand ready to enter the mysterious and unrevealed sanctuary of the eternal God and Goddess. In this sacred space we fear not death, and welcome those who have passed over into our circle. We walk the mystic pathways of the universe and delight in union with unintelligible images. We acknowledge their astral energy like the stars that shine in the night sky, and yet as the new day dawns so too do we rejoice in the timeless cycles of death and life, darkness into light.

12. Cakes and ale: The HP cuts open a pomegranate and says: 'Eat of the seeds of Death.' The fruit is passed to all the participants, and each partakes of the seeds. The HPS cuts open an apple and says: 'Eat of the fruit of life.' A piece of apple is passed to all the participants. All share, hold hands and chant quietly: 'Darkest time, darkest night, no more fear, no more fright.' The chanting fades out slowly.
13. Thank the God and Goddess.
14. Close the quarters as follows:
    - East: 'Guardians of the Watchtowers of east, ancient ones of Air, thank you for joining us in our working tonight. As the Wheel of the Year rolls on, moving forward from darkness into light, may your winds of change blow favourably and bring renewal and rebirth. Sylphs of Air, we thank you and bid you hail and farewell.'
    - North: 'Oh great spirits of Fire. I, a child of the Underworld, thank thee for thy presence here this night and humbly bid thee hail and farewell.'
    - West: 'Powers of the west and of Water, we lovingly thank thee for thy presence and energy in our ritual. We thank thee for washing us clean of old fears and anxieties and that your birthing waters have brought forth new life and hope tonight. Fare thee well and blessed be.'
    - South: 'We offer thanks for your protection from the black ever-rolling abyss, and with your aid we have faced and conquered our fears. As the Mother Earth turns so we regenerate to love, light and life. So mote it be.'
15. Close the circle.

An Ostara (Easter) version – Walking Bear and Niteshade

Everyone present will gather in the circle, standing wherever they want to. The high priest and high priestess (who should be wearing green) will stand in the centre of the circle, on either side of the altar.

The high priest begins the ritual with the following words: 'We have all gathered here to celebrate Spring in all its beauty. May it bring with it a renewal of the positive aspects of our lives. We welcome Spring with open arms and hearts.'

Focusing

The high priestess leads everyone through this, asking participants to envisage a green ball of light moving through the body, centring on the heart chakra. The overriding emphasis must be on opening the heart to Spring, both physically and on a higher level.

Casting the circle

Drumming begins at this point, and the high priest asks everyone to take a step forward and to envisage a bright green, fresh and invigorating light streaming from the sword as he casts the magickal circle. He says:

> I call upon light and Air at the east to illuminate and enliven this circle.
> I call upon light and Fire at the north to illuminate and warm this circle.
> I call upon light and Water at the west to illuminate and cleanse
>   this circle.
> I call upon light and Earth at the south to illuminate and strengthen
>   this circle.
> The circle is cast; only love shall enter and leave.
> So mote it be.

Quarters

Starting in the east, the quarters are invoked as follows:
- Air: 'I call upon you, Elemental Air, to attend this rite and guard this circle, for as we breathe and think, we are kith and kin.'
- Fire: 'I call upon you, Elemental Fire, to attend this rite and guard this circle, for as we consume life to live, we are kith and kin.'
- Water: 'I call upon you, Elemental Water, to attend this rite and guard this circle, for as we feel and our hearts beat, we are kith and kin.'
- Earth: 'I call upon you, Elemental Earth, to attend this rite and guard this circle, for as we are body and strength, we are kith and kin.'

Handing out of eggs

The high priest and high priestess walk around the circle handing every person a dyed green egg. Permanent markers are also passed around.
   The high priestess then says the following:

> What you hold in your hand is a simple egg, but it is also an ancient symbol of rebirth – just as Spring is the time of rebirth. Everyone think of

some positive personal aspect of their character that needs re-energising or is perhaps totally lacking – something they feel that they should focus on. Write what you hope for on the egg, or draw a symbol for it. Later we will dance and focus on these eggs, empowering them. You have a few minutes.

Welcome of Goddess and God, collecting of eggs and dancing/chanting

The high priest and high priestess face each other across the altar, and the high priestess says:

> Oh, Goddess of the Earth be amongst us now, in your aspect as Maiden of the forest, the fair one who brings joy and new life to break the Winter's stillness and silence.
>
> Oh, Laughing God of the green wood with your pipes and cloven hooves, shepherd of creatures free and wild, join us here with your warmth. Let life be born anew.
>
> Friends, let us all place in this cauldron the symbols of our Spring desire that we have brought to this place.

The high priest walks around with the cauldron collecting the eggs, and the high priestess says: 'May the strength of the old enter into new life and arise once more.'

At this point the drumming stops. Led by the high priest and high priestess, everyone begins to dance around the circle, chanting: 'Spring is upon us; let us rejoice.'

When the time is right the high priest will ground the group, and the high priestess concludes with the following words: 'Oh, great ones of the forest and field, make our desires strong and give new life where it is required. Blessed be.'

Thanking of God and Goddess

Drumming begins again. The high priest and high priestess once again face each other across the altar, and the high priestess says: 'Oh, God of the forests, we thank you for your presence here today. May there always be peace between us. Go now in perfect love and trust.'

The high priest then states: 'Oh, Maiden of the forests, we thank you for your presence here today. May there always be peace between us. Go now in perfect love and trust.'

Consecration of cakes and ale
The high priest and high priestess consecrate the food and walk around the group dispensing it to everyone.

Closing of quarters
Starting in the east, the quarters are closed as follows:
- Air: 'We thank you Elemental Air for being present amongst us today. May we ever more be kith and kin! Blessed be!'
- Fire: 'We thank you Elemental Fire for being present amongst us today. May we ever more be kith and kin! Blessed be!'
- Water: 'We thank you Elemental Water for being present amongst us today. May we ever more be kith and kin! Blessed be!'
- Earth: 'We thank you Elemental Earth for being present amongst us today. May we ever more be kith and kin! Blessed be!'

Closing of the circle
Everyone is once again asked to step forward, and the high priest walks around closing the circle by saying: 'The circle is now open, but never broken. Beings and powers visible and invisible depart in peace. Blessed be!'

Burying of eggs
While everyone disperses the high priest and high priestess will bury all the eggs in a specially prepared hole.

Stara's daily devotion
This devotion is quick and keeps you in touch with internal and external divinity. I find that the best time to do it is early in the morning, when one is feeling fresh. There is no better way to start the day.

At the altar, light the incense and God and Goddess candle. If I need a certain quality from any Elemental for the day ahead I ask for it after the greeting. (For example, if I am having an important business meeting, I would ask the Element of Air for clarity of thought to be able to make the right decisions, and the Element of Earth to keep me grounded and level-headed and not let my emotions get in the way of any decisions I might have to make.)

Facing east, say the following: 'I greet you Element of Air and welcome you into my day.' Feel this Element around you. Breathe in deeply and acknowledge it.

Facing north, say the following: 'I greet you Element of Fire, and welcome you into my day.' Feel the Element of Fire around you – warm and comforting – and acknowledge it.

Facing west, say the following: 'I greet you Element of Water, and welcome you into my day.' Feel the Element of Water around you – cool and compassionate – and acknowledge it.

Facing south, say the following: 'I greet you Element of Earth, and welcome you into my day.' Feel the Element of Earth around you – strong and steadfast – and acknowledge it.

I then greet my deity and pay homage to both the God and Goddess with the following prayer:

> My Goddess (whoever your chosen deity is), I thank you for your support in my life and all the blessings that you have bestowed upon me. Please be with me this day and protect me and mine.
>
> My God (whoever your chosen deity is), I thank you for your support in my life and the blessings you have bestowed upon me. Please be with me this day and protect me and mine.

This devotion varies from day to day. On your deity's day, pay special homage to your god or goddess.

Banishing ritual – Ra-Hotep

Ra-Hotep uses the standard Golden Dawn banishing ritual of the Pentagram, which includes the Kabbalistic Cross, improvising with an Egyptian flavour. I include both for perusal.

The Golden Dawn version

Touch the forehead and say 'Ateh' (Unto thee).
Touch the breast and say 'Malkuth' (The Kingdom).
Touch the right shoulder and say 've-Geburah' (and the Power).
Touch the left shoulder and say 've-Gedulah' (and the Glory).
Clasp the hands upon the breast and say 'le-Olahm, Amen' (to the Ages, Amen).
Turn to the east, make a pentagram (that of Earth) with the proper weapon (usually the wand) and say (vibrate) 'IHVH'.
Turn to the south, do the same but say 'ADNI'.
Turn to the west, do the same but say 'AHIH'.
Turn to the north, do the same same but say 'AGLA'.

Pronounce: 'Ye-ho-wau, Adonai, Eheieh, Agla.'

Extending the arms in the form of a cross say:
    Before me Raphael
    Behind me Gabriel
    On my right hand Michael
    On my left hand Uriel
    For about be flames the Pentagram
    And in the column the six-rayed star.

Repeat the first four lines of the Kabbalistic Cross.

Ra-hotep's version

Declaration:
    Astu Nuk (Behold I am)
    Hekna Ma'at (I command truth)
    Khepr Aftu (Come into being, four quarters)
    Sesetna Temt Na Sekhem Tem Serna Em Aftu.
    (I bind up, I gather together your powers. I order the powers in/of the four quarters.)

Cross of light:
    Entek Pau (Thou art he who is)
    Ta Sutenit (The kingdom)
    Ta Sakhem (The Divine Power)
    Ta Djesar (And the glory)
    Ta Taui En Hah (The world forever)
    Nedj Her (Homage to thee).

The pentagrams:

    East – Khepera Neter Yebeta (stab centre and say 'Nef')
            (Khepera, the god of the east – Air)
    South – Suti Neter Resu (stab centre and say 'Ash')
            (Set, the god of the south – Fire)
    West – Tem Neter Amenta (stab centre and say 'Mu')
            (Tem, the god of the west – Water)
    North – Ra Neter Mehta (stab centre and say 'Ta')
            (Ra, the god of the north – Earth)

Invocation:
> Give the sign of Osiris Slain and say:
>
> Before me Tehuti, Lord of Wisdom, Master Magician
> Behind me Auset, Mighty Goddess of magick
> On my right hand Suti, Red god of thunder and the dry desert heat who destroys illusion
> And on my left hand Heru, the golden hawk, whose Mehit
> And Utchat protect, initiate and perfect me
> For about me flames Sehedj (a heaven of stars)
> And above me shines Tau Nudjer (The Star of God).

Give the sign of Osiris Risen and say:

> Nuk Asar un Nefer (I am Osiris the Good being)
> Above me is my Mother Nut, Mighty Goddess of the Sky
> And below me is my Father Geb, Mighty Lord of the Earth.

Repeat the cross of light.

Child-blessing ritual – SilverMoss

1. Ready the circle with 12 stones (or cast the circle the Wiccan way with a doorway in the north-east).
2. Intone the sacred Druidic pledge before entering the circle: 'The truth against the world.'
3. Close the circle.
4. Speak the circle-blessing invocation:
   > Great voice that calls us in the wind of dawn.
   > Strange voice that stills us in the heat of noon.
   > Heard in the sunset.
   > Heard in the moonlight.
   > And in the stirring of the wakeful night.
   > Speak now in blessing.
5. Transfer the circle into the astral plane with the following words: 'Nid dim ond dew; Nid dew ond dim.' (At a time ... not a time; in a place ... not a place.)
6. Call the quarters in the following order: east – Air; north – Fire; west – Water; south – Earth.
7. Invoke the God.
8. Invoke the Goddess.

9. The head priest opens with the following words: 'We are all gathered here to honour our brother/sister at the celebration of the day of his/her birth.'
10. Face east and say: 'Oh great spirits of Air, I present to thee our brother/sister (child's name). May he/she be blessed with perception and knowledge. So mote it be.'
11. Face north and say: 'Oh powerful spirits of Fire, I present to thee our brother/sister, (child's name). May he/she be blessed with the power and magick of the dragon. So mote it be.'
12. Face west and say: 'Oh mighty spirits of Water. I present to thee our brother/sister, (child's name). May thee bless him/her with patience and prosperity. So mote it be.'
13. Face south and say: 'Oh ancient spirits of Earth, I present to thee our brother/sister, (child's name). May he/she be blessed with wisdom and humility. So mote it be.'
14. Face the child and lift hands upwards.
15. (HP) 'Gracious Horned God, I pray thee bless thy child with justice and a meaningful life. So mote it be.'
16. The high priestess states: 'Lovely Mother Goddess, I pray thee bless thy child with magick and mystery of the moon. So mote it be.'
17. Cakes and ale ceremony follows.
18. The high priest and high priestess thank the God and Goddess.
19. Release the quarters in the following order: south – Earth; west – Water; north – Fire; east – Air.
20. Close the circle.

CHAPTER 10

POETRY AND PATHWORKINGS

Poetry and pathworkings are very popular in modern Paganism and Wicca, as well as in certain New Age circles. They are also known as guided meditations. They are a conscious journey into the subconscious. Led by another person's voice, a journey is undertaken, filled with magickal symbolism and rich in archetypes, designed deliberately as keys to unlock the closed subconscious for magickal purposes.

Unlike meditation with its still inner focus on the unconscious, this is a conscious attempt at tapping into the unconscious, the point that keeps the magickal symbolism hidden.

Creative visualisation is the skill necessary for effective pathworking. Here you visualise something to the point of it becoming a reality. It is 'seeing' what others cannot see. It could be seen to be a structured daydream. One explores the self through the inner subconscious landscape.

Pathworking may be seen as an altered state of consciousness. Such pathworkings are usually done in a group and should be led only by an experienced group leader. It may happen that on the 'journey' one in the group goes into a deep state of trance and can't easily enter ordinary consciousness again. This calls for certain processes to be implemented in order that the individuals participating may experience as little trauma as possible when re-entering the conscious state. If a pathworking is done in a ritual context it should be relevant to the ritual.

Writing and reading a pathworking involves a certain amount of skill. Sentences should be short, and intonation should be carefully structured. The narrator should be familiar with the pathworking, but it is not necessary to remember it by heart. One could listen to a voice on tape as well, but somehow it does not have the same effect. Naturally, there should be as little rustling of paper as possible, and the order of all the pages should be checked beforehand. Soft music (without a beat) is usually used. Such music is designed to put the brain into an alpha or alpha-theta state, i.e. a slower state of contemplation – a state of readiness to receive the symbolism inherent in the language.

Here are some basic pathworkings and a selection of poetry. Please note that all of these should begin with visual relaxation exercises (i.e. slight stretching, deep breathing and relaxation techniques). They should all end with a return to ordinary consciousness, either with a countdown or a memory aid reminding participants of the location where they are sitting or lying.

~ (~

PATHWORKINGS

Play with clay

You find yourself standing on a beach on a remote island. The island is surrounded by blue, blue water. The beach is golden, and you realise that you have never seen such a beautiful beach before. You feel the sand, golden, underneath your feet, and like a child, you push your toes, then your feet, into the warm, warm sand. You feel like laughing with the pleasure of it.

You slowly start walking along the golden sand, feeling the grains and the soft waves lapping at your feet. With each breath you breathe in the wonderful smell of the sea. You feel the mist of water softly caressing you and hear the deep rumble of the waves. The whole experience fills you with joy and happiness.

You notice a figure approaching in the distance ... You await this figure and then notice that it is your guide. The guide moves slowly towards you, also clearly enjoying the beach and all it brings. As the guide gets closer, you become aware of their appearance – the guide is wearing loose, white garments, and walks barefoot. There is a radiance of happiness and joy surrounding your guide, and you feel very comfortable being in their presence.

As your guide reaches you, they ask you to come along – on a wonderful journey – and points in the direction of a small hill. The hill is covered with grass, plants, trees and flowers. The air smells wonderful – there is the clean smell of the sea – and you hear the waves gently rolling onto the beach. Delicate shells line the beach – in wonderful colours.

Your guide takes your hand, and you start walking together towards a path that goes up the hill. Your guide tells you that it will be easy to go up this path. As you start going up, you notice that the path is made from natural slate, and that small streams of water are cascading down it. The water reflects all the colours of light, and sometimes it touches you, warm and soft like silk.

As you go up this hill, your guide explains that it is a very special day today. There is a wonderful surprise in store for you; you will be treated to something really wonderful. Your guide looks so relaxed and full of warmth that you start feeling a childlike anticipation at the surprise in store for you.

You notice your surroundings and see flowers, trees and some wonderfully exotic birds. Here and there you spot something moving between the trees, and you can make out animals – all of them playful and running and skipping. You realise that they seem to notice you, and you start feeling playful, just like them.

You keep on moving up, up, still with your guide. You are getting closer to the summit.

As you get closer, you notice that there is a colourful waterfall in front of you – the source of the water running down the hill. You now see more clearly that it is as thin as a veil, and that this is actually lightly covering an arch-like opening. Through this veil of water you also start to notice that there is light reflected from the other side.

You have now reached this veil of soft, light water, and see that it sparkles with all the colours of the rainbow. You see red, yellow, purple and some colours mixed in a way that you have never seen before. Your guide beckons you to follow – going through the veil.

You put your one hand in the water, and it feels so wonderful, warm and soft. Your guide tells you to go in, that you will breathe easily, and to simply enjoy the feeling of this wonderful blessing of the water. You step in, joined by your guide, and stand under this veil of colour – feeling so warm and even more playful. You feel so refreshed and relaxed.

You and your guide step through the veil to the other side, and you notice that you have dried almost instantly. The most breathtaking scene awaits you. You are at the top of the hill, and overlooking the other side of it. The horizon is wide – blue sea everywhere. Closer by on the island are trees, with a golden beach far below. You think you can see dolphins and even whales far off – all playing in the water, totally undisturbed by your presence.

The sun is soft, as you now follow your guide towards a big tree, which seems to overlook this beautiful scene. The tree casts a cool shadow, almost inviting you closer.

As you get closer to the tree, you notice a soft patch of grass underneath, and something that looks like a colourful pond. You get even closer, and then realise that this is not a pond of water, but one filled with colourful clay – a gift from Mother Earth. Your heart is filled with wonder at this.

Your guide tells you to sit down next to this pond of clay – to sit on the soft, green grass – and then joins you as you sit down. Your guide explains that this pond of clay is for you to create something with. You have received a gift, a power from Earth – simply play and be creative with the clay. You need not worry about the clay bits coming onto your skin or hair – it will easily wash off later.

Your guide puts their hands into the clay, asking you to do the same. You put your hands inside the clay, and it feels warm and inviting, soft and pliable. You give thanks to Mother Earth for providing it for you. You feel the urge to start rolling some clay into a ball and experimenting with it. Now you roll it; now you flatten it. You laugh at the joy of these childlike actions. Your guide looks completely relaxed and encourages you to enjoy yourself. Your guide tells you that this is a special moment of creativity for you, and that even if you have never created anything with your hands, you will notice that you have an automatic ability to do so. We have all been born with this ability. Your guide tells you not to be too serious about what you create – as long as you have fun.

You start scooping together more clay, and an idea starts taking form. You feel young, like a child, without any cares in the world, except to play with your clay. There is as much clay as you need to create your idea.

Every now and then you look at the beautiful view, while you create your idea. Sometimes your guide helps you, and, each time they do, you are filled with childlike wonder at this, that such a being could also experience joy at such a simple task.

I will now leave you to play and explore your creativity: to feel the clay in your hands and to shape it into your idea. You and your guide are having fun, relaxing, enjoying the rewards from Earth. I will come and fetch you a little bit later.

[PAUSE while providing time for creating the idea, and after various intervals make the following points.]

The clay is easy to form, and the colour is just as you want it.

You wipe your hands on your forehead, and do not even notice bits of clay stuck there.

The clay starts taking the form of your idea.

You start putting on the finishing touches – smoothing down here, tucking up there.

You have now finished and look at your creation with pride. It is really beautiful, and came out just the way you wanted it to. Your guide looks at you approvingly – for being able to have fun, and exploring your gifts of imagination and creativity, for being able to shape your idea so clearly.

Your guide now gets up and tells you to stand up and bring your clay creation with you. They tell you to place this gift deep within your heart and mind, to remember how you were able to have fun and give form to your will.

The clay will also wait for you – in any colour that you need, and you can always return to play and create should you want to.

You now start returning, under the direction of your guide. As you get to the veil of water, you put your hand in to feel the water again, and the soft warm touch invites you to step in further, until you are completely immersed. You notice that all the bits of clay are simply being washed away, softly, gently, being given back to nature, until your hands and nails, face and clothes are clean, clean.

You step out of the water. The water dries instantly, and slowly you start moving down the hill, down the path until you reach the beach. Your feet feel the warm sand again, and the soft water from the sea touches your toes.

You turn to your guide, who tells you how pleased they are with you – that you have done well, and that you must always nourish the child, the magick and creativity within you. This place will help you with that. Your guide then turns away and starts walking away from you – walking back along the path they came, until you cannot see them anymore.

You are left, comfortably alone, enjoying the feeling of this wonderful, magick island. You remember your body, waiting for you … on the earth plane. You notice the island one more time, the hill and the golden beach and the blue sea with its playful dolphins and whales.

You become more aware of your body, and feel it pull you back. You return joyfully.

You move your toes slightly; you feel your feet completely now, your legs, your lower torso, upper torso and your hands. You move your hands gently, and now feel your chest. You again notice your breathing. Breathing … you hear sounds around you. You feel your face and eyelids, and slowly open your eyes. You feel very good and relaxed – happy at your accomplishments, remembering what you experienced. You slowly, slowly and gently stretch your body, feeling over your body, making sure that you have returned completely, refreshed and happy.

— MA-RI

So what do you fear?

You find yourself lying on a cold, hard surface. You become aware that you are damp – over your whole body. And you shiver when you realise this. You see that you are wearing only your thin witch's robe now, and that even the cord around your waist is damp.

You sit up. Your bones ache. How did you get here? How long have you been here? Why has it taken these conditions to make you aware that you are in a place you do not like or want to be in? What sort of Earth is this? It is not what you have been used to from the Elementals of Earth.

What caused this breach of memory? The last you remember the sun was shining – life was a place to be lived. You could smell the flowers again. Your newfound sense of liberation on your recent achievements felt justified. Your tiresome questioning of your capabilities was finally put to rest.

And now, here, suddenly without warning, you're cold again. And you feel sad, scared and alone. Is it simply the transition from light to dark? The ability no longer to smell the flowers, and instead smelling the damp acrid smell of musty water?

You get up. You learned a long time ago to follow water to its source, and you begin the journey.

Every muscle in your body aches. Your head aches with the confusion of the whirlwind of events that have surrounded you in the past few days. And, yet, it feels like months – years perhaps.

Does it matter, this time, trying to fit it into a logical sequence?

And you walk. You know not where, but to stay you will surely die. And so you walk, you walk, cold, hungry, tired. The festivities of the day, the mirth of the folk that surrounded you, are but a distant memory as you travel alone in your abyss.

The water drips loudly, and your logic tells you that the sound is simply echoed a hundredfold in the cavernous depth of darkness that you are travelling through.

Your logic further tells you that the sound, simply magnified a hundredfold, does not necessarily mean that you need to fear some sort of rushing torrent underfoot.

And you continue – aware that the air is guiding your intuition. For now, you doubt your intuition. You cannot satisfy the tormented questions that threaten to unbalance your intuition.

And you proceed. Presently, you hear water gently lapping against the shore in the not-too-near distance. And you tread even more cautiously, even though your eyes have become accustomed to the dark.

A strange astral mist swirls lightly and gently at the end of your vision. And you see darkness, and an overwhelming body of dark waters. Moving. Swirling. And it is as though blue steam rises from the surface of the waters.

There is nothing else in sight, and you begin to ponder the source of the light. Suddenly, you hear the gentle licking and splashing of oars. And the rhythmic sound of rowing fills your ears. You strain your eyes to see, aware that you feel no fear, just a numbness, a dazedness. You stare out to where the sound is coming from. And there, approaching you, is a small boat, shrouded in grey mists. And standing at the bow is a hooded figure.

You want to laugh – isn't this the picture-book stuff of the grim reaper? And even though you find this situation so ludicrous, not wanting to believe it, you know you have to believe it. For it is real; it is happening.

You are in a strange, cold, dark place and there is an ominous boat coming towards you. What to do? No panic? You resolve to wait? For what else is there to do? You can't go backwards; you can't go forwards. If you could sink further into the ground you would, and now you cannot even begin to conceptualise floating up and outwards and away.

The figure rows silently and determinedly towards you. It gets to the shore where you are standing – waiting now for the inevitable. It lifts its hood. You are too afraid to look into its face, for all your childhood memories of demon stories come flooding back.

But, again, you have no option. And your eyes take on the challenging stare of the challenger. And you see the most beautiful face of the young Goddess – her silver crescent moon inscribed upon her forehead, her skin white against the backdrop of darkness.

You look into her challenging eyes, too confused to rely on logic now. And your intuition, once again, takes over. You get into the boat. In silence you travel for what is probably an eternity. And you stare at this apparition of pure truth, harmony and beauty.

Rowing, simply rowing and rowing in simplicity and serenity. And you see upon her right hand a single ring – a large ruby. In it time stands still, for the ruby is far older than the Maiden herself. And you look into her face as she looks into you. And she continues to row.

The silent lashing of the water against the oars breaks the stillness. You notice that, although you see no visible lines of age upon her face, deep, deep in her face, at a place you can now only perceive on an intuitive level, you see the marks of time, of anxiety, of anxiousness, of doubt, of self-doubt.

And you are content.

The little boat arrives at its destination. Without asking a question you get out and step upon the shore, the air slightly lighter than before, but still swirling with dark mists. She walks ahead of you, but you feel that even if she did not you would walk on.

And there appears the entrance to a further cavern. With sudden dismay, you realise that you are not coming any closer to the source of light but are in fact going deeper into darkness. You recoil at the logic of that thought. But the slippery dreams of water propel you forward and to not listen to the cacophony of logic now.

The entrance is shrouded with mist so thick that you must physically part it with your hands. And as you do it feels as though you want to choke, and there is no time to even think of what it is that you will see once you have parted the mist.

Then all is clear; all is still. The Maiden is no longer in front of you. Deafening silence, and again, you cannot go backwards, but you can go forwards. The contemplation of this is frightening, but you continue.

A mighty shadow is cast over you as you take your first brave step into total darkness and desperation. And the figure hulks over the entire chamber. You bow down in a submission you did not know you had in you, and cower on the ground. You tremble; you cannot cry or make any sound. The figure sits down on a huge throne-like rock, and there is silence. More silence. Unbearable silence and no answers.

Eventually you dare to raise one eye and peek at the figure. And there, sitting with sunglasses on, smoking a joint is – HADES! – dark, dreaded and feared Lord of the Underworld! He is a simple skeleton – no flesh and blood, no bite, just smile and bark.

Even if you tried to laugh you can't, for the situation is now so bizarre that you would perhaps be admitted. You raise your head and stare. Hades stares back, puffing smoke circles at you. And before you can say anything he answers you thus:

> *I know your question is WHY? And this answer is the answer to the great mystery of life, and death, and rebirth. People are afraid of me, and in their minds they make me out to be the hulk you saw, the fearful shadow against the wall. Their own fear of themselves drives them to their terror and terrible deeds.*

And until they realise that they are terrifying and harming themselves they will never see me for what I am – just simple death. Nothing more, nothing less! Simply just a bag of bones.

And then he is gone ...

[PAUSE]

Gently you feel a touch on your shoulder. You turn. It is the Maiden. You know she comes to take you back to the misty shores again. And you are not afraid. You have met the dreaded Lord of the Dark himself now, and you ponder his words.

[PAUSE]

In the boat you ask why she is here and she replies:

I am Persephone, daughter of Demeter, the great Corn Mother. As her daughter I owned the Earth and all the green things upon it. I owned the fledgling birds, the gentle deer, and the slow, little tortoise. I plucked flowers to my heart's content and lay in the summer breezes until I fell asleep. And I was happy.

But I was not content. And one day Hades came to fetch me.

And I found myself on the cold, dark floor as you did a while ago. I felt fear for the first time. I felt anguish and anxiety. I felt confusion – things I never knew whilst I lived under the protection of Demeter. And like you I came to know the Lord of the Underworld.

And I was content.

I am not happy here, but I am eternally content. And at Spring, when I return to Demeter once again, I know great happiness, but little contentment, for I know I will and must and wish to return to this realm again – where I can turn inside myself and study the ways of the gods. For whilst I was and am above, I forget the ways of the Ancients, concentrating on frolicking only in the sun. While it is not a bad thing, it is only part of the greater whole of experience.

[PAUSE]

And then you are at the shore. You get out of the little boat, and as your first toe touches land you realise that it is not hard and cold, but soft and moist – it is a marshy bog. And the first rays of the morning sun light upon your face, and you salute the Element of Fire.

– DARKWOLF

Cleansing the sea

(This is a short pathworking written as part of a ritual against an oil spill.)

Close your eyes. Relax. Take deep breaths. As you inhale, breathe in white light. Let it flood your lungs. As you exhale, breathe out the day's problems – all your worries and troubles. White light in, burdens out.

Become aware of the sound of waves breaking behind you. Listen to them. Hear the sound of them drawing back into the sea. Hear them as they crash onto the shore. It is the ocean's breath you hear. In, out.

Smell the salt, the kelp. Feel their scent prickle your nose. Feel the sea breeze push against your back – tossing your hair and rippling over your legs. In front of you lies Table Mountain. A soft, fluffy cloud hangs mystically over its peak. Become aware that you are standing on a shore somewhere in the Cape.

You try to move your feet. They feel heavy and gritty. You look down. Your feet are covered with black, sticky sand. You bend to wipe it off with your hands. As you wipe your feet, the dark substance transfers itself to your hands. Now your feet and hands are covered with this tar-like substance.

You decide that you will wash them in the sea. You turn. In front of you a thick, black substance rolls over the waves. As the waves pull back, the shiny, dark liquid remains, soiling the beach. You walk closer to get a better look.

The sand gets darker and more slippery. Your feet slide across the surface. It is difficult to stay in control. The inky mess is between your toes, up your feet, around your ankles. It drips off your hands. You must wash it off.

Thinking it will be easier to paddle in the waves, you step into the water. It is cold. It is dark. It frightens you. In your sudden panic, you slip. A wave floods over you, and the undertow drags you away from the shore.

The inky liquid surrounds you. Now you understand: it is an oil spill. The oil seems to be drawn to you. It embraces you, it hugs too tight. It smothers you. The oil covers every inch of your skin. It fills every pore, invades every crevice.

You try to look to the shore. You cannot see. The oil has trickled into your eyes. You try to swim, to get away from it, but it is too thick. It forms a barrier. It encloses you and holds you tight. You try to scream for help. The oil seeps into your mouth.

You look around for something to hold onto – anything – anything that will lift you out, save you. Through unfocused eyes you see that you are not alone. A sea creature floats nearby. It too has been consumed by the oil. It cannot swim or fly away. It cannot call for help. You try to get to it, to help it, to save it.

Every time you get a little closer, the tide rolls in and you are pushed further away. The oil is everywhere, suffocating you. You now know that alone you cannot help. You stop struggling and try to relax.

You begin to visualise a white light around you. You imagine it growing, growing – pressing on until it reaches the horizons. Everything begins to glow and pulsate in the white light. All is still. All is quiet. Waiting.

Through the white light two shapes approach.

Wings of sinew. Five heads, each Element there. The fifth for spirit pure. A mighty dragon. Tiamat has arrived.

Horses of white spray. Chariot of coral. Reins of kelp. Poisedon has come. You see him raise his mighty trident – hailing the Elements:

Air to blow away impurities, bringing joy and light;
Fire to burn the impurities; to bring liveliness and freedom;
Water to cleanse, love and compassion restored;
Earth to protect, peace to return.

They swirl around and around the tips of his trident, building up power, raising the energy higher and higher.

He unleashes them into the sea.

Tiamat releases her mighty power, destroying the waste that lies before her.

(You are free. All are free.)

Chant:

'Tiamat, Poseidon hear our plea
consume the oil
cleanse our sea'.

– NATALIE

Storm swept

It is a wild and stormy night and you find yourself at the bottom of a valley. You cannot see anything around you, and you feel the first stirrings of alarm. For a moment you stand rooted to the spot, unsure if you should stay or walk forward.

Eventually, you gather up your courage and gingerly take a step. You concentrate fiercely on what the ground feels like underneath your bare feet, for with the slightest misstep you could be sent tumbling. The soil is wet and clings to your body. Your hair is soaked and you can feel the water streaming off your hair and face onto your shoulders. The rain is cold and you feel chilled to the bone. You know that you must find some sort of shelter in order to survive this night.

You take another tentative step, inching your way forward carefully, arms outstretched so that you don't walk into any obstacle. Your right hand touches something and moving forward you discover that it is a tree. You cannot tell what variety it is, as you can only use your sense of touch and hearing and your intuition as to which way you should go forward. For a moment you rest against the tree, thankful for its solid presence in a world, from your perspective, gone mad. After a moment you sit down at the base of the tree, feeling the muddy water swirling against your buttocks and legs as you rest your back against the tree. You can feel the tree's rough bark through your soaked robe and it comforts you.

The only sound you can hear is that of the wind howling past you, occasionally buffeting your body. It feels cold against your body and you start shivering. You know you cannot remain here long; you need to find shelter. As your eyes strain to pierce the blackness around you, you catch a glimmer of light. You blink, unsure if it is your imagination playing tricks on you. As you peer intently into the darkness, you see the light again. Hope begins to rise in you and you stand up and carefully inch your way towards the glimmer of light.

The earth beneath your feet is muddy as you walk cautiously with your arms outstretched. You keep your eyes fixed on where the light is becoming more apparent and it lifts your spirits.

The closer you walk to the light, the more carefully you tread. The light has taken on a faint blue glow and you know that it is your guide on this wild, stormy evening. Soon the light is closer and you can see that it is the figure of your guide, swathed in blue from head to toe, holding a staff in its hand. The figure is hooded so you cannot tell whether it is male or female.

As you stop in front of the figure, it raises its hand and beckons you forward. You step closer and it turns and starts to walk into the storm. Hastily you walk after it, knowing that you are safe with your guide.

You concentrate on following your guide, two or three steps behind it. Suddenly it stops and its hand beckons you forward. You walk past your guide and see before you a humble cottage; the door is open and a fire burns merrily in the hearth. You hurry towards it; conscious of how cold and wet you are, you seat yourself before it, stretching out your hands towards the flames for warmth.

You look behind you and see that your guide has disappeared. As you look around the little cottage, you notice there is someone sitting quietly in the shadows. Hastily you stand up and start to apologise for just walking in. The figure indicates for you to sit down and then stands up. It is a venerable old man, his snowy white beard stretches to his waist, he has sparkling green eyes and his smile is warm and merry.

He asks you your name in a deep resonant voice and you tell him, warmed by his friendliness. He hands you a blanket in which to wrap yourself and tells you to sit in the chair by the fire. He disappears for a moment and then reappears with a bowl, spoon and cup, which he hands to you, and then seats himself before the fire. Hungrily you pick up the spoon and start to eat. The bowl contains a rich, savoury stew, seasoned with herbs you have never tasted before. The cup, you discover, contains a honeyed mead which warms you from within. As you put down the empty bowl and cup you find that you are completely dry and warm. You look to your host and thank him. He smiles in return and asks what you were doing out on such a wild and stormy night. You tell him that you don't know the reason, that you were warm and snug, safe at home before finding yourself out in the storm and that you were brought here by a guide.

His eyes show a deep interest, and unbidden you describe the guide to him, that it was hooded and swathed in blue from head to toe, holding a staff in one hand, that it not only spoke to you, but brought you to him. He nods his head and then begins to speak, explaining that he has retreated to this hut to be closer to his gods, and that he has been persecuted and hunted all his life for his special talents. You nod your head in understanding, for you too have known persecution. It may not have been life threatening, but nonetheless you have been persecuted for your beliefs, by people who for the most part are well-intentioned.

Silence descends for a moment and you can hear the wild storm outside and the fire crackling merrily in the hearth. You feel warm and dry and comfortable. Your host asks you if you would like to read as you wait for the storm to end. You signify your assent eagerly and he smiles, stands up and goes to the bookcase, which you only notice now in one corner of the cottage. He stands there for a moment and then takes down a book. As he hands it to you, you see the cover is made of a deep, rich, red material, the likes of which you have never seen before. There is no title, which puzzles you. You open the book and, leaning forward a little, you look at the first page.

With amazement, you see that it is the story of your life. As you turn the pages, you see that it contains everything that you have ever done in your life, all the good and bad. You blush with embarrassment and your host laughs gently and says: 'Child, did you not know that nothing is hidden from your God?'

It suddenly dawns on you that you are sitting in the presence of your God! You throw yourself at his feet and, overwrought, cannot say a word. He stretches out one hand and rests it on your head in a gentle benediction, and says: 'Child, would you not be more comfortable seated in front of the fire on the chair?' You hear the amusement in his voice and, embarrassed, you comply with his request.

He looks at you intently and then begins to speak to you, of all that you have done, and all that you will do, and tells you that you have been brought here to realise that he is, above all else, not to be feared, rather to be respected and loved and listened to, like a friend, an adviser, a parent, a teacher. As you listen to his deep resonant voice, you begin to understand that your relationship with your God has always been different, that you have spoken to him as a friend, that you have asked for advice and he has given it, that you have been chastised with love wisdom, as a parent would do, and that he has taught you throughout your life, either with or without your knowledge. Above all, you realise that your God has loved and does love you. With this understanding, your heart opens and you finally realise that your path is true to him, that you will willingly and with love do anything that he asks you to do. As you sit in front of the flames dancing joyously in the hearth, you also understand that part of that divine flame is within you, that it has always been within you, and you are filled with joy.

He smiles as he sees understanding dawn in your heart. You sit and talk freely, without inhibition, with your God. He tells you the one thing that you need to know at this moment in your life, and you feel yourself surrounded with compassion and love, knowledge and wisdom.

Slowly, the sound of the wind drops and then you notice that the storm has passed. Your God looks at you and smiles and says: 'Child, it is time for you to go forth from this place. Know that I am ever with you.'

You stand and walk towards the door, joy singing through your whole being. You are not sad to be leaving, for you know, without any doubt, that he is always with you and always has been.

You walk out into the dawn and hear bird song as nature stirs. You give thanks and find yourself back in the place where you began your journey.

– ANTHEA

~ (~

Life force

Close your eyes. Take a deep breath. Relax. Continue to breathe in and out slowly and deeply. Feel the tension in your muscles flowing out. Let your muscles relax. Breathe in, breathe out. Try to keep your mind free of thought. Focus on the darkness before your eyes. Breathe in, breathe out.

You notice some small, faint points of light in the distance. You start to drift towards them. As the points of light get closer and brighter, you look around and see more and more points of light. Some are faint, some are bright. Look around you. You are surrounded by millions and millions of stars. You are floating in space. You are looking at the universe. Feel how weightless you are, floating through space. Everything is completely silent, apart from the regular sound of your breathing.

You see a bright star far ahead of you. You drift towards it, passing through the cosmos. As you get closer, it gets brighter and brighter. Now you see a planet orbiting this sun. It is Earth, seen from outer space. You see the blue of the Earth's oceans and the white swirls of cloud covering her surface. See how beautiful Mother Earth is. Feel the love you have for your home, and know that you are of her. As you drift down towards Earth, you pass through some clouds. Soft wisps brush your face, caressing your cheeks.

As you break through the clouds, you're flying now, soaring over deep green forests, majestic mountains capped with pure white snow, and golden yellow fields. Feel the wind in your face. Feel how it blows through your hair. You feel the warm sun on your skin. Feel how its light energy penetrates deep into your body. You hear the rustling of feathers. You turn to see a large eagle soaring through the air beside you. It is perfect in its strength and beauty.

Below you, you see a coastline, the waves breaking on the shore. The ocean is the deepest, clearest blue, like a sapphire gem. You dive down towards it. See the water rushing closer and closer. And splash! You are through the surface, diving into the warm, clear water. There you see many fish swimming – red, blue, yellow, orange, pink – all colours. They are swimming next to you, above you, below you, all around you. Feel the gentle surge of the tides, the moon's influence swaying you back and forth.

You see a school of dolphins swimming ahead and join them. Feel how the water rushes past your face as you race through the waves, jumping and diving in and out of the water. The dolphins are twisting and turning, dancing through the water. One brushes up against you. In the instant that you feel the cool, smooth touch, you sense the dolphin's ecstatic joy. You realise that this joy comes from being alive, from knowing happiness and love. You realise that we are all related; we are all from the same source.

After a time, you see a sandy beach, and leave the water. Walk along the beach and feel the sand beneath your feet. It has been warmed by the sun. You see a pathway running between some trees, a short distance away. You follow the path, into the shade.

As you leave the sound of the crashing waves behind, you hear the breeze gently rustling the leaves of the trees all around you. You see that the path ends at the foot of a huge tree. Go and sit beneath the tree, on the soft, green grass.

Sit with your back against the tree. Sense the life force flowing through the tree, up the tall trunk to the branches high above. Feel the energy tingle and pulse under the bark of the tree trunk. Can you feel how it warms your back? Can you feel the energy flowing from the tree? Feel it in your back, flowing down your arms and legs. Feel how your fingers and toes get warm and tingle. Know that this is the life force that is in all things. Know that because of this force, we are all of the Divine.

Sit quietly under the tree for a while. Listen to what the tree has to tell you. Perhaps the tree will tell you one of its stories, gathered over the hundreds of years it has spent here. Perhaps the tree will share some words of wisdom with you. In return, touch the tree with your fingertips and visualise your energy flowing back into the tree. Visualise this energy flowing up the trunk, into the branches, filling the tree with some of your life energy.

Close your eyes and concentrate on your breathing. Breathe in, breathe out. Feel yourself coming back to this present reality, revitalised and full of energy.

When you are ready, open your eyes.

– ANNETTE

Hecate pathworking

(I usually use this pathworking at the dark moon, especially if I am trying to use a magickal working or divination method with which I am not too familiar.)

You are standing in a clearing in a forest. It is dark, and in the distance you hear the lone cry of a wolf. The wind is sighing in the trees above you. The sky is an inky black, dotted with stars. There is no moon. In your clearing the only light is that of a small fire in the centre of the glade. You are standing in front of the fire, dressed in a black robe, sprinkling incense into the flames. The smoke from the incense rises and seems to swirl around you. The soothing smell of the incense fills your mind. Very soon the smoke seems to be swirling in a pillar around you. All else fades from your vision. All you see is the silvery-grey mist of the incense smoke. Breathing is easy. You begin to feel yourself drifting. Your breathing eases, and you drift into the realm of dreams.

As the mist begins to dissipate, you find yourself standing in front of an entrance to a cave. On either side of the entrance is a standing torch. The torch to the left is shaped like a serpent. The body of the serpent is coiled around a slender axis, and has three heads, each facing in a different direction. A blue flame burns in the centre of the three heads. The torch to the right is the body

POETRY AND PATHWORKINGS

of a great bear, cast in silver, its arms outstretched, and in between its paws a purple flame burns.

You look at the entrance to the cave. Before you stands a young girl. She is dressed in a loose Grecian-type dress, clasped at the shoulders with silver pins. Her golden hair is piled loosely on top of her head. Her green eyes are filled with a light coming from deep within her. Her skin is smooth and unblemished. She giggles, and beckons you to follow her. Turning on her heel, she walks into the cave. You follow her. Your feet seem compelled to move. The cave is warm, and lit with torches in brackets on the walls.

The cave is deep, and as you are led forward, you come to a doorway in one of the walls. The door is made of silver and carved with symbols that are at once strange and yet familiar to you. The girl stops at the door. You knock and turn to see what your companion is doing. The girl has gone. As the door opens, a woman in a green dress, similar to that of the girl, stands before you. She is pregnant, her face is glowing with health and she takes your hand and leads you into the room. All around the room are flowers in full bloom.

Freshly baked bread and fruit are on a wooden table. You feel her energy and power flowing from her hand into you – a clean, strong energy that seems to make you feel at home. You know this woman; you are of her womb. As she looks into your eyes, this knowledge fills you. She smiles and leads you to a doorway at the back of the room. The door is made of oak, carved with magickal symbols and inlaid with crystals.

You knock and turn to say farewell to the woman, but she is not there.

The door opens, and before you stands an old woman. Her silvery hair falls loose about her shoulders. Her face is lined and mysterious. You can see that in her prime she must have been a great beauty. Her eyes, a fiery green, seem to look deep into your soul, and know you. She seems to know a secret. She takes your hand and leads you to an open fire, over which an enormous black cauldron is suspended. She seats you by the fire, dips a ladle into the cauldron, and offers the liquid to you to drink. You do so, tasting honey, and cinnamon, allspice, and dandelion. Your throat tingles, and your entire body seems to glow with warmth. She sits in front of you, and begins to speak. Listen to what she says to you.

[LONG PAUSE]

When she has had her say, she lays her hands on your head, and says: 'I am Hecate, she of the three faces; she who is Maiden, Mother and Crone. In my cauldron all life comes to rest. I hold the key and am the door to all the mysteries of life. I am she who is the great magician, the mother of magick and witchCraft.

I will illuminate the mystery for you and teach you my way. I am Hecate. Hear me and do as I say ...'

[PAUSE]

She breathes on you, her breath sweet and warm on your face. You sense a rising heat from deep within. The warmth within you grows, filling you, threatening to overflow. Her power is now yours; her knowledge is yours; her mystery is no longer hidden from you.

She smiles and says that now it is time to go. Smoke rises from the cauldron, and again swirls around you like a pillar. You feel yourself being drawn back to the present, to your natural space. You start hearing yourself breathe again; slowly the mist dissipates, and you return to your normal space, breathing naturally, and you are ready to open your eyes.

— SHANE

The council

You are standing in an enclosure in a forest. It is twilight, and the dense, dark trees seem blackened – blackened, smoky. They are an ash-like substance to your touch. You step back in distress as you look at the sootiness on your hand.

What has caused this blackness? This ash? This charcoal touch? What disaster came to this place and how recently? Why did this beautiful enclave deserve such a scourging? What did it do wrong? In fact, did it do something to be burnt in such a way?

[PAUSE]

You start to walk. Up above your head – high above – you notice the sun's rays raining through the leaves at the top of the thick brush. The leaves are still green, untouched by the burning monster.

You pace forward, reluctant to move into the smoky desolation, but eager to move on, for you have learned a long time ago that the only way to get through dense darkness is ... to take the first step. Nay, you were in fact taught that the only way to get through dense darkness is to plunge into it. Only then can you see the light.

[PAUSE]

You move forward with intent – glad that at least you have been reminded about the unchangeability of the sun. And you chide yourself for not remembering that it is always there – high in the heavens, even when you can't see it behind the clouds. And you reprimand yourself again for the fact that you had to look for the sun to believe it was there and to take from its strength.

[PAUSE]

Ahead, it seems quite gloomy. The dense trees narrow into a pathway; they seem to bend over each other into an arch – a long, tall, dark, thin, brittle, willow-like arch; a forest-arch of burnt trees.

You proceed further, further, further. The path is narrowing still. Brittle twig-like fingers grope at you, and your spine shudders with the unknown. You can go no further.

A small wooden door blocks your way at the end of the enclave of arched trees. It, too, is arched and panelled in thick wood.

There is a brass knocker on the door. Instinctively, you reach for it, but you let the moment go and look backwards whence you came. It is now dark. There are no stars able to penetrate the smoky black dome of the arched trees. You reach for the knocker again – this time with intent. Before you touch it, the door swings open slowly. You peer inside but you can see nothing. You push the heavy little door with both hands. It will not budge. You push against it with your left shoulder. It swings open dramatically and you land against it with your back. You turn your head and see torches lighting another narrow path.

[PAUSE]

You start to walk. It is sandy and soft underneath your feet. You notice gnarled roof formations all around you. You are walking down a tunnel inside the base of a gigantic tree. Twisted, tangled and tormented roots are interwoven with huge clumsy, clingy, blind earthworms. They crawl chaotically and slowly and deliberately and masterfully over each other and roots alike.

Your skin crawls with anticipation and you make every attempt to hurry down the sandy path without letting your body brush against either side of the tunnel. You can feel the sand in your shoes – feel the grit between your toes, caught mercilessly between your shoes and your socks. It is hindering, but there is no time to stop, for you have noticed in a backward glance that the torches that light your path are extinguishing themselves by some invisible force once you pass by their light.

Another big, arched, wooden door is ahead. There is no knocker and no handle this time. You reach the door and press your ear to it. Muffled noises inside indicate some anguished activity.

There is distress in that room; there is pain. You do not want to enter, but neither do you want to begin the climb back into total darkness, for the last torch was extinguished while you were making out the activity behind the door.

[PAUSE]

You sit down to wait, with your back to the door. You wonder what to do, but you are not concerned, for you have travelled many paths, and there is always a guide. It occurs to you now that this time a guide is a long time coming. A slight sense of panic engulfs you at this realisation. You call on your breathing skills to assuage the panic. You breathe in deeply, breathe out deeply – in, out. You enter a state of calm.

After a while you become aware of a sound – the rustling of cloth. You peer with intent into the darkness ahead. There, coming towards you in a cumbersome manner, is a man, carrying a small candle in a rusty tin. The tin has holes in it. The tin, though humble in appearance and clutched with such forbearing by this man, is, you recognise, otherworldly. The man is wearing a tattered cloak that whirls around him. It is the colour of sackcloth. His shoes are like elfin boots with pointed, curly toes. The lining of the cloak is purple with golden stars and crescent moons.

He carries a large staff in his other hand. His short, curly locks frame a wizened and puckered face.

He strides towards the door. For a moment you think that he has not seen you and that he will step on you. Too late: he is upon you. He peers down at you; he acknowledges you.

You know him. You know him. You know him. The master of so many timeless mists of your dreams. The Lord of the Underworld where you sink to when you must rise up from yourself. The mighty being who you know has accompanied you on painful soul-searching journeys.

He pushes open the door – effortlessly. The billows of his cloak waft over you.

You scramble in on your knees under the cloak. You have not waited to be invited in, for this is a place where, to access your higher self, there can be no doubts about what is yours for the taking and what is not. He strides into a large oval room and comes to a standstill in the middle. His staff rests at his side. He has extinguished the flame from the candle and put the lantern at his feet. In a dramatic gesture he gathers his cloak from around you, and thereby exposes you – still crouching on your knees.

You are in the middle of an area filled with rustic tables in an oval formation. Behind these tables sit men and women. Each person has an inkpot filled with black ink, a feather quill, some parchment and a candle. Some have their heads in their hands. Others are writing furiously. Clearly, nobody is aware of either you or the magician. You turn to the magician and ask who these people are. He whispers that these people are the Elders of the forest and the elected leaders of the Forest People. These are the folk who dwell within its nether regions – beings who, with any burning, are destroyed just as the brittle bark is. They also represent the Council of the Forest – a representation of all woodland creatures, who need a voice if coexistence is to be peaceful.

You gasp. They don't look like elders, council members or wise folk. No, they look ordinary, just like you. There is a young boy over there, scarcely fifteen. He is writing intensely. Weren't elders supposed to be old?

There is a beautiful woman over there, covered in blackness – the colour of the night forest. Isn't she too pretty to be an elder?

And over there is a very ordinary looking person – why is he here?

You ask what they are doing. They have come down here for shelter from the great burning scourge, and they are here to seek counsel from the group mind. They come not to blame each other for the burning; nor do they come to dwell on that which has betrayed them, for all have been touched; all have been burnt. All have lost collectively with the scourging of the forest. All may lose their homes in the upper green foliage.

All have to find an answer together.

The one who set the first flame alight features visibly in all the minds' eyes.

[PAUSE]

The magician stands now, arms and legs outstretched in the great life-affirming pentagram. You follow him into his ability to look into each of those minds' eyes. Each has the ability to see a single aspect of the truth, an aspect of what really happened. But in order to heal the pain, all those aspects must be united. The magician holds his staff high and with his other hand opens his cloak. As it opens, an array of glittery celestial objects emanate outwards. The magician focuses his will on them and directs them to the minds of the councillors. You watch in awe as you see their minds open into circular orbs – opening and opening – until the third eye is opened.

Colour, colour all around the members – yellow, pink, purple, blue, azure, green, gold, silver, indigo – all rippling out and out and out, until they are all enmeshed into one emblazoned protective circle around the members. All the members now focus on the myriad of colours emanating from their third eye, and the magician focuses on all the colours coming together. You fear now, for surely, when this moment comes to you, you will not be able to withstand the beauty and the power, for you are still outside this circle, pondering logic. The magician points his finger towards you, and from a crimson, emblazoned ring, an orb shoots towards you – a colour that you have never seen. It explodes all over you, and, as the pieces start filtering downwards, you are lifted onto them as though you are as light as a feather. To lift you higher – higher and higher and higher still – above the members to the colours that their third eyes are generating. You are floating on these celestial pieces, looking down.

And you catch the eye of the magician, who, with arms outstretched, points his finger at you once again. And this time a tiny black dart lurches towards you – towards your forehead. Before you have time for fear, it pierces your mind to get at your third eye.

[PAUSE]

Stillness. Silence. No logic, no thought. No pain, no emotion. No sadness, no happiness. Just stillness.

And you sit, quietly suspended in the lotus position, staring ahead. Wherever the celestial pieces float, you too must float. You no longer see the magician. There is only you and your Spirit. There is only your truth and integrity.

And you know that it is not relative, for you are all co-joined in the celestial colours and circles around you. And there is peace – the understanding that many third eyes are making absolute truth. There is peace in the understanding that when we raise ourselves above the level of logic, and we no longer get embroiled in the peripheries of pain, we do not strive to understand the macro, for we are the macro. We no longer have an ego that forces us to want to know which building block we are in – in the macro. But realise that it is only the whole that justifies our existence. Us – the little sums of the whole.

And you decide to use this awakening to find clarity on a recent painful issue and to receive the healing that must come from such clarity. And so you start to search your depths, and you take an issue that is causing you much anguish at the moment. And you bring it up – up, up, up. There. To the third eye.

Then suddenly the magician plucks it from you rather rudely and takes it to the centre of the room. As you watch, he throws it into the spirals of colour and celestial circles. You understand that all the pain and discomfort and anguished thought on the matter have a place to go – to the group mind, who, together and in unity, can cope with all the pain.

And then you watch the magician take the Elements from everyone's solutions and, like dough, knead a ball of healing and brightness in the room. He pushes,

POETRY AND PATHWORKINGS

pokes, prods and rolls. He starts to juggle with this ball – your ball and the others'. This motion does not disturb your peace. He juggles. And he juggles. And he grins as he does so. His erect legs bend and buckle to catch and kick the torrent of balls that he is now juggling. He is a master. The magician is a master at moulding pain and the energy that you afford that pain. He masterfully recreates the pain. And opens his cloak. The balls tumble down into huge velvet pockets. As they drop in, tiny, little creatures emerge from the recreated balls. Elfin-like, gnomes, faeries and sprites, salamanders and undines – little lords and ladies. They fly out, giggling gleefully about their recreated incarnation. From energy in pain to energy in creation, they dart around the room, playing games with each other and making mischief with the magic.

The magician suddenly dismisses them, like pesky flies. And they dart off to the councillors – and to you. Look what's coming your way. See how tiny, how fragile and delicate. Does it have wings? Are they veined? Look at the little shoes. Or is yours perhaps naked? What colour is its hair? Does it have freckles? Its delicacy and fragility it now hands over to you. It commits its little life to you now. You are now its master or mistress. Its delicate selfhood is the representation of the delicate life force that the magician has recreated. It can be squashed, just as positive energy towards your own healing can be squashed by your self-doubt and the sad need to maintain and dwell on the pain.

But you know that you and this little creature will be friends for a very long time, for you have spawned it. You are able to look down at the gathering now. As you do so, the magician catches your eye and throws some small golden stars to you. They form descending steps, and you move out of your lotus position, close your eyes and make your way down the starry steps. You now see the councillors writing, and you smile when you see the same golden stars emanating from their paper – now circling around their heads.

And then, in unison, everyone puts down their quills and summons the magician for the verdict. He comes. You realise that the solution to the problem of the great burning has come. And nowhere is blame to be seen, or even vague anger. For with spirits healed and third eye open, the solution has come.

You realise that your clan is not present, and that this great lesson learned inside the oval room should be taken back to them. You hasten to the door and pull it open. The chamber out and up is black, but you have learned to take the first step before thinking that you cannot see. And so, true to your life experience, you take that step. Yet again, the door shuts firmly behind you. There stands the magician. He sends forth a thunderbolt – one you have only ever seen in your dreams. It guides your way, like a slow missile. It penetrates the small door that leads back into the blackened arch of trees on the outside. Pull it out. Hold it in your right hand and pull open the door. It is truly dark now, but the thunderbolt still glows faintly. Do not look back. Continue to walk, holding the thunderbolt and feeling the little creature energising you within.

When you are ready, open your eyes, stretch gently and come back to consciousness in this room.

— DARKWOLF

Meditation for astral space

Lie down, or sit comfortably in a position where you can relax your body completely and allow your mind to respond to these words.

Breathe comfortably, in and out, focusing on the sound of your breath, inhaling and exhaling, feeling the rhythmical rise and fall of your chest as you breathe.

Relax your entire body, starting from your feet, your calves, the thighs, the abdomen, the chest, the arms, the neck and your spine. Feel at one with yourself and the surrounding Elements, knowing that you are a part of the whole, that which sustains you. Merge your essence with the ether around you, but in all this remember that you are a unique individual, breathing in and breathing out, listening to the sound of your breathing in the silence.

Now imagine that you have a stainless steel orb in your pelvis. Inside the orb is a spinning, radiant red light. Remove the lid from the orb and allow the brilliance of this red light to radiate from your pelvis. Allow this light to grow and extend from your body as far as it can.

In your abdomen, you have another steel orb. Open the orb, and a bright orange light emerges. Stretch this light to its maximum outside of your body. At your solar plexus, open the next orb, allowing the brilliant yellow light to radiate; all the while remaining conscious of the already glowing red and orange lights below. In your chest there is another steel orb, and you open it. A beautiful green light shines out, and this grows to its full potential. At your throat, you open the next orb, and this time a blue light is revealed, brilliantly shining and glowing from your neck. Move up to your forehead, and uncover the next orb. This orb has a rich purple light piercing out of it. Radiate this light so that it extends as far as it can around your head. At the crown of your head, the last orb awaits opening. As you open it, a brilliant white light shines very suddenly up and out to the universe, extending to the far reaches of the cosmos in a cone shape, up and out, encompassing all. Be aware of all the colours simultaneously in their bands, pulsing and throbbing out of you, clear and brilliant – radiating like a pure rainbow.

As you look down, you find yourself standing on a coloured rainbow of equal brilliance. This rainbow stretches out in front of you, like a pathway, for as far as you can see. Begin to walk on this road of colour, stepping from one colour to the next. As you step on each colour, focus on how the colour feels to you, and what associated emotions are aroused. First on the green ... to the orange ... to the purple ... to the yellow ... to the blue ... and then to the red band. You walk along this road until you come to a very special place – a beautiful space in Nature – which is safe and secure from the outside world.

In front of you is a body of water. What does this body of water look like? Is it the sea? Or is it a small river lapping at your feet? Or is it a giant lake? Know that this is the quenching water for emotional needs. When you are feeling down, or angry, or anxious, know that you can come to this special place and drink of this water and you will feel refreshed. Look at the intense blue colour of the water and immerse your hand in it. Feel the coolness of the water on your hand as it gently flows or laps onto your fingers. You feel calm and serene – as if this water fills your body from your fingertips through to your toes.

Stand up and see that your feet are firmly planted on the ground. Look around you. See what is on the ground. Is there grass? Just soil? Leaves? Rocks? The ground is solid and supports your weight with ease. Rub your toes into the soil and experience the firmness of the substance beneath you. It is tangible and solid. This ground provides us with stability and security, and looks after our material needs – it sustains us in our everyday life. Feel the sand run between your toes and imagine being filled with the solidity of the soil from your head to your feet, providing absolute firm security in you.

Stretch out your arms and feel the cool breeze blow over you. Breathe in this cool air, and out, drinking it in and absorbing it into your fibre. Feel the air as it moves gently over your skin and goes right to the depths of your being through your lungs. This air penetrates everything and clears your mind. It blows away the old cobwebs from your mind, and leaves you feeling refreshed and able to think clearly. It stimulates your intelligence and clears away confusion. Breathe in this air and feel the cloudy patches in your mind dissolve.

Look up and see the sun shining on you – a huge yellow light, so bright that you can feel its intensity as it burns down on you. You are suddenly aware of this huge star's potential as a burning fireball, and the flames that are leaping from it excites something in your being. A spark is created in you. Every time you look at the sun in this very special place, you feel the life force of this spark within you. The fire that drives you to achieve what you desire, which energises and motivates you to carry out your thoughts and wishes. Allow the sun to bake down onto your face and body and experience the warmth and radiance on your skin. Imagine being filled up with the fire as it courses through your veins and provides heat to every centre of your body. You are radiating life's energies with your wet hands stretched out into the cool air, your feet firmly planted on the Earth, and the fire within you burning in tandem with the sun.

Feel what it's like to be well balanced within these Elements and comfortable knowing that they are there to help you draw on their energies when you find that you lose this balance. All you need to do is come back to this special astral place that you have chosen, and experience the sensations that you are experiencing now, bathing in the Elements as you need them.

Off to the right-hand side, you see a chest. What does the chest look like to you? You wonder what is inside the chest, and you step up to it to open it. As you open it slowly, you see that inside are two candles on candle holders and a box of matches. Lift these up and examine them closely. The first candle is gold in colour and is fairly stout and solid. Take this candle and see the gold light shining off the flame and surrounding you with a fine gold mist. Be aware of the strength that you experience with this gold light and know suddenly that you are not alone. You feel the presence of something greater with you, something awesome and powerful and brighter than the sun. Feel comfortable with this godly strength surrounding you and know that you can indeed accomplish much in your life with this mighty presence around you.

Take up the next candle. This candle is just as sturdy as the first one, except that it is shining silver in colour. Set this candle to the left of the gold one and light it. A brilliant silver light emanates from the candle, and you are aware once again that you are not alone. A beautiful, serene presence surrounds you, and you are aware of this presence wrapping itself around you in love, nurturing you and filling your soul. Know that this is the presence that each of us seeks within us – the divine aspect of the Goddess. Bathe in her glorious silver light and allow the mist to settle around you and become part of you.

The two candles together are now glowing brightly and together they blend into one – the power of the God and the Goddess wraps itself around you in love as you realise that you are an integral part of this awesome power. Something awakens inside your spirit, which immediately identifies and connects with this sensation, and you suddenly feel as if you have come home.

Go back to the chest and open it further. Inside the chest is a small, black velvet bag. Take it out and open it. Inside the bag are some small stones of different colours. Stand by the water's edge and pick up the blue stone. Toss it into the water and thank the Element of Water for its love. Take a brown stone and reach down and bury it under the sand, thanking the Earth for its stability. Take a yellow stone and throw it as hard as you can into the wind, thanking the Air for its cleansing clarity. Take out the red stone and hold it up to the sun and thank it for its burning rays of passion, strength and courage. Place the stone on some rocks or stones nearby to bake in the heat. Inside the bag is a portion of gold and a portion of silver glitter. Throw the gold glitter over the gold candle and watch it as it falls. Do this in offering and give thanks to the God. Take the silver glitter and throw it gently over the silver candle, watching as it falls and as it catches the light on its way down, twinkling and sparkling. Give thanks to the Goddess.

Every time that you need to, for whatever reason, return to this secret astral place. Light the two candles and absorb their radiance. Experience the energies of the Water, the Earth, Air and Fire as needed. Each time you need something new to put in your special astral place search for it in the chest and it will be there. Spend time away here, for this is your refuge, a world away from worlds. But don't forget to leave a gift for the Elements and for the Great Spirit – they will keep giving to you as long as you give back a token of appreciation and love to them.

Extinguish the candles with your fingertips and prepare to leave this special place. The end of the rainbow is still visible to you as it gently touches the ground near your feet. Step onto it and begin the walk back up the coloured pathway and far into the distance. You have found a very special place to which you can return any time, but now it is time to step back into the world in which we live.

You are walking along the rainbow pathway, when you suddenly become aware that the colours are starting to dim. The radiance around you, generated by the steel orbs, is suddenly withdrawn into the centre of your being, and the steel orbs close, from the top of your head, your throat, your chest, your stomach, your abdomen and finally your pelvis. The rainbow at your feet becomes fainter and fainter until it disappears altogether.

When you are ready and the rainbow has disappeared, you may open your eyes and return to this time.

– JO-ANNE

POETRY

Dragon's Isle

There once lived a Dragon, a creature as old as time
He was content to live in peace, he was the last of his kind
The men admired him from afar, brought gifts to honour him
Everything was good, though he was fierce, love was with him
For the bond they shared none could explain
Another nation did not care, all they brought was pain
A black cloud of terror came in legions of death
With a mad church behind them and brimstone in their breath
With machines of war they came from the East
Their Devil's servant they proclaimed the magnificent beast
'Death to the Dragon,' their foul voices cry
'A merciless death the loving demon must die'
Blinded by greed men followed, without asking why
They swore to rule all Pagans when the Dragon's blood rains
    from the sky
And magick will disappear when they rule with fear
Their minds harbour thoughts of power, their madness will
    not clear
A war reigned in heaven, black clouds gathered round
The Dragon fought with valour, the horn of death did sound
The beast was struck with the spear of a saint
The blood on his hands like scarlet red paint
The Dragon tumbled with a mighty cry of pain
As he crawled across the isle, his blood the soil to stain
Along the shore he rests his head finally
In the grim, scarlet water he died in tranquillity
But the blood-stained soil forever chiselled in our memories
As the tribes lift their voices in sorrow to the skies
What followed was a time so dark and vile
Hence the story, the legend of the Dragon's Isle

— SILVERMOSS

Ode de Herne

I am the eternal flame that illuminates the night
I am the power and magic of the rite
I am the treasure that sparks ambition
I am the mystic light of the Pelen Tan
I have gone before and shall be hereafter
I am the essence of life and laughter
I who lay the great elk to sleep
I who give the willow tears to weep
For no rock falls from a mountain if I do not
    push it
And no tree grows if I do not plant it
For it is the seed of life that layeth within me
And I am the magic that makes you see
For I am Herne, God of the Hunt;
Cernunnos, Lord of Animals

– SILVERMOSS

The storm
(from Requiem for Shaun)

Mighty waves crashing underneath
Fine rain pouring from above
Brooding darkened clouds gathering
Angry thunder clattering

White beach sand – swirling
Surf – churning, twirling
Coward sun hidden
All swimming here forbidden

Thunder growling tensely
I miss you so immensely
Daylight now to end
In you I lost a friend

Running out of metaphors
Wondering how it came to this
Kelp whipping in the waters
Lullabies for Neptune's daughters

And when they handed out the when and why
The answers passed by you and I

Open up and open wide
Welcome in the violent tide
Fear not all the angry waves
It's the anger, not the love, that saves.

— FIERY OAK

Primal lover

the darkness cloaked me
like a thick blanket that once my mother's tucked me in
i could not breathe, could not see in the dark
and the archetypes of my surroundings
banged in my head
trying to get out, trying to be said
the blood pulsed in my ears
running behind my eyes
and in the deep red recesses
i could feel your breath
wet and dripping
fresh from the hunt, fresh for my fetch
and i see your fangs
as red as my brains
head to the skies
two howls connecting
wind under your paws
sweeping me with
again
again
again
to the ways of my pack
pounding behind me
you carried my longing
snarling
at my inhibitions
to travel the winds
now in silence
and i looked through your eyes
red slits in the dark
and your wet breath was my birthright
sovereign consort in this realm
and you never speak
of your unconditional love
your inane protection
to the pack travelling obediently
independently, loved

my divine god has touched me
in a way known only to me

— DARKWOLF

Pagan protest

Do you understand
That I will not be confined.
I will not be restricted
By your expectations and conventions.
I will not chain my soul and conform
To fit your rigid ideals.

I will not say what you want me to say,
I will be free and embrace my destiny.
I will not be what you want me to be.
I'm out there where angels fear to tread,
It's the only way I know.
I will taste everything.

Savour kinky sweetness,
Delight in the bizarre,
Sing, dance and kiss the sky.
Your restrictions stunt my growth.
Your rules and lack of imagination
curtail my creativity and inspiration.

I will not bow my head in submission,
Meek and cowed for all to see
and seek relief in.
I will not fit into your neat grey pattern
to fulfil your complacency.
Gaily clad, I will whirl like a dervish in the sunshine.

I will stand on my mountain under the shining moon,
And howl like a wolf.
I will hold my head up high,
Hair streaming, laughing like a banshee.
With my last breath —
I will call out my Pagan protest.

— DAYALA STARDANCER

The triad

One moonlight night I had a dream
The Golden Orb hung in the heavens
Pregnant with possibilities
I found myself hiding –
Sheltered in a dark, damp copse
Peering into a clearing, with misty breath
I watched the Ancients dance
Singing filled the winter night
A clear, sweet, bell-like tinkle
Water in a running brook
Chanting – the low, deep rustle of leaves
Crooning, crackling, cackle of fire flames
Through the dim and smoky light
And the scent of perfumed wood
A mystical haze –
That belonged not to our world
Round and round the fire – in harmony
Three figures spun
In ancient ritual
Maiden –
Garbed in lily white
Floating and ethereal in purity
Hair like spun gold –
Crowned with tiny flowers
Beauty personified
She was whirling and laughing –
Innocence alive
Mother –
Ample and seductive
Lithe sensuous movements
Like a harem dancer
At the peak of sexuality
Green velvet flowing round her ankles
She had a smile so warm and comforting
Crone –
Twisting and turning
Bent in black

Gnarled, knotted hand gripping a stick
Wise, lined face peering from a hood
She had eyes bright with wisdom
I watched the spiral dance – entranced
The flickering fire
Warm, comforting, sleep-inducing
I woke up in bed
The moon shining her blessing through my window –
And the wind whispered,
'The Old Religion is still alive.'
— DAYALA STARDANCER

My moon child

Child of the moon, fluid and sensitive.
Ruled by Artemis, Hecate and Hera.
Deep and unfathomable they say.
What secrets lie behind those eyes?

All the days of love, laughter and pain,
wrapped in the soft cocoon you spun.
I know you by the waxing and waning,
the eternal rhythm of your emotions.

The world sees the tough outer shell
the lunar path a touch of insanity in you.
I know the deep caring passionate soul,
as you follow in the moon's astral path.
New moon sees new beginnings in you,
new ideas are born, it is time to plant.
Full moon sees the power with you,
harness the power it is time to reap.

Child of the moon, this is your destiny,
to follow this path through all of time.
Scatter your dreams, love and magic,
so I can ride a moonbeam with you.

— AMBER MOON

the tear

once in a neon dreamland, i dreamed a song
of a witch who spun a tower over me
as she whirled in flashback ecliptic aftermath,
androgyne future with a hand in the past.
once in a neon dreamland, i dreamed a video
of white limousines with hierarchical gods,
the lightning played the perfect hologram wall mural
thundered in a sky without rain.

once in a neon dreamland, i dreamed a story
of fire eating the sidewalk shows at the mad hatter's
party.

once in a neon dreamland, i dreamed a dream
of desert and devils and gauntlets and duels.

once in a neon dreamland, i dreamt a journey
of beltaine wreaths and costumed ferrymen
clothed in the enchanted mists of ancient rite
as merlinian myth meets the rocky horror picture show
once in a neon dreamland, i dreamt a bubble
of princes and heroes and chauffeured transvestites
in techno bewonderment of laser-filled dance floors

once in a neon wasteland, i dreamt a dance
of snaked plastic strips entwined in grateful fingers

— J ISEN

Should I end up in heaven

Should I, by mistake, end up in heaven
(heaven forbid)
I shall walk down streets, white and gold,
And notice the faces of people, clone-like, staring,
At me with eyes, hostile and cold –
And I shall hold my athame high and daring,
Searching for peace, the fire, the soil on the ground,
But the elements of life are nowhere to be found.
Should I, by some horrid mistake, end up in heaven ...
I shall suddenly feel a breeze, soft and cool,
And watch how clouds gather from nowhere,
As the drops fall, a clone stands like a fool
Watching me strip until I alive and bare
Wash away the disappointment and pain,
And sing, and dance, and laugh in the rain.
Should I, by some very horrid mistake, end up in heaven ...
There shall be a silence, which I have never known,
And notice the absence of the spirits of old –
No trees, no stones, no animals – clones alone ...
And in wild rage I shall open the gates, silver and cold.
And howl and chant into the open sky around,
And they shall gather and enter, free and unbound –
And fires shall erupt, water will flow,
Spirit will be and wind will blow.
And the clones will smell the brewing mead –
And run as the antlers protrude from my head.

— RAINSPIDER

Dawn and dusk

Dawn bears baskets filled with gifts
Of laughter, joy and love
She offers to us free of charge
The Bounty from above

Inviting us to sample
Her fresh abundant wares
So reach inside and take your pick
It's known to heal all cares

Dusk brings empty vessels
For worries, cares and strain
She offers to us free of charge
Release from all the pain

So tidy up your cupboard
Be careful what you keep
For getting rid of baggage
Will make you free to sleep.

— DEBBIE DE VILLIERS

Black

Black, oh so Black
The Cell is Foul and Black
Black minds – Knowing only Black
Heavy – Dense – Suffocating
Surrounded by Nothing but Blackness
No exit – No escape
Bearing down – All encroaching Blackness
Black Death – The Only Solution

Thick – Coagulating – Stinking Black Blood
Oozing from the Demon's Maw, now Black in Death
The flow is Weak and Black
The smell too, is Black
It settles into a Pool – Thick and Black
The Stench is Foul – Filling the Air
Almost Gaseous
Can't Breathe – Sickening – Offensive – Cloying Black

The Pit is Dark, Deep and Black
Black Slime coating the Sides
Black Moss Centuries Old
Black unimaginable, scheming Creatures
Cold, Black, Loathsome and Black
Indescribably Evil, and Black
They Writhe – Twist – Creep – Crawl
In the Everlasting dank Blackness

Deep – Deep Blackness
Souls in Torment – Black Minded
Black Thoughts – Black Deeds – Black Intentions
How do we Flee from their Blackness?
No Hope – No Light – No Distraction – Only Black
Their Black Connivances – Words and Ideas – Are nothing but Black
No use – utter hopelessness – Must we succumb to their Blackness?
NEVER!

– EPONA MOONDANCER

Untitled

You are not enclosed within your bodies,
nor confined to houses or fields.

That which is you dwells above the mountain
and roves with the wind

It is not a thing which crawls into the sun for warmth
or digs holes into the darkness for
safety,

But a thing free, a spirit that envelopes the Earth
and moves in the ether.

And what is word knowledge but a shadow
of wordless knowledge?

Your thoughts and my words are waves from a seated memory
that keeps record of our yesterdays

And of the ancient days when the Earth
knew not us or herself.

Thrice Blessed Be

— DEE

CHAPTER 11

THE SPIRIT OF AFRIKAANS

An exciting recent development has been the publication of the first book on Paganism in Afrikaans. Jade Groen, a practitioner for a number of years, and a gifted healer, has written a book titled *Spinnelap* (spider cloth). Its essence is that of a patchwork quilt, torn to shreds, patched up by the golden threads of magick.

It is a breakthrough book because it deals in particular with the Afrikaner woman's psyche and healing. In a sense it is a sort of Pagan *Women Who Run with the Wolves*-type book. It is not so much about Paganism per se, describing its various paths and rituals, nor is it a handbook on spells. It is a book that informs woman about her inherent, forgotten wisdom through her buried European Pagan roots and how she can reconnect by tapping into such ancient Pagan custom, tradition and lore. Groen uses the Pagan Wheel of the Year to explain the psychology of change, and liberally adds spells for cleansing and healing. As explained earlier, the soul, the spirit, the psyche of the white South African (particularly the South African with an Afrikaans background), is spiritually impoverished, hungry, and desirous of a spirituality that can quell this hunger, and Paganism is a legitimate option. Groen explores these ideas thoroughly. It is an earthy book, dealing with moon and seasonal cycles, energy teachings, trusting intuition, and exploring their role in the healing of the Afrikaans woman's soul. I personally think it is a radical book for the audience it is aimed at and I say 'bravo'!

Many South African practitioners are Afrikaans in origin. They mix the languages of English and Afrikaans freely, and many English Pagan words have found an Afrikaans identity. Here are a few words that have become acceptable already:

Witch	=	Heks
Witches	=	Hekse
Druids	=	Druide
Shamanism	=	Sjamanisme
Celtic	=	Keltiese
Pagan	=	Pagaan
Paganism	=	Paganisme
Ritual	=	Rituele/Seremonies
Cauldron	=	Ketel/Potjie
Goddess	=	Godin

Already some of the most beautiful liturgy has been translated into Afrikaans. Here is the 'Charge of the Goddess', adapted from the original version by Doreen Valiente. The English version is included for perusal, and is translated by Angelique Raeven.

Charge of the Goddess

Whenever ye have need of anything, once in the month, and better it be when the moon is full, then shall ye assemble in some secret place and adore the spirit of me, who am Queen of all witches. There shall ye assemble, ye who are fain to learn all sorcery, yet have not won its deepest secrets; to these will I teach things that are yet unknown. And ye shall be free from slavery; and as a sign that ye be really free, ye shall be naked in your rites; and ye shall dance, sing, feast, make music and love, all in my praise.

For mine is the ecstasy of the spirit, and mine also is joy on Earth; for my law is love unto all beings.

Keep pure your highest ideal, strive ever towards it; let naught stop you or turn you aside. For mine is the secret door which opens upon the land of Youth and mine is the cup of the wine of life, and the Cauldron of Cerridwen, which is the Holy Grail of immortality. I am the gracious Goddess, who gives the gift of joy unto the heart of man. Upon Earth, I give the knowledge of the spirit eternal; and beyond death, I give peace and freedom, and reunion with those who have gone before. Nor do I demand sacrifice, for behold I am the Mother of all living, and my love is poured out upon the Earth.

I who am the beauty of the green Earth, and the white Moon among the stars, and the mystery of the waters, and the desire of the heart of man, call unto thy soul. Arise, and come unto me.

For I am the soul of Nature, who gives life to the universe. From me all things proceed, and unto me all things must return; and before my face, beloved of Gods and of men, let thine innermost divine self be enfolded in the rapture of the infinite. Let my worship be within the heart that rejoiceth; for behold, all acts of love and pleasure are my rituals. And therefore let there be beauty and strength, power and compassion, honour and humility, mirth and reverence within you.

And thou who thinkest to seek for me, know that thy seeking and yearning shall avail thee not unless thou knowest the mystery; that if that which thou seekest thou findest not within thee, then thou will never find it without.

For behold, I have been with thee from the beginning; and I am that which is attained at the end of desire.

Die Stem van die Godin

Wanneer julle enigiets benodig, vergader in 'n heilige en verskuilde plek. Daar kan julle my ontvang, elke maand met die vol Maan. Spreek met my – die Godin van die hekse!

Julle sal vry wees van slawerny, en as 'n teken, sal julle nakend wees in my eer. Julle sal dans, sing, musiek en liefde maak, tot my eer. Want Ek is die ekstasie van die gees, en geluk op aarde, want my gawe is liefde aan alle wesens.

Hou rein jou hoogste ideale, streef altyd daarna. Laat niks jou keer, of wegwys nie. Want Ek is die geheim wat die deur na ewige jeug oopmaak, en Ek is die beker van wyn van lewe, en die ketel van Kerridwen, die Heilige Graal van onsterfbaarheid.

Ek is die genadige Godin wat die geskenk van blydskap aan die harte van alle mense bied. Op aarde dra Ek kennis vir die ewige siel; en na die dood bied Ek vrede en vryheid, en reünie met die wat julle vooruitgegaan het. Ek soek geen offerande nie, want aanskou – Ek is die Moeder van alle lewe en giet my liefde uit oor die aarde.

Ek is die skoonheid van die groen aarde en die wit Maan tussen die sterre, en die geheime van die waters en die begeertes in die harte van mense.

Laat jou siel uitroep! Staan op, en kom na my; want Ek is die gees van die natuur wat lewe skenk aan die heelal.

Uit my vloei alle dinge, en na my keer alle dinge terug. In my aangesig, geliefde van mense en Gode, laat jou innerlike goddelikheid omvou word in die verkeer met die oneindige.

Laat Ek vereer word in die hart wat verheug is, want Ek beskou alle dade van liefde en verblydenis as my rituele. Laat daar skoonheid en sterkte wees, krag en menslikheid, eerbaarheid en ontmoed, vrolikheid en eerbiedigheid in jou binneste wese.

~ (~

In parts of the community where Afrikaans is the lingua franca, rituals are conducted in that language. Many of these would be directly translated from the English version. Here is a quote from Jade Groen's book (pages 253–55). I include the Afrikaans version and the translation. It describes the first time she cast a circle using Afrikaans and how the beauty and richness of the Afrikaans language came home to her.

Afrikaans is Gemaak vir Majiek

Die eerste sirkels wat ek gestrooi het, was met 'n Engelse boek in my hand. Ek was te besig om alles van majiek to leer om dit nog te vertaal ook. 'n Aansienlike hoeveelheid energie stroom deur 'n mens as jy 'n sirkel strooi en en jy moet nog jou kop bymekaar hou. Toe ek uiteindelik vir die eerste keer in Afrikaans sirkel strooi, was dit 'n groot deurbraak. Die trane het geloop. Ek het nog nooit vantevore Moeder Natuur so vereer nie. Nog nooit was my Moedertaal vir my so mooi nie. Die krag van die Afrikaanse woorde was merkbaar sterker, die majiek meer Aards en tasbaar. Haar woorde het my gerusgestel op 'n vlak waar niks my vantervore nog gesus het nie.

Daardie volmaanaand het ek besef watter magiese mag daar in ons beeldskone, Aardse taal opgesluit is. Net soos elke rituele gebaar iets betekenisvol simboliseer, is elke woord wat ons uitspreek se kernbetekenis van belang. Die hekse van ouds het hulle woorde getel. Die magiese gebruik van die Germaanse rune-alfabet is geskoei op die begrip dat letters en woorde oor die mag van verwesenliking beskik. Die *Woord/Wurd/Urd/Erda/Aarde/Wyrd* is majiek want dit is die skeppingswoord en Afrikaanse woorde is baie-baie majiek omdat daar nog nie so erg met ons Moedertaal gepeuter is nie. Veral nie met die begrippe uit die Aardgelowige voedingsbodem nie. Volgens die mitologie het ons Oermoeders magiese letters in die spinnerak vir die eerste alfabet gebruik. Die Wyrd ou Vroue het die klanke aanmekaar geweef in Taalmateriaal. Hierdie majiek het onlangs gebeur met Afrikaans, die mooiste taallap op Aarde.

Afrikaans, die wonderbaarlike taal – wat uit Europa stam, maar wat die naam het van die oerkontinent waar sy wortel gevat het. Die taal wat eens op 'n tyd 'n kombuistaal was – ag, hoe lekker, daar in die hart van die huis. Afrikaans, so jonk maar tog so onderdruk en as 'n taal van onderdrukking gebruik. Dit kan nou die taal van ware vroulike geestelike bevryding word as ons die stilte wil breek; as ons die groot Vrou wil vryspreek. Majiek Afrikaans kan in Afrikabodem wortelskiet om 'n nuwe werklikheid te skep, om die Afrikaner se negatiwiteit te omskep, om Suid-Afrika oor te toor in 'n land van melk en liefde en heuning – ja juis in Afrikaans, want sy is jonger, soos 'n meisie, sy het meer krag soos 'n maagd, en sy spreek van liefde vir Moeder Aarde.

Ons liewe Afrikanervolk kon dit nog nooit regkry om saam te stem of te staan as een stam nie. Die enigste ding wat ons in een web vasspin, is ons taal. Ons kan ons eie nuwe spinnerak van selfbeskikking in ons kordate kombuistaal spin. Ons kan ons harte heelmaak. Ons kan ons siele vryspreek in Afrikaans. Ons kan ons wêreld oortoor in Afrikaans.

Onthou, daar is 'n kritieke tipe massa: Die punt wat positief meer as negatief gaan weeg en die bordjies gaan verhang. Die punt waar 'n volgehoue positiewe bewussyn die negatiewe gedagtestroom verdryf. So, dink net wat is alles moontlik as elke liewe vrou elke volmaan vir vyf minute 'n Nuwe Wêreld voor haar geestesoog oproep ...

Kom susters, moenie skaam wees nie. Gebruik jou hartlike huistaal om volmaan vrede vir alle vroue op die aardbol te stuur. Roep die engele en jou geesgidse in Afrikaans. Praat met die gees van die see en die riviere en die rots en die dier in Afrikaans. Eer jou skepper in asemrowende Afrikaans. Laat die vroulike geesdrif in Afrikaans uit borrel. Skep nuwe heilige geskrifte en gedigte en joernale van jou geesteservarings in jou kombuistaal. Maar bowenal, bowenalles al, spin 'n nuwe gesonde stuk materiaal met Afrikaanse spinnedrade. Koester jou Moeder in jou hart op Afrikaans. Luister na die Aardklop. Hoor hoe haar hart klop. Praat met Haar, prys Haar en vertel Haar hoe lief is jy vir Haar in jou Moedertaal. Sit salf aan Haar mynwonde en lawe Haar hartkloppings met Groen Afrikaans. Vra al die afgestorwe spesies in Afrikaans om vergifnis. Weef Haar vlaktes weer oop sonder grensdrade. Weef Haar dat sy weer wemel van natuurlike wesens. Weef Haar diere spekvet, wild en vry. Weef Haar woude weer ruig, Haar fonteine suiwer, Haar lug skoon, Haar oseane weer veilig vir walvisse. Weef 'n bekoorlike lap vir Haar lyf sodat ons weer veilig op Haar kan woon.

Weef 'n skitterende sterk bewussynsrak vir al ons Aardkinders waarop ons kan lag en dans en skyn onder die maan. Kom ons vier weer ons wonderbaarlike bestaan. Stel ons toekoms blink voor ons geestesoog voor. Kom susters, laat ons ons wêreld oortoor!

Afrikaans is Made for Magick

The first circle I cast was while I was holding an English book in my hand. I was way too busy learning all about magick to waste time translating it. An enormous amount of energy pulses through one when casting a circle, and one needs to focus. When I eventually cast my first circle in Afrikaans, it was a great breakthrough. The tears were rolling. Never before had I honoured Mother Nature to this extent. Never before did my mother tongue sound so beautiful. The power of the Afrikaans words were remarkably stronger, the magick more Earthy and tactile. The words reached and calmed a part of me never reached before.

That night of the full moon, I realised what magickal strength was locked within our beautiful language. Just as each ritual gesture symbolises something meaningful, the root meaning of each word spoken is of importance. The witches of old counted their words. The magickal use of the Germanic rune alphabet is based upon the understanding that letters and words contain the power of actualisation. The *Word/Wurd/Urd/Erda/Earth/Wyrd* is magickal because it is the Word of Creation and Afrikaans words are very, very magickal because our mother tongue has not yet been tampered with too badly – especially not with the Nature-based spirituality concepts. According to myth, our Ancestral Mothers used magickal letters from spider webs for the first alphabet. The old women of the Wyrd weaved the sounds into language-fabric. This magick happened recently to Afrikaans, the most beautiful language-fabric on Earth.

Afrikaans, the marvellous language – which stems from Europe, but adopted the name from the ancient continent where she was rooted. The language that was once considered a kitchen language – ah, how cosy, there in the heart of the home. Afrikaans, so new but already suppressed and used as a language of oppression. Now it can become the language of true female spiritual freedom, if we want to break the silence; if we want to absolve the Great Woman. Magickal Afrikaans can germinate in African territory to become a new reality, to transform the Afrikaner negativity, to bewitch South Africa into a land of milk and love and honey. Yes, precisely in Afrikaans, because she is younger, like the Maiden, and because she has more power like the Mother, and she talks of love for Mother Earth.

Our dear Afrikaner people can't manage to agree or stand united as one tribe. The only thing that weaves us into one web is our language. We can spin our own new web of dispensation in our bold kitchen-language. We can heal our hearts. We can free our souls in Afrikaans. We can re-conjure our world in Afrikaans.

Remember, the point at which critical mass occurs: The point where positive outweighs negative and tilts the scale: The point where a positive consciousness drives out a negative train of thought. Therefore, just think what could be possible if each and every woman visualises her New World for five minutes each full moon.

Come, my sisters, don't be shy. Use your home language to send full-moon peace to all women on Earth. Call the angels and your spirit guides in Afrikaans. Talk to the Spirits of the Sea and the River and the Rock and the Animal in Afrikaans. Honour your Maker in breathtaking Afrikaans. Let the feminine enthusiasm flow from you in Afrikaans.

Create your own sacred writings and poems and journals of your spiritual experiences, in your kitchen-language. But above all, above everything, weave a new healthy piece of fabric from Afrikaans threads. Cherish your Mother in your heart, in Afrikaans. Listen to the pulse of the Earth. Listen to Her heartbeat. Talk to Her, praise Her and tell Her how much you love Her in your mother-tongue. Administer ointment to her mining wounds and soothe her palpitations in Green Afrikaans. Beg forgiveness from all the extinct species, in Afrikaans. Weave open Her plains again, without boundaries. Weave Her so that once again She teems with natural creatures. Weave Her animals healthy, wild and free. Weave Her forests lush, Her fountains pure, Her air clean, Her oceans once again safe for whales. Weave an enchanted cloth for Her body so we can exist safely upon Her once again.

Weave a stunningly strong web of consciousness for all our children of the Earth, whereupon we can laugh and dance and shine beneath the moon. Come let us celebrate our wonderful existence once again and visualise our bright future. Come, my Sisters, let us re-conjure our world.

CONCLUDING THOUGHTS

The Pagan scene in South Africa is a rich and eclectic tapestry. It has come a long way in a short space of time. It is difficult to say exactly when the neo-Pagan movement in South Africa began, but certainly it became public approximately eight years ago. At last, Paganism had a face and an e-mail address, and people who were interested had somewhere to turn for information.

Previous attempts to start something similar had failed. Perhaps the time was not right. Finally, the Goddess granted permission, and from here other credible organisations were spawned. Hiving off from these were smaller groups that weren't interested in the administrative tasks of public ventures. Together with already existing covens and solitary practitioners, they helped to spread the religious ideology of Paganism. Despite the rapid spread, the Pagan movement in South Africa is still fairly small. Estimates are around 50 000 practitioners (the white population is at approximately 5.8 million). However, many people find that they are Pagan without even knowing it, and, as more and more literature becomes available, it seems that an increasing hunger for knowledge is being satisfied.

In my opinion, the main influence on the public neo-Pagan movement in South Africa was the formation of the Pagan Federation of South Africa. It was the catalyst for change in the Pagan status quo, providing a forum for criticism and a 'home' for South African Pagans. That the organisation played a formative role in shaping the face of Paganism is undeniable. Whatever the criticism and praise of the organisation and whatever the personality differences within its leadership, it was after all the only public Pagan body available at the time. It was the only Pagan animal that had an e-mail address, a PO Box number and a secretary to answer queries. So, any Pagan with a social streak had little choice.

For a short, sweet time we all played together. Many of the well-known public faces today started off in the PFSA. But, inevitably, natural leaders soon emerged and went their own way, collected a following and started their own legitimate groups. This illustrated the need for different approaches and styles to meet the large and growing Pagan community's needs.

Although a few individuals (representing one or two groups, perhaps) remain insular and will not network with other groups, the majority of members of the organisations mentioned in Chapter 2 mix freely and easily with each other, especially at the Sabbats.

The early days of the public Pagan scene were akin to a birthing process – birth pains, ecstatic joy, wonder, sleepless nights, and so on. A few years ago the crawling stage began. New groups developed and the right to establish oneself as a separate entity to the 'mother body' was big on the agenda. Today, at least in the main cities, you can pick and choose which Beltaine festival you would like to attend. Paganism has progressed from absolute obscurity to a household name and is now entrenched in South African civil and religious society. Perhaps not in Pofadder or the Hex River Valley yet, but this is nothing to worry about. Paganism has a momentum of its own. When the time is right, the Goddess will send her ambassador.

So, where do we go from here? Whether you lead a group, an organisation, a coven or yourself, all are representatives of the Goddess. Whether you are new to all of this, have been pondering for a while or are too shy to turn to anyone, there is someone who will listen. While we don't evangelise in any way, we are there for the true seeker.

As South African Pagans, we are not the poor cousins of Pagans anywhere else in the world. At one stage we thought this was the case. Perhaps some of us still think so. However, evidence from many of our colleagues now living in Australia, the USA and Britain bears testimony to the fact that our Craft practice and interpretation are comparable in standard.

There are only a handful of leaders in South Africa, and they themselves have had no mentors. They have had to learn through the Internet, relying on their intuition and travelling overseas intermittently. So, the road to establishing a credible reputation has been filled with obstacles. However, now that this is a fait accompli, and we can take our rightful place among international Pagan movements, we need to be critical of ourselves – always remembering that South African neo-Paganism has a much shorter history than that of its overseas counterparts.

Tradition in South Africa is very eclectic and is still growing. My first teacher, for example, had only a little training from someone in England, and therefore the training I offered my students was very eclectic. As they grew and became teachers themselves, their training syllabus became even more eclectic, and so the eclecticism continues to progress. Quite exciting really, as it has been refined into traditions of its own.

Although the Aquarian Tabernacle Church and the Correllian Tradition can be described as 'imported' traditions, and some Pagans might feel that their coven is able enough to form their own lineage or tradition, these imported traditions lend us the necessary depth for which we are looking at the moment. Eclecticism may be exciting, dynamic, rewarding, racy and creative, but it often falls short on depth.

With the advent of the ATC and the Correllian Tradition, the dynamics will shift a little. While they are not South African traditions, the syllabus does take on a South African flavour.

Eclecticism also applies to the varied approaches to magick. Most notable is the crossover between high and low magickal techniques. In my experience, an experienced practitioner would have no trouble comparing the making of a poppet while sitting in front of the Triangle of Art, or combining the use of certain techniques from magickal orders, such as the IOT. In some circles there are crossovers between traditional African healing techniques and Wiccan customs, and in certain cases Sangoma magick is combined with Wiccan magick.

Certainly, there are individuals and covens that try to be very 'traditional' and become quite rigid in their practice. This is most notably a Gardnerian trait. But this approach does not reflect the beliefs and practices of the majority. The majority of practitioners are very flexible in their magickal practice. The degree of spontaneity that I have witnessed at countless circle workings is an indication of this flexibility as well as a willingness to learn.

The eclectic nature of South African Paganism doesn't mean that it is undefined and disjointed. Through all the talks and trials, through the tribulations and triumphs, through the teasing and temptations, we all subscribe to a Goddess of four faces:
- The Maiden – representing fun
- The Mother – illustrating compassion
- The Crone – representing wisdom
- The Enchantress – symbolising mystery

Among other things, these are the values that we all hold dear to ourselves.

The interviews, spells and rituals in this book reflect the varied styles and approaches to the subject. The short and long spells and rituals and the succinct and lengthy interviews all reflect the jigsaw puzzle that is South African Pagan thought and practice. Despite the lack of tradition and teachers, these practitioners have got on and done it.

The large majority of those interviewed view themselves as witches working within the parameters of Wiccan Craft and ethics. Nearly all consider themselves Pagan, but qualify that term with the word 'witch'.

Most practitioners interviewed, although they have a great amount of book knowledge, would cross and have crossed the line into magickal practices that are not necessarily Wiccan.

Most of them work as solitary practitioners, but they also operate in 'working groups' from time to time. A number of them have children and are raising their children as Pagans until they are old enough to choose for themselves. All involve their children in circle work.

It is my belief that Paganism will continue to grow in numbers, as it is very appealing to people across the board. My appeal to current Pagan leadership is to recognise that there is enough work from the Goddess for all of us. There is a role for every organisation. Each one has different views, aims and objectives, so let's fulfil them.

REFERENCES

Anodea, Judith, *The Truth About Neo-Paganism*. Llewellyn Publications, 1999.
ATC, *The ATC Redbook of Wiccan Liturgy*. Washington: ATC, 1999.
The British Druid Order, Information package (undated).
Buckland, Raymond, *Buckland's Complete Book of Witchcraft*. Llewellyn Publications, 1995.
'The Correllian Tradition'. http://telepathicmedia.com/correlliantemple/.
'Correspondences'. http://www.geocities.com/Athens/2962/bos/corres/direct.html.
Crowley, Vivianne, *Principles of Paganism*. Thorson, 1996.
Farrar, Janet and Stewart, *Eight Sabbats for Witches*. Phoenix, 1981.
Groen, Jade, *Spinnelap*. Cape Town: Future Managers, 2001.
Jackson, N.A., *Call of the Horned Piper*. Capall Bann Publishing, 1995.
Jennings, Pete, *The Norse Tradition: A Beginner's Guide*. Headway, 1998.
Laubscher, B.J.F., *The Pagan Soul*. Howard Timmins, 1975.
Pagan Africa, Issue 2, December 1997; Issue 2, August 1998; Issue 5, December 1998/January 1999; Issue 6, April 1999; Issue 7, August/September 1999; New Millennium Issue, January 2001.
Steyn, Chrissie, *Worldviews in Transition: An Investigation into the New Age Movement in South Africa*. UNISA, 1994.
Thiele, Christian, 'Sangomas under siege'. http://www.dispatch.co.za/1999/07/10/features/LP1.HTM.
Thorpe, S.A., *Shamans, Medicine Men and Traditional Healers*. UNISA, 1993.